The RSC Shakespeare

William Shakespeare

THE TAMING OF THE SHREW

Edited by Jonathan Bate and Eric Rasmussen

Introduction by Jonathan Bate

The Modern Library
New York

CONTENTS

INTRODUCTION

THE "TAMING" AND THE "SHREW"

The Taming of the Shrew: is Kate (or should we call her Katherina?) really a "shrew" and is she really "tamed"?

The novelist Vladimir Nabokov once wrote that "reality" is a word that only has meaning when it is placed between quotation marks. The physicist's "reality" is not the same as the biochemist's, the secular humanist's as the religious fundamentalist's. Dare one say that woman's is not the same as man's? In a culture where the conception of inherent sexual difference is regarded as a mere prejudice, as a forbidden thought (regardless of the "reality" revealed by molecular biology and neuroanatomy), *The Taming of the Shrew* is not likely to be one of Shakespeare's most admired plays. Its presentation of female subordination presents the same kind of awkwardness for liberal sensibilities that the representation of Shylock does in the post-Holocaust world. At face value, the play proposes that desirable women are quiet and submissive, whereas women with spirit must be "tamed" through a combination of physical and mental abuse. Necessary tools may include starvation, sense deprivation, and the kind of distortion of "reality" that is practiced in totalitarian regimes.

Thus O'Brien to Winston Smith in George Orwell's *1984:* "How many fingers am I holding up?" In this "reality" the correct answer is not the actual number but the number that the torturer says he is holding up. There is a precise analogy on the road back to Padua, after Kate has undergone her taming in the secluded country house where no neighbor will hear her cries:

PETRUCHIO   I say it is the moon.
KATE   I know it is the moon.
PETRUCHIO   Nay, then you lie. It is the blessèd sun.
KATE   Then, God be blessed, it is the blessèd sun.
But sun it is not, when you say it is not,

> And the moon changes even as your mind.
> What you will have it named, even that it is,
> And so it shall be so for Katherine.
> HORTENSIO   Petruchio, go thy ways, the field is won.

She has been bent to her husband's will. She is now ready to demonstrate that she is prepared to love, serve, and obey him. She knows her place: "Such duty as the subject owes the prince / Even such a woman oweth to her husband." She offers to place her hand beneath her husband's foot. The shrew is tamed.

The younger dramatist John Fletcher, who was Shakespeare's collaborator in his final years, clearly thought that this harsh ending needed a riposte. He wrote a sequel, *The Woman's Prize; or, The Tamer Tamed,* in which Kate has died and Petruchio remarried, only to find his new wife giving him a taste of his own medicine by means of the time-honored device of refusing to sleep with him until he submits to her will. Kate's sister Bianca plays the role of colonel in a war between the sexes which the women win, thus proving that it was an act of folly for Petruchio to tyrannize over his first wife in Shakespeare's play.

In Shakespeare's time, it was absolutely orthodox to believe that a man was head of the household, as the monarch was head of state and God was head of the cosmos. "My foot my tutor?" says Prospero in *The Tempest* when his daughter, Miranda, presumes to speak out of turn: if the man was the head, the girl-child was the foot, just as in *Coriolanus* a plebeian is nothing more than the "big toe" of the commonwealth. Kate's readying of her hand to be trodden upon turns the analogy between social and bodily hierarchy into a stage image. But she is going much further than she should: the wife was not supposed to be beneath the foot, she was supposed to be the heart of the household. Instead of crowing in his triumph, Petruchio says "kiss me, Kate" for the third time, giving Cole Porter a title for his reimagining of the story in the cheerful mode of a musical.

Nabokov placed the word "reality" in quotation marks not because he was a cultural relativist, but because he was an aesthete. That is to say, he did not believe that art was merely a reflection, a mirror, of a preexistent "reality." Art shapes the way in which we perceive ourselves and the world. "Falling in love" is not only the work of molecular change in the brain, but also a set of behaviors learned from the romantic fictions of page, stage—now screen—and cultural memory. One of the tricks of great art is to draw attention to its own artificiality and in so doing paradoxically assert that its "reality" is as real as anything in the quotidian world of its audience. Shakespeare's taste for plays-within-the-play and allusions to the theatricality of the world, Mozart's witty quotations of the clichés of operatic convention, and Nabokov's magical wordplay all fulfill this function.

Sometimes, though, the opposite device is used: an artist puts quotation marks around a work in order to say "Don't take this too seriously, don't mistake its feigning for 'reality.'" *The Taming of the Shrew* is such a work: the opening scenes with Christopher Sly place the entire play within quotation marks. The "induction" presents a series of wish-fulfillment fantasies to a drunken tinker: the fantasy that he is a lord, that he has a beautiful young wife, that scenes of erotic delight can be presented for his delectation, and that a company of professional players will stage "a kind of history" for his sole benefit, in order to frame his mind to "mirth and merriment" while teaching him how to tame a shrewish wife. But Sly is not a lord and the "wife" who watches with him is not a woman but a crossed-dressed boy—which reminds us that in Shakespeare's working world the Kate who is humiliated by Petruchio was also not a woman but a cross-dressed boy-actor. The effect of the frame is to distance the action and so to suggest that it does not present the "reality" of proper marital relations. If Sly is not a lord and the pageboy not a wife, then this is not how to tame a shrew.

In the surviving script of the play, Sly and the pageboy disappear after the first act, presumably because Shakespeare's acting company was not large enough to waste several members of the cast sitting in the gallery as spectators all the way through. But in an anonymously published play of 1594 called *The Taming of a Shrew*, which is a source, adaptation, reconstruction or variant version of Shakespeare's play, the Christopher Sly "frame" is maintained throughout the action by means of a series of brief interludes and an epilogue. This version ends with the tinker heading for home with the claim that the play has taught him how to tame a shrew and thus to handle his own wife. But the tapster knows better: "your wife will course [thrash] you for dreaming here tonight." The hungover Sly is in no position to tame anybody; he will return home and be soundly beaten by his wife. Kate's speech propounds the patriarchal ideal of marriage, but in *A Shrew* the union of Sly and his wife reveals this ideology's distance from "reality." Its implied resolution, with the woman on top, intimates that "real" housewives are not silent and obedient, and plays cannot teach husbands to tame them into submission.

We do not need the epilogue of the anonymously published play to see that Shakespeare's ending is more complicated and ironic than first appears. Having been outwitted in his courtship of Bianca, Hortensio marries the widow for her money. The latter shows signs of frowardness and has to be lectured by Kate. The first half of Kate's famous submission speech is spoken in the singular, addressed specifically to the widow and not to womankind in general: "*Thy* husband is thy lord, thy life, thy keeper, / Thy head, thy sovereign: one that cares for thee." The contextual irony of this is not always appreciated: in contradistinction to Kate's prescriptions, in the particular marriage to which she is referring it will be the wife, the wealthy widow, who provides the "maintenance." Hortensio will be spared the labors of a breadwinner. According to Kate, all a husband asks from a wife is love, good looks, and obedience; these are said to be "Too little payment for so great a debt." But the audience knows that in this case the debt is all Hortensio's. Besides, he has said earlier that he is no longer interested in woman's traditional attribute of "beauteous looks"—all he wants is the money. Kate's vision of obedience is made to look oddly irrelevant to the very marriage upon which she is offering advice.

Then there is Kate's sister. Petruchio's "taming school" is played off against the attempts by Lucentio and Hortensio to gain access to Bianca by disguising themselves as schoolmasters. In the scene in which Lucentio courts her in the guise of a Latin tutor, the woman gives as good as she gets. She is happy to flirt with her supposed teacher over Ovid's erotic manual *The Art of Love*. This relationship offers a model of courtship and marriage built on mutual desire and consent. Bianca escapes her class of sixteenth-century woman's usual fate of being married to a partner of the father's choice, such as rich old Gremio. If anything, Bianca is the dominant partner at the end. She is not read a lecture by Kate, as the widow is, and she gets the better of her husband in their final onstage exchange. Like Beatrice in *Much Ado About Nothing*, she more than matches her man in the art of wordplay. One almost wonders if she would not be better matched with the pretended rather than the "real" Lucentio, that is to say the clever servant Tranio who oils the wheels of the plot and sometimes threatens to steal the show.

The double plot is a guarantee that, despite the subduing of Kate, the play is no uncomplicated apology for shrew-taming. But is Kate really subdued? Or is her submission all part of the game that she and Petruchio have been playing out? It is their marriage, not the other ones, that compels the theater audience. A woman with Kate's energies would be bored by a conventional lover such as Lucentio. She and Petruchio are well matched because they are both of "choleric" temperament. Their fierce tempers are what make them attractive to each other and charismatic to us. They seem to know they are born for each other from the moment in their first private encounter when they share a joke about oral sex ("with my tongue in your tail"). "Where two raging fires meet together" there may not be an easy marriage, but there will certainly not be a dull match and a passive wife. In the twentieth century the roles seemed ready made for Richard Burton and Elizabeth Taylor.

THE CRITICS DEBATE

What you have just read is *one* critical interpretation of the play. But there are many other possible answers to the awkward questions raised by its title, action, resolution, and framing, so for the sake of balance the remainder of this introduction will offer an overview of some of them.

The critical debate about *The Taming of the Shrew* begins at the end: is Kate's notorious last speech delivered ironically? Is she genuinely tamed, or is she playing a game of her own, retaining her psychological independence? A related question concerns the play's style. Is it a farce, a form in which we are not encouraged to take it very seriously when people are slapped around? Or is it a sophisticated social comedy, the ironic texture of which directs our attention to what one critic calls the social illness of a materialistic patriarchy?

Historically attuned commentators have related the play to contemporaneous debates about the nature and role of the sexes, and the disruption caused to society by unruly, "shrewish" or "scolding" women. In early modern England there was a criminalization of female unruliness. As Sir William Blackstone later explained in his *Commentaries on the Laws of England*,

> A common scold, *communis rixatrix*, (for our law-Latin confines it to the feminine gender) is a public nuisance to her neighbourhood. For which offence she may be indicted; and, if convicted, shall be sentenced to be placed in a certain engine of correction called the trebucket, castigatory, or cucking stool, which in the Saxon language signifies the scolding stool; though now it is frequently corrupted into ducking stool, because the residue of the judgement is, that, when she is so placed therein, she shall be plunged in the water for her punishment.[1]

The equivalent punishment in Scotland was the "scold's bridle," a form of muzzle designed to stop the foul, gossipy, or malicious mouth of the woman. What is striking in this context, feminist critic Lynda Boose suggests, "is that the punishments meted out to women are much more frequently targeted at suppressing women's speech than they are at controlling their sexual transgressions": "the chief social offences seem to have been 'scolding,' 'brawling,' and dominating one's husband. The veritable prototype of the female offender of this era seems to be . . . the woman marked out as a 'scold' or 'shrew.' "[2] Public humiliation as much as physical discomfort was the purpose of the "cucking"/"ducking" stool and the "scold's bridle." They were shaming devices: "The cucking of scolds was turned into a carnival experience, one that literally placed the woman's body at the center of a mocking parade. Whenever local practicalities made it possible, her experience seems to have involved being ridden or carted through town."[3] The Skimmington Ride in Thomas Hardy's novel *The Mayor of Casterbridge* (1884) is a late example of this practice.

The question, though, is how to relate the play to such customs. In one sense, a drama performed on the public stage is close kin to a mocking parade. In another sense, it is very different, since we know that it is only a game and that the female victim is only an actor. And within the world of the play, the humiliation of Kate is more private than public. Furthermore, Petruchio's actions are intended to be preemptive: unlike many of the women who were ritually punished for their behavior, she is not an unruly *wife*.

The starting point of the modern female spectator's response to the play is likely to be Kate's own emotion: rage. Why should a daughter submit to her father's will? Why should women accept the way they are treated by men? In an influential feminist reading of Shakespeare, the critic Coppélia Kahn has no doubt about the play's historical authenticity:

> The overt force Petruchio wields over Kate by marrying her against her will in the first place and then by denying her every wish and comfort, by stamping, shouting, reducing her to exhaustion, etc., is but a farcical representation of the psychological realities of marriage in Elizabethan England, in which the husband's will constantly, silently, and invisibly, through custom and conformity, suppressed the wife's.[4]

Yet at the same time, she credits Shakespeare with the intelligence to see the irrationality of such behavior:

> Shakespeare does not rest with showing that male supremacy in marriage denies woman's humanity. In the most brilliant comic scene of the play [4.3], he goes on to demonstrate how it defies reason. Petruchio demands that Kate agree that the sun is the moon in order to force a final showdown. Having exhausted and humiliated her to the limit of his invention, he now wants her to know that he would go to any extreme to get the obedience he craves. Shakespeare implies here that male supremacy is ultimately based on such absurdities, for it insists

that whatever a man says is right because he is a man, even if he happens to be wrong.[5]

The purpose of theater is not usually to endorse or to dissent from a moral position or a sociological phenomenon. It is to show—comically, tragically, farcically, thoughtfully—how human beings interact with each other. Shakespeare's greatest resource is his language and what attracts him to Katherina as a character for realization on the stage is what attracts Petruchio to her: her lively language. How would his original audience have responded to that language? First and foremost, they would have enjoyed it and laughed with it. If they began to reflect upon it, they would have been pulled in contradictory directions. There may well have been an element perhaps of fear and loathing: "From the outset of Shakespeare's play, Katherine's threat to male authority is posed through language; it is perceived as such by others and is linked to a claim larger than shrewishness—witchcraft—through the constant allusions to Katherine's kinship with the devil."[6] But equally, among the more sophisticated, there could have been a relish in the subversion of norms. Translating this into the language of modern feminist criticism,

> Kate's self-consciousness about the power of language, her punning and irony, and her techniques of linguistic masquerade, are strategies of italics. . . . Instead of figuring an essentialized woman's speech, they deform language by subverting it, that is, by turning it inside out so that metaphors, puns, and other forms of wordplay manifest their veiled equivalences: the meaning of woman as treasure, of wooing as a civilized and acceptable disguise for sexual exploitation, of the objectification and exchange of women.[7]

Mastery of language was an extremely important idea in Shakespeare's time. The pedagogy of Renaissance humanism was fundamentally concerned with the cultivation of the powers of speech and argument as the means of realizing our potential as rational beings. Within the play, Petruchio's subduing and refinement of Kate operates in parallel to the purported efforts of the supposed tutors to teach the sisters classical literature and the art of the lute. "By learning to speak the pedagogue's language of social and familial order, Kate shows herself to be a better student of standard humanist doctrine than her sister."[8]

Paradoxically, there is a sense in which Petruchio liberates Kate from her own demons:

> Petruchio directs Kate to the dark center of her psyche and dramatizes her fears so that she may recognize them. He shows her what she has become, not only by killing her in her own humour but also by presenting her with a dramatic image of her own emotional condition: he acts out for her the drama of her true self held in bondage by her tyrannical, violent self. What is internal . . . Petruchio makes external.[9]

> Petruchio's method is to suppose (and he is correct) or assume qualities in Katherina that no one else, possibly even the shrew herself, ever suspects. What he assumes as apparently false turns out to be startlingly true. His "treatment" is a steady unfolding of her really fine qualities: patience, practical good sense, a capacity for humor, and finally obedience, all of which she comes gradually to manifest in a spirit chastened but not subdued.[10]

The suggestion, then, is that beneath the surface of the brutal sex farce is a different story in which two intelligent but temperamental people learn how to live together. A variant on such an interpretation is to suggest that Petruchio's "taming" may be an elaborate game:

> The audience's realization that Petruchio is game-playing, that he is posing behind the mask of a disorderly male shrew and is having considerable fun exploiting his role, is the key to a romantic reading of the play. Thus Kate is tamed not by Petruchio's whip but by the discovery of her own imagination, for when she learns to recognize the sun for the moon and the moon for the dazzling sun she is discovering the liberating power of laughter and play.[11]

As a wife she submits, but as a player in the game she is now a full and skillful partner. Most important, she is helping to create her own role as an obedient spouse, and the process of creation gives her pleasure. Her obedience is not meekly accepted, but embraced and enjoyed.[12]

Like a good humanist husband, he has been his wife's teacher; and like an actor, he has taught her to assume a new role. When Kate learns to mimic as well as he, these two easily transcend the roles and hierarchies that govern their world.[13]

By this account, Petruchio injects a dose of realism into the romantic ideas about love that comedy habitually perpetuates. It has been said that he

drags love out of heaven, and brings it down to earth. To the chivalrous, love is a state of worship; to him, it is a problem of wiving. Its object is not primarily a search for spiritual bliss in the contemplation of the beloved. It seeks merely a guarantee of domestic comfort. . . . A condition of this is, naturally, that he must be master of what is his own. Courtship is merely incidental to the attainment of this ease and settlement.[14]

Perhaps Kate, too, participates willingly and actively in the game. The submission speech has often been read in the light of this possibility:

Far from reiterating old platitudes about the inferiority of women, however, what Kate actually says reflects a number of humanist assumptions about an ideal marriage popularized by Tudor matrimonial reformers. If we wish to see a real vision of subjugated woman, we should turn to the parallel speech of Kate in the anonymous A Shrew . . . [who] recites a medieval argument about women's moral inferiority. . . . Shakespeare makes no reference to moral inferiority in women. His emphasis instead is on reciprocity of duties in marriage, based on the complementary natures of man and woman.[15]

We cannot really take that speech at face value. Much of this comedy is an unspoken dialogue between Katherina and Petruchio; and we have to take her speech in the context of the whole play, not as a set-piece on the woman's place. We should read Katherina's final speech as the parallel, and answer, to Petruchio's rhetoric. The mode of speech adopted by each is hyperbole.[16]

Kate's "act" at the end is, therefore, far more ethical than Bianca's "act" throughout the play, although both women pretend to be good. They do not simply exchange roles, for then Kate would appear as false as Bianca has been. Through the use of parodic speech, Shakespeare makes Kate shatter the façade of female hypocrisy that . . . Bianca put into practice.[17]

The very nature of Kate's performance *as* performance suggests that she is offering herself to Petruchio not as his servant, as she claims, but as his equal in a select society . . . those who, because they know that man is an actor, freely choose and change their roles in order to avoid the narrow, imprisoning roles society would impose on them.[18]

The conclusion to be drawn from such a reading is that the very artfulness of game-playing—of theater—offers a form of release from the pressures of patriarchal, mercantile society:

The Taming of the Shrew does not fully resolve the marital problems raised in the play, nor does it resolve the problems of patriarchy raised by the shrew character and the plot that conventionally tamed her. Instead, it reasserts marital hierarchy parodically at the end and allows the shrew and her husband to escape from their mercantile world through art.[19]

The danger of reading Petruchio's actions positively in this way is that one might find oneself glossing over the violence he threatens and performs. There is a long stage tradition of giving him a whip, which—unless one starts becoming very Freudian—is hardly conducive to the idea that Kate is complicit in everything that happens to her.

The questions of performance and role-playing raised by Kate's final speech are often read in the light of the induction:

> In *The Taming of a Shrew* . . . the Sly-narrative is not a prologue but an extended dramatic framework: Sly and his attendants are kept on stage more or less throughout, and are given several further comments on and interventions in the action of the play.[20]

> The transformation of Christopher Sly from drunken lout to noble lord, a transformation only temporary and skin-deep, suggests that Kate's switch from independence to subjection may also be deceptive and prepares us for the irony of the denouement.[21]

This emphasis on disguise and illusion is equally evident in the Bianca plot:

> Bianca can play her role in a courtship, and her role in a business transaction, without revealing her true face. But the play . . . goes on for one scene after marriage, and Lucentio learns to his dismay what lay behind that romantic sweetness. On the other hand, Petruchio has been concerned with personality all along. The taming plot presents in a deeper, more psychological way ideas that are handled superficially and externally in the romantic plot. Education is one such idea. . . . Petruchio . . . really does teach Kate, and teaches her that inner order of which the music and the mathematics offered to Bianca are only a reflection.[22]

But it is above all the Sly framework that establishes a self-referential theatricality in which the status of the shrew-play *as* a play is enforced. The female characters in the play are boy-actors assuming a role, parodied and highlighted by the page playing Sly's "wife." Thus "in the induction, these relationships of power and gender, which in

Elizabethan treatises, sermons, homilies, and behavioural handbooks were figured as natural and divinely ordained, are subverted by the metatheatrical foregrounding of such roles and relations as culturally constructed."[23] "Katherina's mind is worked on by Petruchio as Sly's is by the Lord, producing a similar sense of dislocation. . . . Finally she [too] acquires a new identity."[24]

Every production of every Shakespeare play is different from every other. The very process of adaptation and reinterpretation is what keeps the work alive. Shakespeare's endurance is dependent on cultural evolution in the light of new circumstances, new beliefs and values. But perhaps of all the plays *The Taming of the Shrew* is the one in which almost everything hangs on a few essential director's and actor's decisions: what to do about the induction, how to play the two sisters and the two courtships off against each other, how playful to make the taming, how sincere to make the submission.

ABOUT THE TEXT

Shakespeare endures through history. He illuminates later times as well as his own. He helps us to understand the human condition. But he cannot do this without a good text of the plays. Without editions there would be no Shakespeare. That is why every twenty years or so throughout the last three centuries there has been a major new edition of his complete works. One aspect of editing is the process of keeping the texts up to date—modernizing the spelling, punctuation and typography (though not, of course, the actual words), providing explanatory notes in the light of changing educational practices (a generation ago, most of Shakespeare's classical and biblical allusions could be assumed to be generally understood, but now they can't).

Because Shakespeare did not personally oversee the publication of his plays, with some plays there are major editorial difficulties. Decisions have to be made as to the relative authority of the early printed editions, the pocket format "Quartos" published in Shakespeare's lifetime, and the elaborately produced "First Folio" text of 1623, the original "Complete Works" prepared for the press after his death by Shakespeare's fellow-actors, the people who knew the plays better than anyone else. In the case of *The Taming of the Shrew*, there is no Quarto text, so all modern editions follow the Folio.

Scholars still debate the nature of the relationship between *A pleasant conceited historie, called The taming of a shrew As it was sundry times acted by the Right honorable the Earle of Pembrook his seruants* (1594) and Shakespeare's *The Taming of the Shrew* as published in the First Folio. The main action shares a similar plot line with parallel but sometimes differently named characters (Sly and Kate are the only names shared by the two plays; in *A Shrew*, Kate has two sisters not just one, and the setting is Athens rather than Padua). Four possibilities have been advanced:

1. Shakespeare used the previously existing *A Shrew*, which he did not write, as a source for *The Shrew*.

2. *A Shrew* is a reconstructed version of *The Shrew*; that is, what has sometimes been called a "Bad Quarto," an attempt by actors (or conceivably a stenographer in the audience) to reconstruct the original play from memory and sell it.

3. Both versions were written legitimately by Shakespeare himself; that is, one of the plays, presumably *A Shrew*, is an earlier draft of the other.

4. The two plays are unrelated other than by the fact that they are independently derived from another play which is now lost. This is the so-called "*Ur-Shrew*" theory (in reference to the idea of an "*Ur-Hamlet*," a lost play behind Shakespeare's *Hamlet*).

(1) would be in accordance with his practice elsewhere (as when, for example, he used the anonymous *King Leir* as a source for *King Lear*) and with his early reputation as a patcher of other men's plays. But if (2) or (3) were correct, there might well be a case for staging the "frame" in the more complete form in which it is found in *A Shrew*. (2), the "Bad Quarto" theory, has found the highest level of support among modern scholars, despite the fact that the differences of plot, language, character, and name are far greater than in the plays usually so classified, such as the First Quarto of *Hamlet*. Explanation (4) has little support, since it adds an unnecessary additional hypothesis about a lost play.

The existence of the anonymous *Taming of a Shrew* Quarto of 1594 raises the question of whether the original performances of Shakespeare's play would have maintained the Christopher Sly "frame" throughout the action. Some modern editions and productions incorporate the Sly sequences from the latter part of the action, on the grounds that his disappearance from the Folio after the first act is dramatically unsatisfying. In accordance with our editorial policy of respecting the Folio wherever possible, we do not do so. We do, however, print the relevant sequences of the old play (modernized but unannotated) at the end of the play, giving readers the chance to think about them and performers the option to play them. In order to facilitate discussion of the distinctiveness of Kate's crucial "submission" speech, we also include a text of the equivalent speech from *A Shrew*.

The following notes highlight various aspects of the editorial process and indicate conventions used in the text of this edition:

Lists of Parts are supplied in the First Folio for only six plays, not including *The Taming of the Shrew*, so the list here is editorially supplied. Capitals indicate that part of the name used for speech headings in the script (thus "Christopher sly, a drunken beggar/tinker").

Locations are provided by the Folio for only two plays, of which *The Taming of the Shrew* is not one. Eighteenth-century editors, working in an age of elaborately realistic stage sets, were the first to provide detailed locations ("another part of the city"). Given that Shakespeare wrote for a bare stage and often an imprecise sense of place, we have relegated locations to the explanatory notes at the foot of the page, where they are given at the beginning of each scene where the imaginary location is different from the one before. In the case of *The Taming of the Shrew*, the induction takes place in the hall of a lord's house that is assumed to be in England but that is then theatrically transformed into Padua and related Italian locations.

Act and Scene Divisions were provided in the Folio in a much more thoroughgoing way than in the Quartos. Sometimes, however, they were erroneous or omitted; corrections and additions supplied by editorial tradition are indicated by square brackets. Five-act division is based on a classical model, and act breaks provided the opportunity to replace the candles in the indoor Blackfriars playhouse which the King's Men used after 1608, but Shakespeare did not necessarily think in terms of a five-part structure of dramatic composition. The Folio convention is that a scene ends when the stage is empty. Nowadays, partly under the influence of film, we tend to consider a scene to be a dramatic unit that ends with either a change of imaginary location or a significant passage of time within the narrative. Shakespeare's fluidity of composition accords well with this convention, so in addition to act and scene numbers we provide a *running scene* count in the right margin at the beginning of each new scene, in the typeface used for editorial directions. Where there is a scene break caused by a momentary bare stage, but the location does not change and extra time does not pass, we use the convention *running scene continues*. There is inevitably a degree of editorial judgment in making such calls, but the system is very valuable in suggesting the pace of the plays.

Speakers' Names are often inconsistent in Folio. We have regularized speech headings, but retained an element of deliberate inconsistency in entry directions, in order to give the flavor of Folio. Thus Sly is always so-called in his speech headings, but "Beggar" or "drunkard" in entry directions.

Verse is indicated by lines that do not run to the right margin and by capitalization of each line. The Folio printers sometimes set verse as prose, and vice versa (either out of misunderstanding or for reasons of space). We have silently corrected in such cases, although in some instances there is ambiguity, in which case we have leaned toward the preservation of Folio layout. Folio sometimes uses contraction ("turnd" rather than "turned") to indicate whether or not the final "-ed" of a past participle is sounded, an area where there is variation for the sake of the five-beat iambic pentameter rhythm. We use the convention of a grave accent to indicate sounding (thus "turnèd" would be two syllables), but would urge actors not to overstress. In cases where one speaker ends with a verse half-line and the next begins with the other half of the pentameter, editors since the late eighteenth century have indented the second line. We have abandoned this convention, since the Folio does not use it, nor did actors' cues in the Shakespearean theater. An exception is made when the second speaker actively interrupts or completes the first speaker's sentence.

Spelling is modernized, but older forms are very occasionally maintained where necessary for rhythm or aural effect.

Punctuation in Shakespeare's time was as much rhetorical as grammatical. "Colon" was originally a term for a unit of thought in an argument. The semicolon was a new unit of punctuation (some of the Quartos lack them altogether). We have modernized punctuation throughout, but have given more weight to Folio punctuation than many editors, since, though not Shakespearean, it reflects the usage of his period. In particular, we have used the colon far more than many editors: it is exceptionally useful as a way of indicating how many Shakespearean speeches unfold clause by clause in a developing argument that gives the illusion of enacting the process of thinking in the moment. We have also kept in mind the origin of punctuation in classical times as a way of assisting the actor and orator: the comma suggests the briefest of pauses for breath, the colon a middling one and a full stop or period a longer pause. Semicolons, by contrast, belong to an era of punctuation that was only just coming in during Shakespeare's time and that is coming to an end now: we have accordingly only used them where they occur in our copy-texts (and not always then). Dashes are sometimes used for parenthetical interjections where the Folio has brackets. They are also used for interruptions and changes in train of thought. Where a change of addressee occurs within a speech, we have used a dash preceded by a full stop (or occasionally another form of punctuation). Often the identity of the respective addressees is obvious from the context. When it is not, this has been indicated in a marginal stage direction.

Entrances and Exits are fairly thorough in Folio, which has accordingly been followed as faithfully as possible. Where characters are omitted or corrections are necessary, this is indicated by square brackets (e.g. "[*and Attendants*]"). *Exit* is sometimes silently normalized to *Exeunt* and *Manet* anglicized to "remains." We trust Folio positioning of entrances and exits to a greater degree than most editors.

Editorial Stage Directions such as stage business, asides, indications of addressee and of characters' position on the gallery stage are only used sparingly in Folio. Other editions mingle directions of this kind with original Folio and Quarto directions, sometimes marking them by means of square brackets. We have sought to distinguish what could be described as *directorial* interventions of this kind from Folio-style directions (either original or supplied) by placing them in the right margin in a different typeface. There is a degree of subjectivity about which directions are of which kind, but the procedure is intended as a reminder to the reader and the actor that Shakespearean stage directions are often dependent upon editorial inference alone and are not set in stone. We also depart from editorial tradition in sometimes admitting uncertainty and thus printing permissive stage directions, such as an *Aside?* (often a line may be equally effective as an aside or a direct address—it is for each production or reading to make its own decision) or a *may exit* or a piece of business placed between arrows to indicate that it may occur at various different moments within a scene.

Line Numbers in the left margin are editorial, for reference and to key the explanatory and textual notes.

Explanatory Notes at the foot of each page explain allusions and gloss obsolete and difficult words, confusing phraseology, occasional major textual cruces, and so on. Particular attention is given to nonstandard usage, bawdy innuendo, and technical terms (e.g. legal and military language). Where more than one sense is given, commas indicate shades of related meaning, slashes alternative or double meanings.

Textual Notes at the end of the play indicate major departures from the Folio. They take the following form: the reading of our text is given in bold and its source given after an equals sign, with "Q" indicating a reading from the 1594 First Quarto text of *The Taming of a Shrew,* "F" from the First Folio of 1623, "F2" a correction introduced in the Second Folio of 1632, "F3" a correction from the Third Folio of 1664 and "Ed" one that derives from the subsequent editorial tradition. The rejected Folio ("F") reading is then given. Thus for Act 2 scene 1 line 250: "**2.1.250 askance** = Ed. F = a sconce." This means that we have preferred the editorial emendation "askance" which makes sense of the line "Thou canst not frown, thou canst not look askance," whereas "a sconce" makes none and must be a scribal or printing error.

KEY FACTS

MAJOR PARTS (*with percentages of lines/number of speeches/scenes on stage*): Petruchio (22%/158/8), Tranio (11%/90/8), Kate (8%/82/8), Hortensio (8%/70/8), Baptista (7%/68/6), Lucentio (7%/61/8), Grumio (6%/63/4), Gremio (6%/58/6), Lord (5%/17/2), Biondello (4%/39/7), Bianca (3%/29/7), Sly (2%/24/3), Vincentio (2%/23/3), Pedant (2%/20/3).

LINGUISTIC MEDIUM: 80% verse, 20% prose.

DATE: Usually considered to be one of Shakespeare's earliest works. Assuming that Quarto *The Taming of a Shrew*, registered for publication May 1594, is a version of the text rather than a source for it (see below), the play is likely to predate the long periods of plague closure that inhibited theatrical activity from summer 1592 onward, but there is no firm evidence for a more precise date.

SOURCES: The Induction's scenario of a beggar transported into luxury is a traditional motif in ballads and the folk tradition; the shrewish wife is also common in fabliaux and other forms of popular tale, as well as classical comedy; Socrates, wisest of the ancients, was supposed to be married to the shrewish Xanthippe; the courtship of Bianca is developed from George Gascoigne's *Supposes* (1566), itself a prose translation of Ludovico Ariosto's *I Suppositi* (1509), an archetypal Italian Renaissance comedy suffused with conventions derived from the ancient Roman comedies of Plautus and Terence. Some scholars suppose that *The Taming of a Shrew* (1594) is a badly printed text of an older play that was Shakespeare's primary source, but others regard it as an adaptation of Shakespeare's work; it includes the Christopher Sly frame, the taming of Kate (with a differently named tamer) and a highly variant version of the Bianca subplot.

TEXT: The 1623 Folio is the only authoritative text; it seems to have been set from manuscript copy, possibly a scribal transcript that retains some of the marks of Shakespeare's working manuscript. The 1594 Quarto *Taming of a Shrew* must be regarded as an autonomous work, but it provides a source for emendations on a few occasions where it corresponds closely to *The Shrew*.

THE TAMING OF
THE SHREW

LIST OF PARTS

Christopher SLY,
a drunken
beggar/tinker

A LORD

HOSTESS

A PAGE named
Bartholomew

Players

Huntsmen

Servants

⎫ in
⎬ the
⎭ Induction

BAPTISTA Minola, a gentleman of
Padua

KATE (Katherina), his elder
daughter, the "shrew"

BIANCA, his younger daughter

PETRUCHIO, a gentleman from
Verona, suitor to Kate

LUCENTIO, in love with Bianca
(disguises himself as "Cambio,"
a Latin tutor)

VINCENTIO, Lucentio's father, a
merchant from Pisa

GREMIO, an aged suitor to Bianca

HORTENSIO, friend of Petruchio and
suitor to Bianca (disguises
himself as "Litio," a music tutor)

TRANIO, Lucentio's servant

BIONDELLO, a boy in the service of
Lucentio

GRUMIO ⎫ Petruchio's
CURTIS ⎬ servants

A PEDANT

A WIDOW

A TAILOR

A HABERDASHER

Servants and Messengers
(Petruchio has servants named
NATHANIEL, JOSEPH, NICHOLAS, PHILIP,
and PETER)

[Induction] Scene 1   *running scene 1*

Enter Beggar and Hostess, [the beggar is called] Christopher Sly

SLY   I'll pheeze you, in faith.

HOSTESS   A pair of stocks, you rogue!

SLY   You're a baggage, the Slys are no rogues. Look in the
               chronicles, we came in with Richard Conqueror: therefore
5   *paucas pallabris*, let the world slide. Sessa!

HOSTESS   You will not pay for the glasses you have burst?

SLY   No, not a denier. Go by, Saint Jeronimy, go to thy
               cold bed and warm thee.

HOSTESS   I know my remedy: I must go fetch the thirdborough.
                                                              [Exit]

10 SLY   Third, or fourth, or fifth borough, I'll answer him by
               law. I'll not budge an inch, boy. Let him come, and kindly.
                                                    [He] falls asleep

Wind horns. Enter a Lord from hunting, with his train

LORD   Huntsman, I charge thee tender well my hounds.
               Brach Merriman, the poor cur is embossed,
               And couple Clowder with the deep-mouthed brach.
15   Saw'st thou not, boy, how Silver made it good
               At the hedge-corner, in the coldest fault?
               I would not lose the dog for twenty pound.

Induction Scene 1   *Location: rural England*   1 pheeze fix, get even with   **2 A . . .
stocks** i.e. I'll put you in the stocks (instrument of punishment in which the arms or legs were
confined)   **3 baggage** good-for-nothing woman, harlot   **4 chronicles** historical account
Richard Conqueror Sly may confuse Richard Coeur-de-lion (Lionheart) with William the
Conquerer   **5 *paucas pallabris*** "few words" (corruption of the Spanish)   **Sessa!** Be off! (cry
used in hunting)/be quiet   **6 burst** broken   **7 denier** tenth of a penny   **Go . . . Jeronimy** Sly
confuses Saint Jerome with Hieronimo, a character in Thomas Kyd's *The Spanish Tragedy* who
cautioned himself with "Hieronimo, beware! Go by, go by!"   **8 cold bed** perhaps a beggar's
bed, the damp ground   **9 thirdborough** parish constable   **10 by law** in court   **11 kindly** by
all means   **12 charge** order   **tender well** take good care of   **13 Brach** bitch-hound (given
that **Merriman** would seem a more suitable name for a male dog, some editors emend to
"breathe"—i.e. "give breathing space to"—thus also improving the grammar)   **cur** dog
embossed exhausted, foaming at the mouth   **14 couple** leash together   **deep-mouthed**
brach bitch with a loud bark   **15 made it good** i.e. picked up the scent   **16 coldest fault**
when the scent was lost

FIRST HUNTSMAN   Why, Belman is as good as he, my lord.
He cried upon it at the merest loss,
20   And twice today picked out the dullest scent.
Trust me, I take him for the better dog.
LORD   Thou art a fool. If Echo were as fleet,
I would esteem him worth a dozen such.
But sup them well and look unto them all:
25   Tomorrow I intend to hunt again.
FIRST HUNTSMAN   I will, my lord.
LORD   What's here? One dead, or drunk? See,   *Sees Sly*
doth he breathe?
SECOND HUNTSMAN   He breathes, my lord. Were he not warmed
with ale,
This were a bed but cold to sleep so soundly.
30   LORD   O monstrous beast, how like a swine he lies!
Grim death, how foul and loathsome is thine image.
Sirs, I will practise on this drunken man.
What think you, if he were conveyed to bed,
Wrapped in sweet clothes, rings put upon his fingers,
35   A most delicious banquet by his bed,
And brave attendants near him when he wakes,
Would not the beggar then forget himself?
FIRST HUNTSMAN   Believe me, lord, I think he cannot choose.
SECOND HUNTSMAN   It would seem strange unto him when he
waked.
40   LORD   Even as a flatt'ring dream or worthless fancy.
Then take him up and manage well the jest:
Carry him gently to my fairest chamber
And hang it round with all my wanton pictures;
Balm his foul head in warm distillèd waters

---

19 **cried . . . loss** howled upon discovering the scent when it had been completely lost
merest total   22 **fleet** swift   24 **sup** feed   **unto** after   29 **bed but cold** cold bed in which
31 **Grim . . . image** in his drunken stupor Sly resembles a corpse   32 **practise on** trick
34 **sweet** delightful/perfumed   35 **banquet** light meal   36 **brave** fine   37 **forget himself**
behave inappropriately/forget who he was   38 **cannot choose** is bound to   39 **strange**
odd/wonderful   40 **fancy** fanciful thought/imagining   43 **hang it round** adorn it   **wanton**
lively   44 **Balm** anoint, bathe   **foul** dirty/unattractive   **distillèd** fragrant

45   And burn sweet wood to make the lodging sweet:
        Procure me music ready when he wakes,
        To make a dulcet and a heavenly sound.
        And if he chance to speak, be ready straight
        And with a low submissive reverence
50   Say 'What is it your honour will command?'
        Let one attend him with a silver basin
        Full of rose-water and bestrewed with flowers,
        Another bear the ewer, the third a diaper,
        And say 'Will't please your lordship cool your hands?'
55   Someone be ready with a costly suit
        And ask him what apparel he will wear.
        Another tell him of his hounds and horse,
        And that his lady mourns at his disease.
        Persuade him that he hath been lunatic,
60   And when he says he is, say that he dreams,
        For he is nothing but a mighty lord.
        This do, and do it kindly, gentle sirs.
        It will be pastime passing excellent,
        If it be husbanded with modesty.
65 FIRST HUNTSMAN   My lord, I warrant you we will play our part,
        As he shall think by our true diligence
        He is no less than what we say he is.
    LORD   Take him up gently and to bed with   *Some carry out Sly*
            him,
        And each one to his office when he wakes.   *Sound trumpets*
70   Sirrah, go see what trumpet 'tis that sounds.
                                    [*Exit a Servingman*]
        Belike, some noble gentleman that means,
        Travelling some journey, to repose him here.
    Enter Servingman
        How now? Who is it?

---

45 **sweet** scented   47 **dulcet** sweet   48 **straight** straight away   49 **low** humble   **reverence** bow/servitude   53 **ewer** jug containing water for handwashing   **diaper** cloth   58 **disease** illness/derangement   60 **is** must be (mad)   62 **kindly** naturally   63 **passing** exceedingly   64 **husbanded** managed   **modesty** care/moderation   65 **warrant** assure   66 **As** so that   69 **office** duty, role   70 **Sirrah** sir (used to an inferior)   71 **Belike** perhaps

SERVINGMAN   An't please your honour, players
75   That offer service to your lordship.
          Enter Players
          LORD   Bid them come near.— Now, fellows, you are
             welcome.
          PLAYERS   We thank your honour.
          LORD   Do you intend to stay with me tonight?
          SECOND PLAYER   So please your lordship to accept our duty.
80   LORD   With all my heart. This fellow I remember,
             Since once he played a farmer's eldest son.
             'Twas where you wooed the gentlewoman so well:
             I have forgot your name, but, sure, that part
             Was aptly fitted and naturally performed.
85   FIRST PLAYER   I think 'twas Soto that your honour means.
          LORD   'Tis very true, thou didst it excellent.
             Well, you are come to me in happy time,
             The rather for I have some sport in hand
             Wherein your cunning can assist me much.
90   There is a lord will hear you play tonight;
             But I am doubtful of your modesties,
             Lest over-eyeing of his odd behaviour —
             For yet his honour never heard a play —
             You break into some merry passion
95   And so offend him, for I tell you, sirs,
             If you should smile he grows impatient.
          FIRST PLAYER   Fear not, my lord, we can contain ourselves
             Were he the veriest antic in the world.
          LORD   Go, sirrah, take them to the buttery,   *To a Servingman*
100   And give them friendly welcome every one.
             Let them want nothing that my house affords.
                                   Exit one with the Players

---

74 An't if it   79 So please if it please   duty services   84 fitted suited (to you)   87 happy
fortunate   88 rather for more so because   89 cunning professional skill   91 doubtful
apprehensive about   modesties propriety, self-control   92 over-eyeing of observing/staring
at   94 merry passion fit of laughter   96 impatient angry   98 veriest antic most complete
buffoon   99 buttery storeroom for provisions   101 want lack   affords has to offer

Sirrah, go you to Barthol'mew my page,
And see him dressed in all suits like a lady.
That done, conduct him to the drunkard's chamber,
105   And call him 'madam', do him obeisance.
Tell him from me, as he will win my love,
He bear himself with honourable action,
Such as he hath observed in noble ladies
Unto their lords, by them accomplishèd:
110   Such duty to the drunkard let him do
With soft low tongue and lowly courtesy,
And say, 'What is't your honour will command,
Wherein your lady and your humble wife
May show her duty and make known her love?'
115   And then with kind embracements, tempting kisses,
And with declining head into his bosom,
Bid him shed tears, as being overjoyed
To see her noble lord restored to health,
Who for this seven years hath esteemèd him
120   No better than a poor and loathsome beggar:
And if the boy have not a woman's gift
To rain a shower of commanded tears,
An onion will do well for such a shift,
Which in a napkin being close conveyed
125   Shall in despite enforce a watery eye.
See this dispatched with all the haste thou canst.
Anon I'll give thee more instructions.   *Exit a Servingman*
I know the boy will well usurp the grace,
Voice, gait and action of a gentlewoman:
130   I long to hear him call the drunkard husband,
And how my men will stay themselves from laughter

---

103 **all suits** every aspect (puns on sense of "outfits")   105 **do him obeisance** bow/be
submissive   106 **as he will** if he wishes to   107 **bear** must conduct   **honourable action**
dignified behavior   109 **by them accomplishèd** performed by them (the ladies)   110 **duty**
reverence   111 **tongue** voice   **lowly** humble   116 **with . . . bosom** bowing his head to his
chest   119 **esteemèd him** believed himself to be   122 **commanded tears** tears on command
123 **shift** purpose/trick   124 **napkin** handkerchief   **close conveyed** secretly carried   125 **in
despite** notwithstanding anything   126 **dispatched** carried out   127 **Anon** shortly
128 **usurp the grace** take on the elegance   131 **how** to see how   **stay** prevent

When they do homage to this simple peasant.
I'll in to counsel them. Haply my presence
May well abate the over-merry spleen
135   Which otherwise would grow into extremes.   [*Exeunt*]

[Induction Scene 2]   *running scene 1 continues*

Enter aloft the drunkard [Sly] with Attendants, some with apparel,
basin and ewer, and other appurtenances, and Lord

SLY   For God's sake, a pot of small ale.

FIRST SERVINGMAN   Will't please your lordship drink a cup of
sack?

SECOND SERVINGMAN   Will't please your honour taste of these
conserves?

THIRD SERVINGMAN   What raiment will your honour wear today?

5   SLY   I am Christophero Sly, call not me 'honour' nor
'lordship'. I ne'er drank sack in my life: and if you give me
any conserves, give me conserves of beef: ne'er ask me what
raiment I'll wear, for I have no more doublets than backs, no
more stockings than legs, nor no more shoes than feet —
10   nay, sometime more feet than shoes, or such shoes as my
toes look through the over-leather.

LORD   Heaven cease this idle humour in your honour!
O, that a mighty man of such descent,
Of such possessions and so high esteem,
15   Should be infusèd with so foul a spirit!

SLY   What, would you make me mad? Am not I
Christopher Sly, old Sly's son of Burtonheath, by birth a

---

133 in go in   Haply perhaps/hopefully   134 spleen i.e. mood, impulse (the spleen was
thought to be the seat of laughter)   **Induction Scene 2**   *running scene 1 continues*
most editions assume a shift of location from "outside an ale-house" to "a bedroom in the lord's
house," but the text suggests that the location of the whole induction is the lord's house, the
only move being from outside (the main stage) to the bedroom (above space)   1 small weak
(hence cheap)   2 sack Spanish white wine   3 conserves confections, sweetmeats
4 raiment clothing   7 conserves of beef salted beef   8 doublets close-fitting jackets
11 look . . . over-leather i.e. peep through holes   12 idle humour mad whim   15 spirit
temperament/mood/fiend   17 Burtonheath possibly Barton-on-the-heath, a village near
Stratford-upon-Avon

pedlar, by education a cardmaker, by transmutation a bear-
herd, and now by present profession a tinker? Ask Marian
20   Hacket, the fat ale-wife of Wincot, if she know me not: if she
say I am not fourteen pence on the score for sheer ale, score
me up for the lying'st knave in Christendom. What, I am not
bestraught! Here's—

THIRD SERVINGMAN   O, this it is that makes your lady mourn!
25   SECOND SERVINGMAN   O, this is it that makes your servants droop!
LORD   Hence comes it that your kindred shuns your house,
As beaten hence by your strange lunacy.
O noble lord, bethink thee of thy birth,
Call home thy ancient thoughts from banishment
30   And banish hence these abject lowly dreams.
Look how thy servants do attend on thee,
Each in his office ready at thy beck.
Wilt thou have music? Hark! Apollo plays,   *Music*
And twenty cagèd nightingales do sing.
35   Or wilt thou sleep? We'll have thee to a couch
Softer and sweeter than the lustful bed
On purpose trimmed up for Semiramis.
Say thou wilt walk, we will bestrow the ground.
Or wilt thou ride? Thy horses shall be trapped,
40   Their harness studded all with gold and pearl.
Dost thou love hawking? Thou hast hawks will soar
Above the morning lark. Or wilt thou hunt?
Thy hounds shall make the welkin answer them
And fetch shrill echoes from the hollow earth.

---

18 **cardmaker** maker of cards, instruments for combing wool   **transmutation** change of
condition   **bear-herd** keeper of a performing bear   19 **tinker** pot-mender   20 **ale-wife**
woman who keeps an ale-house   **Wincot** village four miles south of Stratford-upon-Avon
21 **on the score** in debt   **score** tally kept by marking notches on a piece of wood   **sheer**
weak/drunk without food   **score . . . for** reckon me to be   23 **bestraught** out of my mind
25 **droop** become despondent   27 **As** as if   29 **ancient** former   30 **dreams** delusions
33 **Apollo** Greek god of music   36 **lustful** arousing desire   37 **trimmed up** decked out
Semiramis legendary queen of Assyria, famous for her voluptuousness   38 **bestrow** scatter
(probably with rushes)   39 **trapped** adorned/fitted out   41 **hawking** hunting with hawks
43 **welkin** sky

45   FIRST SERVINGMAN   Say thou wilt course, thy greyhounds are as
          swift
       As breathèd stags, ay, fleeter than the roe.
       SECOND SERVINGMAN   Dost thou love pictures? We will fetch thee
          straight
       Adonis painted by a running brook,
       And Cytherea all in sedges hid,
50   Which seem to move and wanton with her breath,
       Even as the waving sedges play with wind.
       LORD   We'll show thee Io as she was a maid,
       And how she was beguilèd and surprised,
       As lively painted as the deed was done.
55   THIRD SERVINGMAN   Or Daphne roaming through a thorny wood,
       Scratching her legs that one shall swear she bleeds,
       And at that sight shall sad Apollo weep,
       So workmanly the blood and tears are drawn.
       LORD   Thou art a lord, and nothing but a lord.
60   Thou hast a lady far more beautiful
       Than any woman in this waning age.
       FIRST SERVINGMAN   And till the tears that she hath shed for thee
       Like envious floods o'errun her lovely face,
       She was the fairest creature in the world,
65   And yet she is inferior to none.
       SLY   Am I a lord? And have I such a lady?
       Or do I dream? Or have I dreamed till now?
       I do not sleep: I see, I hear, I speak,
       I smell sweet savours and I feel soft things.
70   Upon my life, I am a lord indeed

---

45 course hunt the hare   **46 breathèd** exercised, strong-winded   **roe** small deer   **48 Adonis**
in classical mythology, a beautiful huntsman, pursued by **Cytherea** (Venus); when he was
killed by a boar while hunting, she changed him into an anemone   **49 Cytherea** more
commonly known as Venus, the goddess of love   **sedges** coarse grass growing by rivers
50 wanton grow playful/flourishing/lustful   **52 Io** in classical myth, a girl raped by Jove/
Jupiter, then turned into a heifer   **maid** virgin   **53 beguilèd** bewitched/deceived   **surprised**
attacked   **54 lively** lifelike   **55 Daphne** in classical mythology, a girl pursued by the god
Apollo; she prayed for help and was turned into a laurel tree   **58 workmanly** skillfully
61 waning degenerate/declining from the perfection of Eden   **63 envious** cruel   **65 yet** even
now

And not a tinker nor Christopher Sly.
Well, bring our lady hither to our sight,
And once again, a pot o'th'smallest ale.

SECOND SERVINGMAN   Will't please your mightiness to wash your
hands?

75   O, how we joy to see your wit restored!
O, that once more you knew but what you are!
These fifteen years you have been in a dream,
Or when you waked, so waked as if you slept.

SLY   These fifteen years! By my fay, a goodly nap.

80   But did I never speak of all that time?

FIRST SERVINGMAN   O, yes, my lord, but very idle words,
For though you lay here in this goodly chamber,
Yet would you say ye were beaten out of door,
And rail upon the hostess of the house,

85   And say you would present her at the leet,
Because she brought stone jugs and no sealed quarts:
Sometimes you would call out for Cicely Hacket.

SLY   Ay, the woman's maid of the house.

THIRD SERVINGMAN   Why, sir, you know no house nor no such
maid,

90   Nor no such men as you have reckoned up,
As Stephen Sly and old John Naps of Greece
And Peter Turph and Henry Pimpernell
And twenty more such names and men as these
Which never were nor no man ever saw.

95   SLY   Now lord be thankèd for my good amends!

ALL   Amen.

Enter [the Page dressed as a] lady, with Attendants

SLY   I thank thee. Thou shalt not lose by it.

PAGE   How fares my noble lord?

---

75 **wit** senses   76 **knew but** only knew   79 **fay** faith   80 **of** in   84 **rail upon** rant, complain
about   **hostess . . . house** landlady of the inn   85 **present . . . leet** bring accusations
against her at the manorial court (**leet**)   86 **stone . . . quarts** unlike **sealed quarts, stone jugs**
had no official mark upon them guaranteeing they contained the specified amount of ale
88 **woman's . . . house** landlady's maid   90 **reckoned up** listed   91 **Greece** possibly a
corruption of "Greet," a small village not far from Stratford   95 **amends** recovery

SLY   Marry, I fare well, for here is cheer enough. Where
       is my wife?
100   PAGE   Here, noble lord. What is thy will with her?
      SLY   Are you my wife and will not call me husband?
      My men should call me 'lord'. I am your goodman.
      PAGE   My husband and my lord, my lord and husband,
      I am your wife in all obedience.
105   SLY   I know it well.— What must I call her?
      LORD   Madam.
      SLY   Al'ce madam, or Joan madam?
      LORD   'Madam', and nothing else. So lords call ladies.
      SLY   Madam wife, they say that I have dreamed
110   And slept above some fifteen year or more.
      PAGE   Ay, and the time seems thirty unto me,
      Being all this time abandoned from your bed.
      SLY   'Tis much. Servants, leave me and her alone.
                                             [*Exeunt Attendants*]
      Madam, undress you and come now to bed.
115   PAGE   Thrice-noble lord, let me entreat of you
      To pardon me yet for a night or two,
      Or, if not so, until the sun be set.
      For your physicians have expressly charged,
      In peril to incur your former malady,
120   That I should yet absent me from your bed:
      I hope this reason stands for my excuse.
      SLY   Ay, it stands so that I may hardly tarry so long. But I
      would be loath to fall into my dreams again. I will therefore
      tarry in despite of the flesh and the blood.
      Enter a Messenger
125   MESSENGER   Your honour's players, hearing your amendment,
      Are come to play a pleasant comedy,

---

99 **Marry** by the Virgin Mary   **fare** am getting along (plays on the sense of "food and drink")
cheer hospitality (plays on the sense of "food and drink")   102 **goodman** husband
107 **Al'ce** Alice   112 **abandoned** banished   119 **In . . . malady** due to the risk of bringing on
your old illness   121 **stands for** is valid as   122 **it stands** my penis is erect   **hardly** plays on
the idea of erectile hardness   124 **despite** spite   126 **pleasant** merry

For so your doctors hold it very meet,
Seeing too much sadness hath congealed your blood,
And melancholy is the nurse of frenzy:
130   Therefore they thought it good you hear a play
And frame your mind to mirth and merriment,
Which bars a thousand harms and lengthens life.

SLY   Marry, I will, let them play it. Is not a comonty a
Christmas gambold or a tumbling trick?

135   PAGE   No, my good lord, it is more pleasing stuff.

SLY   What, household stuff?

PAGE   It is a kind of history.

SLY   Well, we'll see't. Come, madam wife, sit by my side
and let the world slip, we shall ne'er be younger.   *They sit*

Flourish

[Act 1 Scene 1]   *running scene 2*

Enter Lucentio and his man Tranio

LUCENTIO   Tranio, since for the great desire I had
To see fair Padua, nursery of arts,
I am arrived for fruitful Lombardy,
The pleasant garden of great Italy,
5   And by my father's love and leave am armed
With his good will and thy good company,
My trusty servant, well approved in all,
Here let us breathe and haply institute
A course of learning and ingenious studies.
10   Pisa, renownèd for grave citizens,

---

127 **meet** fitting   131 **frame** adjust   132 **bars** prevents   133 **comonty . . . gambold** Sly's
mispronunciation of "comedy" and "gambol" (entertainment)   134 **tumbling trick** acrobatic
trick   135 **stuff** matter (Sly responds to the literal sense of "furnishings")   137 **history** story
139 **slip** slide by   **1.1**   *Location: Padua   Lucentio* name suggests "light," making him a
fitting partner for "Bianca" (the white/fair)   2 **Padua** city in northern Italy   **nursery**
training ground (the university of Padua was one of the oldest in Europe)   3 **for** in
Lombardy Padua is not in Lombardy, which is probably, however, intended here to denote all of
northern Italy   5 **leave** permission   7 **approved** tested, proved   8 **breathe** rest   **haply**
perhaps/fortunately   **institute** begin   9 **ingenious** intellectual   10 **grave** learned

Gave me my being and my father first,
A merchant of great traffic through the world,
Vincentio come of the Bentivolii.
Vincentio's son, brought up in Florence,
15   It shall become to serve all hopes conceived,
To deck his fortune with his virtuous deeds:
And therefore, Tranio, for the time I study,
Virtue and that part of philosophy
Will I apply that treats of happiness
20   By virtue specially to be achieved.
Tell me thy mind, for I have Pisa left
And am to Padua come, as he that leaves
A shallow plash to plunge him in the deep
And with satiety seeks to quench his thirst.
25   TRANIO   *Mi perdonato*, gentle master mine.
I am in all affected as yourself,
Glad that you thus continue your resolve
To suck the sweets of sweet philosophy.
Only, good master, while we do admire
30   This virtue and this moral discipline,
Let's be no stoics nor no stocks, I pray,
Or so devote to Aristotle's checks
As Ovid be an outcast quite abjured.
Balk logic with acquaintance that you have
35   And practise rhetoric in your common talk,
Music and poesy use to quicken you;
The mathematics and the metaphysics,
Fall to them as you find your stomach serves you.

---

11 **Gave . . . first** i.e. both I and my father were born there   12 **great traffic** extensive trade
13 **come of** descended from   **Bentivolii** a powerful Italian family who were, in fact, from
Bologna rather than Pisa   14 **Vincentio's . . . deeds** it is appropriate that Vincentio's son,
who was brought up in Florence, should fulfill the expectations of him by adding to his fortune
with acts of virtue   19 **treats of** concerns   23 **plash** pool   24 **satiety** excess   25 *Mi*
perdonato "pardon me" (Italian)   26 **affected** disposed   31 **stoics** rigorous individuals
practicing abstinence and endurance   **stocks** stupid, senseless people   32 **Aristotle** Greek
philosopher   **checks** recommendations of moral restraint   33 **As** that   **Ovid** Roman poet,
author of *The Art of Love*   **abjured** rejected   34 **Balk** argue, quibble over   35 **common**
everyday   36 **quicken** enliven   38 **Fall** to apply yourself/begin eating   **stomach serves you**
inclination/appetite requires

No profit grows where is no pleasure ta'en:
40   In brief, sir, study what you most affect.
LUCENTIO   Gramercies, Tranio, well dost thou advise.
If, Biondello, thou wert come ashore,
We could at once put us in readiness,
And take a lodging fit to entertain
45   Such friends as time in Padua shall beget.
But stay a while, what company is this?
TRANIO   Master, some show to welcome us to town.

Enter Baptista with his two daughters, Katherina and Bianca, Gremio
a pantaloon, Hortensio suitor to Bianca. Lucentio [and] Tranio stand by

BAPTISTA   Gentlemen, importune me no farther,
For how I firmly am resolved you know:
50   That is, not to bestow my youngest daughter
Before I have a husband for the elder.
If either of you both love Katherina,
Because I know you well and love you well,
Leave shall you have to court her at your pleasure.
55   GREMIO   To cart her rather. She's too rough for me.   *Aside?*
There, there, Hortensio, will you any wife?
KATE   I pray you, sir, is it your will   *To Baptista*
To make a stale of me amongst these mates?
HORTENSIO   'Mates', maid? How mean you that? No mates for
you,
60   Unless you were of gentler, milder mould.
KATE   I'faith, sir, you shall never need to fear:
Iwis it is not halfway to her heart.
But if it were, doubt not her care should be

---

39 No . . . ta'en a version of Horace's famous statement that "he who has mixed usefulness
with pleasure has gained every point"   40 affect like   41 Gramercies many thanks
42 wert were to   45 beget create   *Bianca* Italian for "white"   *pantaloon* in Italian comedy,
the foolish old man   48 importune urge   50 bestow give in marriage   55 cart her drive
her around in a cart (usual punishment for a prostitute)   rough violent/uncontrollable
56 will you do you want   58 stale bait/laughing-stock/prostitute (puns on the chess term
"stalemate")   mates fellows (plays on the sense of "husbands")   62 Iwis indeed   not . . .
heart i.e. marriage is not something I even consider   63 her care my chief desire

To comb your noddle with a three-legged stool
65   And paint your face and use you like a fool.

HORTENSIO   From all such devils, good lord deliver us!

GREMIO   And me too, good lord!

TRANIO   Husht, master! Here's some good   *Aside to Lucentio*
pastime toward;
That wench is stark mad or wonderful froward.

70   LUCENTIO   But in the other's silence do I see   *Aside to Tranio*
Maid's mild behaviour and sobriety.
Peace, Tranio!

TRANIO   Well said, master. Mum, and gaze   *Aside to Lucentio*
your fill.

BAPTISTA   Gentlemen, that I may soon make good
75   What I have said, Bianca, get you in,
And let it not displease thee, good Bianca,
For I will love thee ne'er the less, my girl.

KATE   A pretty peat! It is best
Put finger in the eye, an she knew why.

80   BIANCA   Sister, content you in my discontent.
Sir, to your pleasure humbly I subscribe:
My books and instruments shall be my company,
On them to look and practise by myself.

LUCENTIO   Hark, Tranio, thou may'st hear Minerva speak.

85   HORTENSIO   Signior Baptista, will you be so strange?
Sorry am I that our good will effects
Bianca's grief.

GREMIO   Why will you mew her up,
Signior Baptista, for this fiend of hell,
90   And make her bear the penance of her tongue?

BAPTISTA   Gentlemen, content ye, I am resolved.—
Go in, Bianca.—   [*Exit Bianca*]

---

64 noddle head   65 paint i.e. redden with scratching   use treat   68 toward about to begin
69 wonderful froward remarkably obstinate   73 Mum hush   78 peat pet   79 Put . . . why
make herself cry if she could think of an excuse   80 content you be satisfied   81 pleasure
will   subscribe submit   84 Minerva goddess of wisdom   85 strange distant, unfriendly
86 effects causes   88 mew her up confine her   89 for on account of   90 her i.e. Bianca
her i.e. Kate's (sharp)

And for I know she taketh most delight
In music, instruments and poetry,
95 Schoolmasters will I keep within my house
Fit to instruct her youth. If you, Hortensio,
Or Signior Gremio, you, know any such,
Prefer them hither, for to cunning men
I will be very kind, and liberal
100 To mine own children in good bringing up.
And so farewell.— Katherina, you may stay,
For I have more to commune with Bianca.   *Exit*

KATE   Why, and I trust I may go too, may I not? What,
shall I be appointed hours, as though, belike, I knew not
105 what to take and what to leave? Ha?   *Exit*

GREMIO   You may go to the devil's dam. Your gifts are so
good, here's none will hold you.— Their love is not so great,
Hortensio, but we may blow our nails together, and fast it
fairly out. Our cake's dough on both sides. Farewell. Yet for
110 the love I bear my sweet Bianca, if I can by any means light
on a fit man to teach her that wherein she delights, I will
wish him to her father.

HORTENSIO   So will I, Signior Gremio. But a word, I pray.
Though the nature of our quarrel yet never brooked parle,
115 know now, upon advice, it toucheth us both — that we may
yet again have access to our fair mistress and be happy rivals
in Bianca's love — to labour and effect one thing specially.

GREMIO   What's that, I pray?

HORTENSIO   Marry, sir, to get a husband for her sister.

120 GREMIO   A husband? A devil.

HORTENSIO   I say a husband.

---

93 for because   98 Prefer recommend   cunning skillful   102 commune discuss
104 appointed hours given a timetable   belike perhaps   106 dam mother   gifts qualities
(ironic)   107 here's . . . you no one here will detain you   Their love i.e. women's love
108 blow our nails wait patiently/waste time   fast . . . out manage to survive/endure it as
cordially as we can   109 Our . . . sides i.e. we have both failed   110 light on come across
112 wish recommend   114 brooked parle tolerated conversation/negotiation   115 advice
consideration   toucheth concerns   117 labour and effect work for and bring about

GREMIO   I say a devil. Think'st thou, Hortensio, though her
father be very rich, any man is so very a fool to be married to
hell?

125   HORTENSIO   Tush, Gremio, though it pass your patience and
mine to endure her loud alarums, why, man, there be good
fellows in the world, an a man could light on them, would
take her with all faults, and money enough.

GREMIO   I cannot tell, but I had as lief take her dowry with
130   this condition: to be whipped at the high cross every
morning.

HORTENSIO   Faith, as you say, there's small choice in rotten
apples. But come, since this bar in law makes us friends, it
shall be so far forth friendly maintained till by helping
135   Baptista's eldest daughter to a husband we set his youngest
free for a husband, and then have to't afresh. Sweet Bianca!
Happy man be his dole! He that runs fastest gets the ring.
How say you, Signior Gremio?

GREMIO   I am agreed, and would I had given him the best
140   horse in Padua to begin his wooing that would thoroughly
woo her, wed her and bed her and rid the house of her!
Come on.   *Exeunt both [Gremio and Hortensio].*

Tranio and Lucentio remain

TRANIO   I pray, sir, tell me, is it possible
That love should of a sudden take such hold?

145   LUCENTIO   O Tranio, till I found it to be true,
I never thought it possible or likely.
But see, while idly I stood looking on,
I found the effect of love in idleness,
And now in plainness do confess to thee,
150   That art to me as secret and as dear

---

125 pass surpass   126 alarums noise (literally, a military call to arms)   127 an if   129 had
as lief would as willingly   130 high cross cross set on a pedestal in the town center   133 bar
in law legal impediment (i.e. Baptista's refusal to let Bianca marry until Kate is married)
it . . . maintained it shall progress in a friendly manner   136 have to't afresh renew our
combat once again   137 Happy . . . dole! Happiness to the winner! (proverbial)   ring alludes
to the jousting game in which competitors tried to lift a ring with their lances (puns on senses
of "wedding ring" and "vagina")   148 love in idleness puns on "love-in-idleness," a pansy
thought to have power to stimulate love   150 secret trusted

As Anna to the Queen of Carthage was,
Tranio, I burn, I pine, I perish, Tranio,
If I achieve not this young modest girl.
Counsel me, Tranio, for I know thou canst.

155   Assist me, Tranio, for I know thou wilt.

TRANIO   Master, it is no time to chide you now.
Affection is not rated from the heart:
If love have touched you, naught remains but so,
Redime te captum quam queas minimo.

160   LUCENTIO   Gramercies, lad. Go forward. This contents:
The rest will comfort, for thy counsel's sound.

TRANIO   Master, you looked so longly on the maid,
Perhaps you marked not what's the pith of all.

LUCENTIO   O, yes, I saw sweet beauty in her face,
165   Such as the daughter of Agenor had,
That made great Jove to humble him to her hand.
When with his knees he kissed the Cretan strand.

TRANIO   Saw you no more? Marked you not how her sister
Began to scold and raise up such a storm
170   That mortal ears might hardly endure the din?

LUCENTIO   Tranio, I saw her coral lips to move
And with her breath she did perfume the air.
Sacred and sweet was all I saw in her.

TRANIO   Nay, then, 'tis time to stir him from his   *Aside*
trance.—
175   I pray, awake, sir. If you love the maid,
Bend thoughts and wits to achieve her. Thus it stands:
Her elder sister is so curst and shrewd

---

151 **Anna . . . Carthage** Dido, Queen of Carthage, confided in her sister Anna that she was in love with Aeneas   157 **rated** driven out through rebuke   159 *Redime . . . minimo* "free yourself from bondage for as little ransom as you can" (Latin, inaccurately quoted, as in the standard Elizabethan grammar textbook, from Terence's play *Eunuchus*)   160 **Go forward** carry on   **This** i.e. what you have said so far   162 **so longly** for such a long time/so longingly   163 **marked not** did not notice   **pith** essence   165 **daughter of Agenor** Europa, daughter of the King of Tyre; she was loved by Jove, who turned himself into a bull in order to abduct her   166 **him** himself   167 **kissed** i.e. knelt on   **Cretan strand** shore of Crete (in fact, Europa was taken to, rather than from, Crete)   176 **Bend** apply, direct   177 **curst** bad-tempered   **shrewd** shrewish, disagreeable

That till the father rid his hands of her,
Master, your love must live a maid at home,
180 And therefore has he closely mewed her up,
Because she will not be annoyed with suitors.
LUCENTIO   Ah, Tranio, what a cruel father's he!
But art thou not advised he took some care
To get her cunning schoolmasters to instruct her?
185 TRANIO   Ay, marry, am I, sir, and now 'tis plotted.
LUCENTIO   I have it, Tranio.
TRANIO   Master, for my hand,
Both our inventions meet and jump in one.
LUCENTIO   Tell me thine first.
190 TRANIO   You will be schoolmaster
And undertake the teaching of the maid:
That's your device.
LUCENTIO   It is; may it be done?
TRANIO   Not possible, for who shall bear your part,
195 And be in Padua here Vincentio's son,
Keep house and ply his book, welcome his friends,
Visit his countrymen and banquet them?
LUCENTIO   *Basta,* content thee, for I have it full.
We have not yet been seen in any house,
200 Nor can we be distinguished by our faces
For man or master. Then it follows thus:
Thou shalt be master, Tranio, in my stead,
Keep house and port and servants as I should.
I will some other be, some Florentine,
205 Some Neapolitan, or meaner man of Pisa.
'Tis hatched and shall be so. Tranio, at once
Uncase thee: take my coloured hat and   *They exchange clothes*
cloak.

179 maid unmarried virgin   180 closely securely   181 annoyed vexed/distracted
183 advised aware   187 for my hand by my hand/for my part   188 inventions meet plans
agree   jump coincide   192 device plot   194 bear play   196 Keep house entertain   ply
his book study   198 *Basta* "enough" (Italian)   full in full   203 port position, dignity
205 meaner lower-ranking   207 Uncase undress   coloured as opposed to the plainer, often
blue, livery worn by Elizabethan servants

When Biondello comes, he waits on thee,
But I will charm him first to keep his tongue.

210 TRANIO   So had you need.
In brief, sir, sith it your pleasure is,
And I am tied to be obedient —
For so your father charged me at our parting,
'Be serviceable to my son', quoth he,
215 Although I think 'twas in another sense —
I am content to be Lucentio,
Because so well I love Lucentio.

LUCENTIO   Tranio, be so, because Lucentio loves.
And let me be a slave, t'achieve that maid
220 Whose sudden sight hath thralled my wounded eye.

Enter Biondello

Here comes the rogue. Sirrah, where have you been?

BIONDELLO   Where have I been? Nay, how now? Where are you?
Master, has my fellow Tranio stolen your clothes? Or you
stolen his? Or both? Pray, what's the news?

225 LUCENTIO   Sirrah, come hither. 'Tis no time to jest,
And therefore frame your manners to the time.
Your fellow Tranio here, to save my life,
Puts my apparel and my count'nance on,
And I for my escape have put on his,
230 For in a quarrel since I came ashore
I killed a man, and fear I was descried.
Wait you on him, I charge you, as becomes,
While I make way from hence to save my life.
You understand me?

235 BIONDELLO   I, sir? Ne'er a whit.

LUCENTIO   And not a jot of Tranio in your mouth.
Tranio is changed into Lucentio.

BIONDELLO   The better for him. Would I were so too!

---

209 **charm** persuade   211 **sith** since   212 **tied** obliged   213 **charged** instructed
220 **Whose sudden sight** the sudden sight of whom   **thralled** enslaved   **wounded** i.e.
pierced by Cupid's arrow   226 **frame** fit   228 **count'nance** manner/appearance
231 **descried** witnessed/denounced   232 **becomes** is suitable

TRANIO   So could I, faith, boy, to have the next wish after,
240   That Lucentio indeed had Baptista's youngest daughter.
    But, sirrah, not for my sake, but your master's, I advise
    You use your manners discreetly in all kind of companies:
    When I am alone, why, then I am Tranio,
    But in all places else your master Lucentio.
245 LUCENTIO   Tranio, let's go. One thing more rests that thyself
    execute: to make one among these wooers. If thou ask me
    why, sufficeth my reasons are both good and weighty.

Exeunt

The Presenters above speak

FIRST SERVINGMAN   My lord, you nod. You do not mind the play.

SLY   Yes, by Saint Anne, do I. A good matter, surely.
250   Comes there any more of it?

PAGE   My lord, 'tis but begun.

SLY   'Tis a very excellent piece of work, madam lady.
    Would 'twere done!   *They sit and mark*

[Act 1 Scene 2]   *running scene 2 continues*

Enter Petruchio and his man Grumio

PETRUCHIO   Verona, for a while I take my leave,
    To see my friends in Padua; but of all
    My best belovèd and approvèd friend,
    Hortensio, and I trow this is his house.
5   Here, sirrah Grumio, knock, I say.

GRUMIO   Knock, sir? Whom should I knock? Is there any man
    has rebused your worship?

PETRUCHIO   Villain, I say, knock me here soundly.

GRUMIO   Knock you here, sir? Why, sir, what am I, sir, that I
10   should knock you here, sir?

---

242 **discreetly** prudently   245 **rests** remains   **that thyself execute** which is for you to carry out   246 **make** become   247 **sufficeth** let it suffice   *Presenters above* i.e. the remaining characters from the Induction   248 **mind** attend to   249 **matter** subject   253 **Would** I wish *mark* attend, observe   **1.2**   *Grumio* connotations of "groom"—i.e. servingman   1 **Verona** city in northern Italy   2 **of all** especially   4 **trow** know/believe   6 **knock** Grumio plays on the sense of "strike (a person)"   7 **rebused** malapropism for "abused"

PETRUCHIO   Villain, I say, knock me at this gate
And rap me well, or I'll knock your knave's pate.

GRUMIO   My master is grown quarrelsome. I should knock
you first,
And then I know after who comes by the worst.

15 PETRUCHIO   Will it not be?
Faith, sirrah, an you'll not knock, I'll ring it.
I'll try how you can *sol-fa* and sing it.

He wrings him by the ears

GRUMIO   Help, mistress, help! My master is mad.

PETRUCHIO   Now, knock when I bid you, sirrah villain.

Enter Hortensio

20 HORTENSIO   How now? What's the matter? My old friend Grumio
and my good friend Petruchio? How do you all at Verona?

PETRUCHIO   Signior Hortensio, come you to part the fray?
Con tutto il cuore, ben trovato, may I say.

HORTENSIO   *Alla nostra casa ben venuto, molto honorata signor*
25 *mio* Petruchio. Rise, Grumio, rise. We will compound this
quarrel.

GRUMIO   Nay, 'tis no matter, sir, what he 'leges in Latin. If this
be not a lawful cause for me to leave his service, look you, sir:
he bid me knock him and rap him soundly, sir. Well, was it fit
30 for a servant to use his master so, being perhaps, for aught I
see, two and thirty, a pip out?
Whom would to God I had well knocked at first,
Then had not Grumio come by the worst.

---

11 **Villain** wicked one/servant   **me** for me   **gate** door   12 **pate** head   13 **I . . . worst** if I hit
you first I know that I shall come off the worst for it   16 **ring** i.e. with a circular knocker or
bell; puns on "wring"   17 **I'll . . . it** i.e. I'll see how you can shriek   *sol-fa* sing a scale
18 **mistress** some editors emend to "masters"   21 **How . . . all** what are you both doing
23 *Con . . . trovato* "with all my heart well met" (Italian)   24 *Alla . . .* Petruchio "Welcome
to our house, most worshipful Petruchio" (Italian)   25 **compound** settle   27 **'leges** alleges
in Latin despite his Italian name, Grumio does not know the difference between Latin and
Italian   30 **use** treat   **aught** anything   31 **two . . . out** i.e. overshooting the mark/not in
his right mind/drunk (thirty-one was a card game, the object of which was to collect cards
with a total value of thirty-one; it was also a term for being drunk)   **pip** one of the spots on a
card

PETRUCHIO   A senseless villain! Good Hortensio,
35   I bade the rascal knock upon your gate
And could not get him for my heart to do it.
GRUMIO   Knock at the gate? O heavens! Spake you not these
words plain, 'Sirrah, knock me here, rap me here, knock me
well, and knock me soundly'? And come you now with,
40   'knocking at the gate'?
PETRUCHIO   Sirrah, be gone, or talk not, I advise you.
HORTENSIO   Petruchio, patience. I am Grumio's pledge.
Why, this' a heavy chance 'twixt him and you,
Your ancient, trusty, pleasant servant Grumio.
45   And tell me now, sweet friend, what happy gale
Blows you to Padua here from old Verona?
PETRUCHIO   Such wind as scatters young men through the
world,
To seek their fortunes further than at home
Where small experience grows. But in a few,
50   Signior Hortensio, thus it stands with me:
Antonio, my father, is deceased,
And I have thrust myself into this maze,
Happily to wive and thrive as best I may.
Crowns in my purse I have and goods at home,
55   And so am come abroad to see the world.
HORTENSIO   Petruchio, shall I then come roundly to thee
And wish thee to a shrewd ill-favoured wife?
Thou'ldst thank me but a little for my counsel.
And yet I'll promise thee she shall be rich,
60   And very rich. But thou'rt too much my friend,
And I'll not wish thee to her.
PETRUCHIO   Signior Hortensio, 'twixt such friends as we
Few words suffice: and therefore, if thou know
One rich enough to be Petruchio's wife —

---

36 heart i.e. life   42 pledge guarantor   43 this' this is   heavy chance sad situation
44 ancient long-standing   45 happy fortunate   49 in a few briefly   53 wive marry
54 Crowns gold coins   56 come roundly speak plainly   57 wish commend   ill-favoured
foul-tempered   58 Thou'ldst you would

65   As wealth is burden of my wooing dance —
        Be she as foul as was Florentius' love,
        As old as Sibyl and as curst and shrewd
        As Socrates' Xanthippe, or a worse,
        She moves me not, or not removes, at least,
70   Affection's edge in me, were she as rough
        As are the swelling Adriatic seas.
        I come to wive it wealthily in Padua,
        If wealthily, then happily in Padua.
GRUMIO   Nay, look you, sir, he tells you flatly what his mind
75   is. Why, give him gold enough and marry him to a puppet or
        an aglet-baby; or an old trot with ne'er a tooth in her head,
        though she have as many diseases as two and fifty horses.
        Why, nothing comes amiss, so money comes withal.
HORTENSIO   Petruchio, since we are stepped thus far in,
80   I will continue that I broached in jest.
        I can, Petruchio, help thee to a wife
        With wealth enough and young and beauteous,
        Brought up as best becomes a gentlewoman.
        Her only fault, and that is faults enough,
85   Is that she is intolerable curst
        And shrewd and froward, so beyond all measure
        That, were my state far worser than it is,
        I would not wed her for a mine of gold.
PETRUCHIO   Hortensio, peace! Thou know'st not gold's effect.
90   Tell me her father's name and 'tis enough,
        For I will board her, though she chide as loud
        As thunder when the clouds in autumn crack.

---

65 burden refrain/bass accompaniment (in a song)   66 Florentius' love in Gower's *Confessio*
Amantis Florentius is a knight who agrees to marry an ugly hag if she helps him solve the
riddle on which his life depends   67 Sibyl ancient prophetess; in classical mythology, Apollo
gave the Sibyl of Cumae as many years of life as she held grains of sand in her hand, but he did
not grant her accompanying youth   68 Xanthippe wife of Socrates, notorious for her bad
temper   69 moves me not does not affect me   not . . . me cannot blunt the edge of my
desire   74 mind opinion/intention   76 aglet-baby small figure ornamenting the tag of a
lace or cord   trot hag   78 so . . . withal so long as money comes with it   79 are . . . in have
gone this far   80 that I broached what I began   85 intolerable intolerably   87 state
financial situation   91 board accost (naval metaphor referring to attacking a ship; plays on
the sense of "have sex with")   92 crack roar, explode

HORTENSIO   Her father is Baptista Minola,
An affable and courteous gentleman.
95   Her name is Katherina Minola,
Renowned in Padua for her scolding tongue.
PETRUCHIO   I know her father, though I know not her,
And he knew my deceasèd father well.
I will not sleep, Hortensio, till I see her,
100   And therefore let me be thus bold with you
To give you over at this first encounter,
Unless you will accompany me thither.
GRUMIO   I pray you, sir, let him go while the humour lasts. O'
my word, an she knew him as well as I do, she would think
105   scolding would do little good upon him. She may perhaps
call him half a score knaves or so. Why, that's nothing; an he
begin once, he'll rail in his rope-tricks. I'll tell you what, sir,
an she stand him but a little, he will throw a figure in her
face and so disfigure her with it that she shall have no more
110   eyes to see withal than a cat. You know him not, sir.
HORTENSIO   Tarry, Petruchio, I must go with thee,
For in Baptista's keep my treasure is:
He hath the jewel of my life in hold,
His youngest daughter, beautiful Bianca,
115   And her withholds from me and other more,
Suitors to her and rivals in my love,
Supposing it a thing impossible,
For those defects I have before rehearsed,
That ever Katherina will be wooed:
120   Therefore this order hath Baptista ta'en,
That none shall have access unto Bianca
Till Katherine the curst have got a husband.

---

101 give you over leave you   **103 humour** whim   **O'** on   **104 an** if   **106 half a score** ten
107 rail rant   **rope-tricks** possibly Grumio's version of "rhetoric" or "rope rhetoric," or
implying tricks deserving of punishment by hanging   **108 stand** resist, withstand   **figure**
figure of speech/rhetorical trick   **110 withal** with   **112 keep** safe-keeping (literally, fortified
tower)   **treasure** plays on the sense of "(Bianca's) vagina"   **113 hold** custody   **115 other**
more others besides   **118 defects** faults   **rehearsed** related   **120 order** measure

GRUMIO   Katherine the curst!
A title for a maid of all titles the worst.
125 HORTENSIO   Now shall my friend Petruchio do me grace,
And offer me disguised in sober robes
To old Baptista as a schoolmaster
Well seen in music, to instruct Bianca,
That so I may by this device at least
130 Have leave and leisure to make love to her
And unsuspected court her by herself.

Enter Gremio and Lucentio disguised

GRUMIO   Here's no knavery! See, to beguile the old folks, how
the young folks lay their heads together! Master, master, look
about you. Who goes there, ha?
135 HORTENSIO   Peace, Grumio, it is the rival of my love.
Petruchio, stand by a while.   *They stand aside*
GRUMIO   A proper stripling and an amorous!   *Aside*
GREMIO   O, very well, I have perused the note.   *To Lucentio*
Hark you, sir, I'll have them very fairly bound —
140 All books of love, see that at any hand —
And see you read no other lectures to her.
You understand me. Over and beside
Signior Baptista's liberality,
I'll mend it with a largesse. Take your paper too,   *Gives Lucentio*
145 And let me have them very well perfumed,   *the note*
For she is sweeter than perfume itself
To whom they go to. What will you read to her?
LUCENTIO   Whate'er I read to her, I'll plead for you
As for my patron, stand you so assured,
150 As firmly as yourself were still in place —
Yea, and perhaps with more successful words
Than you, unless you were a scholar, sir.

---

125 grace favor   **128 seen** skilled   **130 make love to** woo/seduce   **132 Here's no knavery!**
i.e. this does not look like a trick (sarcastic)   **beguile** deceive   **137 proper stripling** fine,
handsome youth   **138 note** presumably, a list of required books   **139 fairly** handsomely
140 at any hand in any case   **141 read . . . lectures** give no other lessons   **143 liberality**
generosity   **144 mend . . . largesse** add to it with a donation   **145 them** i.e. the books
150 yourself . . . place if you yourself were present

GREMIO	O, this learning, what a thing it is!	
GRUMIO	O, this woodcock, what an ass it is!	*Aside*
155 PETRUCHIO	Peace, sirrah!	
HORTENSIO	Grumio, mum.— God save you, Signior Gremio.	
GREMIO	And you are well met, Signior Hortensio.	

Trow you whither I am going? To Baptista Minola.
I promised to inquire carefully
160 About a schoolmaster for the fair Bianca,
And by good fortune I have lighted well
On this young man, for learning and behaviour
Fit for her turn, well read in poetry
And other books, good ones, I warrant ye.
165 HORTENSIO 'Tis well. And I have met a gentleman
Hath promised me to help me to another,
A fine musician to instruct our mistress.
So shall I no whit be behind in duty
To fair Bianca, so beloved of me.
170 GREMIO Beloved of me, and that my deeds shall prove.

GRUMIO And that his bags shall prove.   *Aside*

HORTENSIO Gremio, 'tis now no time to vent our love.
Listen to me, and if you speak me fair,
I'll tell you news indifferent good for either.
175 Here is a gentleman whom by chance I met,
Upon agreement from us to his liking,
Will undertake to woo curst Katherine,
Yea, and to marry her, if her dowry please.
GREMIO So said, so done, is well.
180 Hortensio, have you told him all her faults?
PETRUCHIO I know she is an irksome brawling scold:
If that be all, masters, I hear no harm.

---

154 **woodcock** proverbially stupid bird   157 **you . . . met** I am glad to meet you   158 **Trow you** do you know   163 **Fit . . . turn** suited to her needs (plays on the sense of "suitable for sex")   166 **help me to** assist me in obtaining   171 **bags** money-bags   172 **vent** proclaim   173 **me fair** courteously to me   174 **indifferent . . . either** that is equally good for both of us   176 **agreement . . . liking** our agreeing to his conditions (Hortensio later explains that he and Gremio are to pay for the cost of wooing Kate)   179 **So . . . well** if what you say were to be achieved, it would be all very well

GREMIO   No, say'st me so, friend? What countryman?

PETRUCHIO   Born in Verona, old Antonio's son.

185   My father dead, my fortune lives for me,

And I do hope good days and long to see.

GREMIO   O sir, such a life with such a wife were strange.

But if you have a stomach, to't a' God's name.

You shall have me assisting you in all.

190   But will you woo this wild-cat?

PETRUCHIO   Will I live?

GRUMIO   Will he woo her? Ay, or I'll hang her.   *Aside?*

PETRUCHIO   Why came I hither but to that intent?

Think you a little din can daunt mine ears?

195   Have I not in my time heard lions roar?

Have I not heard the sea, puffed up with winds,

Rage like an angry boar chafèd with sweat?

Have I not heard great ordnance in the field,

And heaven's artillery thunder in the skies?

200   Have I not in a pitchèd battle heard

Loud 'larums, neighing steeds, and trumpets' clang?

And do you tell me of a woman's tongue,

That gives not half so great a blow to hear

As will a chestnut in a farmer's fire?

205   Tush, tush! Fear boys with bugs.

GRUMIO   For he fears none.

GREMIO   Hortensio, hark:

This gentleman is happily arrived,

My mind presumes, for his own good and yours.

210   HORTENSIO   I promised we would be contributors

And bear his charge of wooing whatsoe'er.

GREMIO   And so we will, provided that he win her.

GRUMIO   I would I were as sure of a good dinner.

---

183 **What countryman?** Where are you from?   188 **stomach** appetite   **to't** begin eating, go ahead   191 **Will I live?** i.e. of course   197 **chafèd** irritated   198 **ordnance** artillery 200 **pitchèd** planned   201 **'larums** calls to arms   204 **chestnut . . . fire** chestnuts crackle when they burn   205 **Fear** frighten   **bugs** imaginary terrors   211 **charge** expense

Enter Tranio brave [disguised as Lucentio] and Biondello

TRANIO   Gentlemen, God save you. If I may be bold,
215   Tell me, I beseech you, which is the readiest way
To the house of Signior Baptista Minola?

BIONDELLO   He that has the two fair daughters, is't he you
mean?

TRANIO   Even he, Biondello.

GREMIO   Hark you, sir, you mean not her to—

220 TRANIO   Perhaps, him and her, sir. What have you to do?

PETRUCHIO   Not her that chides, sir, at any hand, I pray.

TRANIO   I love no chiders, sir. Biondello, let's away.

LUCENTIO   Well begun, Tranio.   *Aside*

HORTENSIO   Sir, a word ere you go:
225   Are you a suitor to the maid you talk of, yea or no?

TRANIO   And if I be, sir, is it any offence?

GREMIO   No, if without more words you will get you hence.

TRANIO   Why, sir, I pray, are not the streets as free
For me as for you?

230 GREMIO   But so is not she.

TRANIO   For what reason, I beseech you?

GREMIO   For this reason, if you'll know,
That she's the choice love of Signior Gremio.

HORTENSIO   That she's the chosen of Signior Hortensio.

235 TRANIO   Softly, my masters. If you be gentlemen,
Do me this right: hear me with patience.
Baptista is a noble gentleman,
To whom my father is not all unknown,
And were his daughter fairer than she is,
240   She may more suitors have, and me for one.
Fair Leda's daughter had a thousand wooers,
Then well one more may fair Bianca have,

---

brave finely dressed   **215 readiest** quickest   **219 to —** the implied missing word is "woo,"
though some editors emend to "too?"   **220 What . . . do?** What is it to do with you?
222 chiders quarrelers, rebukers   **223 begun** said   **224 ere** before   **233 choice** chosen/
special   **238 all** altogether   **241 Leda's daughter** Helen of Troy, supposedly the most
beautiful woman in the world

And so she shall. Lucentio shall make one,
Though Paris came in hope to speed alone.

245 GREMIO   What, this gentleman will out-talk us all.

LUCENTIO   Sir, give him head. I know he'll prove a jade.

PETRUCHIO   Hortensio, to what end are all these words?

HORTENSIO   Sir, let me be so bold as ask you,
Did you yet ever see Baptista's daughter?

250 TRANIO   No, sir, but hear I do that he hath two:
The one as famous for a scolding tongue
As is the other for beauteous modesty.

PETRUCHIO   Sir, sir, the first's for me, let her go by.

GREMIO   Yea, leave that labour to great Hercules,
255 And let it be more than Alcides' twelve.

PETRUCHIO   Sir, understand you this of me, in sooth:
The youngest daughter whom you hearken for,
Her father keeps from all access of suitors,
And will not promise her to any man
260 Until the elder sister first be wed.
The younger then is free, and not before.

TRANIO   If it be so, sir, that you are the man
Must stead us all and me amongst the rest,
And if you break the ice and do this feat,
265 Achieve the elder, set the younger free
For our access, whose hap shall be to have her
Will not so graceless be to be ingrate.

HORTENSIO   Sir, you say well, and well you do conceive.
And since you do profess to be a suitor,
270 You must, as we do, gratify this gentleman,
To whom we all rest generally beholding.

---

244 **Though** even if   **Paris** the Trojan prince who snatched Helen from her husband   **speed alone** be the only one to succeed   246 **head** free reign   **jade** worn-out horse   253 **let . . . by** leave her alone   254 **Hercules . . . twelve** in Greek mythology, Hercules (also called **Alcides**) carried out twelve seemingly impossible tasks   255 **let it be** grant that it is   256 **sooth** truth   257 **hearken for** seek to win/inquire after   263 **stead** help   266 **whose hap** he whose good fortune it   267 **Will . . . ingrate** will not be so ill-mannered as to be ungrateful   268 **conceive** understand   270 **gratify** show gratitude to/reward   271 **rest** remain   **beholding** indebted

TRANIO   Sir, I shall not be slack, in sign whereof,
Please ye we may contrive this afternoon
And quaff carouses to our mistress' health,
275   And do as adversaries do in law,
Strive mightily, but eat and drink as friends.
GRUMIO *and* BIONDELLO   O excellent motion! Fellows, let's be gone.
HORTENSIO   The motion's good indeed and be it so,
Petruchio, I shall be your *ben venuto*.   *Exeunt*

[Act 2 Scene 1]   *running scene 3*

Enter Katherina and Bianca   *Bianca's hands tied*

BIANCA   Good sister, wrong me not, nor wrong yourself,
To make a bondmaid and a slave of me.
That I disdain. But for these other goods,
Unbind my hands, I'll pull them off myself,
5   Yea, all my raiment, to my petticoat,
Or what you will command me will I do,
So well I know my duty to my elders.
KATE   Of all thy suitors here I charge thee tell
Whom thou lov'st best: see thou dissemble not.
10   BIANCA   Believe me, sister, of all the men alive
I never yet beheld that special face
Which I could fancy more than any other.
KATE   Minion, thou liest. Is't not Hortensio?
BIANCA   If you affect him, sister, here I swear
15   I'll plead for you myself, but you shall have him.
KATE   O, then belike you fancy riches more:
You will have Gremio to keep you fair.
BIANCA   Is it for him you do envy me so?
Nay then you jest, and now I well perceive

---

273 **contrive** spend, use   274 **quaff carouses** drink toasts   275 **adversaries** opposing
lawyers   276 **Strive** compete   277 **motion** proposal   279 ***ben venuto*** "welcome" (Italian);
sense here is "host"   **2.1   2 bondmaid** slave-girl   **3 goods** ornaments, jewels, love tokens
4 Unbind if you will unbind   **5 raiment** clothing   **9 dissemble** lie   **11 special** particular
13 Minion hussy   **14 affect** love   **17 fair** well dressed   **18 envy** despise

20   You have but jested with me all this while.
      I prithee sister Kate, untie my hands.

KATE   If that be jest, then all the rest was so.   *Strikes her*

Enter Baptista

BAPTISTA   Why, how now, dame? Whence grows this
      insolence?—
      Bianca, stand aside. Poor girl, she weeps.

25   Go ply thy needle, meddle not with her.—
      For shame, thou hilding of a devilish spirit,
      Why dost thou wrong her that did ne'er wrong thee?
      When did she cross thee with a bitter word?

KATE   Her silence flouts me, and I'll be revenged.

Flies after Bianca

30   BAPTISTA   What, in my sight? Bianca, get thee in.

Exit [Bianca]

KATE   What, will you not suffer me? Nay, now I see
      She is your treasure, she must have a husband,
      I must dance barefoot on her wedding day,
      And for your love to her lead apes in hell.

35   Talk not to me. I will go sit and weep
      Till I can find occasion of revenge.   [*Exit*]

BAPTISTA   Was ever gentleman thus grieved as I?
      But who comes here?

*Enter Gremio, Lucentio in the habit of a mean man, Petruchio with
[Hortensio as a musician, and] Tranio, with his boy [Biondello] bearing
a lute and books*

GREMIO   Good morrow, neighbour Baptista.

40   BAPTISTA   Good morrow, neighbour Gremio.
      God save you, gentlemen!

PETRUCHIO   And you, good sir. Pray, have you not a daughter
      Called Katherina, fair and virtuous?

BAPTISTA   I have a daughter, sir, called Katherina.

---

23 **dame** madam (accusatory)   25 **ply thy needle** sew/embroider   **meddle not** have nothing
to do   26 **hilding** good-for-nothing   28 **cross** provoke, thwart   29 **flouts** mocks   31 **suffer**
listen to/permit/endure   33 **dance . . . day** traditionally the fate of an unmarried elder sister
34 **lead . . . hell** proverbially old maids did so because they had no children to lead in heaven
36 **occasion of** opportunity for   *habit* clothing   *mean* humble

45 GREMIO   You are too blunt. Go to it orderly.

   PETRUCHIO   You wrong me, Signior Gremio, give me leave.—
                I am a gentleman of Verona, sir,   *To Baptista*
                That, hearing of her beauty and her wit,
                Her affability and bashful modesty,
50   Her wondrous qualities and mild behaviour,
                Am bold to show myself a forward guest
                Within your house, to make mine eye the witness
                Of that report which I so oft have heard.
                And for an entrance to my entertainment,
55   I do present you with a man of mine,   *Presents Hortensio*
                Cunning in music and the mathematics,
                To instruct her fully in those sciences,
                Whereof I know she is not ignorant.
                Accept of him, or else you do me wrong.
60   His name is Litio, born in Mantua.

   BAPTISTA   You're welcome, sir, and he, for your good sake.
                But for my daughter Katherine, this I know,
                She is not for your turn, the more my grief.

   PETRUCHIO   I see you do not mean to part with her,
65   Or else you like not of my company.

   BAPTISTA   Mistake me not, I speak but as I find.
                Whence are you, sir? What may I call your name?

   PETRUCHIO   Petruchio is my name, Antonio's son,
                A man well known throughout all Italy.

70 BAPTISTA   I know him well. You are welcome for his sake.

   GREMIO   Saving your tale, Petruchio, I pray,
                Let us that are poor petitioners speak too:
                Baccare! You are marvellous forward.

   PETRUCHIO   O, pardon me, Signior Gremio, I would fain be
                doing.

---

45 Go . . . orderly apply yourself to the business with decorum   46 give me leave excuse
me/let me explain myself   48 wit intelligence   51 forward eager/presumptuous   54 for . . .
entertainment as an entrance-fee for my reception   57 sciences fields of learning
59 Accept of accept   60 Litio Second Folio and many later editions emend to "Licio"
throughout   Mantua city in northern Italy   63 turn purpose/needs   71 Saving with
respect for   72 poor petitioners humble suitors   73 *Baccare!* "Stand back!" (mock-Latin)
74 I . . . doing I am eager for action (perhaps plays on the sense of "having sex")

75 GREMIO   I doubt it not, sir. But you will curse your wooing.—
          Neighbour, this is a gift very grateful, I am   *To Baptista*
          sure of it. To express the like kindness, myself, that have been
          more kindly beholding to you than any, freely give unto you
          this young scholar, that hath been long studying   *Presents*
80   at Rheims, as cunning in Greek, Latin, and other   *Lucentio*
          languages, as the other in music and mathematics. His name
          is Cambio. Pray, accept his service.
   BAPTISTA   A thousand thanks, Signior Gremio.
          Welcome, good Cambio.—
85   But, gentle sir, methinks you walk like a stranger.   *To Tranio*
          May I be so bold to know the cause of your coming?
   TRANIO   Pardon me, sir, the boldness is mine own,
          That, being a stranger in this city here,
          Do make myself a suitor to your daughter,
90   Unto Bianca, fair and virtuous.
          Nor is your firm resolve unknown to me,
          In the preferment of the eldest sister.
          This liberty is all that I request,
          That, upon knowledge of my parentage,
95   I may have welcome 'mongst the rest that woo,
          And free access and favour as the rest.
          And toward the education of your daughters
          I here bestow a simple instrument,   *Presents lute and books*
          And this small packet of Greek and Latin books:
100   If you accept them, then their worth is great.
   BAPTISTA   Lucentio is your name? Of whence, I pray?
   TRANIO   Of Pisa, sir, son to Vincentio.
   BAPTISTA   A mighty man of Pisa. By report
          I know him well. You are very welcome, sir.—   *To Hortensio*
105   Take you the lute, and you the set of books,   *and Lucentio*

---

76 **grateful** agreeable   77 **like** same   78 **kindly** fittingly/affectionately   80 **Rheims** northern
French town with a well-known university   82 **Cambio** Italian for "exchange"   85 **walk . . .
stranger** seem like a newcomer/seem as if you are not one of the group/stand aside
92 **preferment** precedence (i.e. offering Kate before Bianca)   94 **upon knowledge** when you
know   101 **Lucentio . . . name?** perhaps Baptista learns this by opening one of the books in
which Lucentio's name is written   103 **mighty** renowned, noble

You shall go see your pupils presently.—
Holla, within!

Enter a Servant

Sirrah, lead these gentlemen
To my daughters, and tell them both
110 These are their tutors: bid them use them well.

[*Exit Servant, with Lucentio and Hortensio,*
Biondello following]

We will go walk a little in the orchard,
And then to dinner. You are passing welcome,
And so I pray you all to think yourselves.

PETRUCHIO   Signior Baptista, my business asketh haste,
115 And every day I cannot come to woo.
You knew my father well, and in him me,
Left solely heir to all his lands and goods,
Which I have bettered rather than decreased.
Then tell me, if I get your daughter's love,
120 What dowry shall I have with her to wife?

BAPTISTA   After my death the one half of my lands,
And in possession twenty thousand crowns.

PETRUCHIO   And for that dowry I'll assure her of
Her widowhood, be it that she survive me,
125 In all my lands and leases whatsoever.
Let specialties be therefore drawn between us,
That covenants may be kept on either hand.

BAPTISTA   Ay, when the special thing is well obtained,
That is, her love, for that is all in all.

130 PETRUCHIO   Why, that is nothing, for I tell you, father,
I am as peremptory as she proud-minded.
And where two raging fires meet together
They do consume the thing that feeds their fury.

---

106 **presently** at once   107 **Holla** a shout to attract attention   111 **orchard** garden
112 **dinner** the main meal of the day, served between eleven and noon   **passing** extremely
114 **asketh haste** is urgent   122 **in possession** i.e. on marriage   123 **assure** . . .
widowhood provide for her after my death/guarantee her rights as a widow   125 **leases**
property that is let   126 **specialities** a special contract   127 **covenants** formal agreements
128 **special** unique/particular   130 **fathor** i.e. father-in-law

Though little fire grows great with little wind,
135   Yet extreme gusts will blow out fire and all:
So I to her and so she yields to me,
For I am rough and woo not like a babe.

BAPTISTA   Well mayst thou woo, and happy be thy speed!
But be thou armed for some unhappy words.

140   PETRUCHIO   Ay, to the proof, as mountains are for winds,
That shakes not, though they blow perpetually.

Enter Hortensio [disguised as Litio], with his head broke

BAPTISTA   How now, my friend? Why dost thou look so pale?

HORTENSIO   For fear, I promise you, if I look pale.

BAPTISTA   What, will my daughter prove a good musician?

145   HORTENSIO   I think she'll sooner prove a soldier.
Iron may hold with her, but never lutes.

BAPTISTA   Why, then thou canst not break her to the lute?

HORTENSIO   Why, no, for she hath broke the lute to me.
I did but tell her she mistook her frets,
150   And bowed her hand to teach her fingering,
When, with a most impatient devilish spirit,
'Frets, call you these?' quoth she, 'I'll fume with them.'
And with that word, she struck me on the head,
And through the instrument my pate made way,
155   And there I stood amazèd for a while,
As on a pillory, looking through the lute,
While she did call me rascal fiddler
And twangling Jack, with twenty such vile terms,
As had she studied to misuse me so.

160   PETRUCHIO   Now, by the world, it is a lusty wench.
I love her ten times more than e'er I did.
O, how I long to have some chat with her!

---

136 So I so I shall behave (like an **extreme gust**)   138 happy . . . speed may the outcome be
happy/fortunate   140 to the proof so as to be invulnerable   *broke* grazed, bleeding
145 prove become/test the skill of   146 hold with resist, withstand   147 break her to teach
her to play   148 broke . . . me i.e. broken the lute over my head   149 frets ridges for guiding
the fingers (Kate shifts the sense to "vexations")   152 fume show anger   154 pate head
155 amazèd perplexed, dumbstruck   156 As . . . pillory as if in the stocks (in which the head
was confined by wooden boards)   157 fiddler lute-player/meddler   158 Jack base fellow
159 studied practiced, planned   160 lusty lively

BAPTISTA   Well, go with me and be not so
          discomfited.   *To Hortensio*
          Proceed in practice with my younger daughter,
165   She's apt to learn and thankful for good turns.
          Signior Petruchio, will you go with us,
          Or shall I send my daughter Kate to you?
PETRUCHIO   I pray you do.   *Exeunt all but Petruchio*
          I'll attend her here,
          And woo her with some spirit when she comes.
170   Say that she rail, why then I'll tell her plain
          She sings as sweetly as a nightingale:
          Say that she frown, I'll say she looks as clear
          As morning roses newly washed with dew:
          Say she be mute and will not speak a word,
175   Then I'll commend her volubility,
          And say she uttereth piercing eloquence:
          If she do bid me pack, I'll give her thanks,
          As though she bid me stay by her a week:
          If she deny to wed, I'll crave the day
180   When I shall ask the banns and when be married.
          But here she comes, and now, Petruchio, speak.
          Enter Katherina
          Good morrow, Kate, for that's your name, I hear.
KATE   Well have you heard, but something hard of
          hearing:
          They call me Katherine that do talk of me.
185 PETRUCHIO   You lie, in faith, for you are called plain Kate,
          And bonny Kate and sometimes Kate the curst,
          But Kate, the prettiest Kate in Christendom,
          Kate of Kate Hall, my super-dainty Kate,
          For dainties are all Kates, and therefore, Kate,
190   Take this of me, Kate of my consolation,

---

163 **discomfited** disheartened   164 **in practice** with your lessons   168 **attend** wait for
172 **clear** serene, faultless   176 **piercing** moving   177 **pack** leave   179 **crave** demand
180 **banns** public proclamations of intended marriages   183 **hard** puns on **heard** (which was
pronounced similarly)   189 **dainties . . . Kates** puns on "cates" (i.e. **dainties**, delicacies)
190 **of** from

Hearing thy mildness praised in every town,
Thy virtues spoke of, and thy beauty sounded,
Yet not so deeply as to thee belongs,
Myself am moved to woo thee for my wife.

195   KATE   Moved? In good time! Let him that moved you hither
Remove you hence. I knew you at the first
You were a movable.

PETRUCHIO   Why, what's a movable?

KATE   A joint stool.

200   PETRUCHIO   Thou hast hit it: come, sit on me.

KATE   Asses are made to bear, and so are you.

PETRUCHIO   Women are made to bear, and so are you.

KATE   No such jade as you, if me you mean.

PETRUCHIO   Alas, good Kate, I will not burden thee,

205   For knowing thee to be but young and light—

KATE   Too light for such a swain as you to catch,
And yet as heavy as my weight should be.

PETRUCHIO   Should be? Should — buzz!

KATE   Well ta'en, and like a buzzard.

210   PETRUCHIO   O slow-winged turtle, shall a buzzard take thee?

KATE   Ay, for a turtle, as he takes a buzzard.

PETRUCHIO   Come, come, you wasp, i'faith, you are too angry.

KATE   If I be waspish, best beware my sting.

PETRUCHIO   My remedy is then to pluck it out.

215   KATE   Ay, if the fool could find it where it lies.

---

192 sounded proclaimed/fathomed   **193 deeply . . . belongs** loudly/in such depth as you
deserve   **194 moved** compelled (Kate shifts to the literal sense)   **195 In good time!** Indeed!
196 you . . . first from the start   **197 movable** piece of furniture/changeable person
199 joint stool low stool made by a joiner ("I took you for a joint stool" was a way of mockingly
apologizing for ignoring someone)   **200 sit on me** i.e. as I am a stool (with sexual innuendo)
201 Asses puns on "arses"   **bear** carry loads (Petruchio plays on the sense of "bear the
weight of a man's body/of a baby")   **204 burden** lie on top of/accuse   **205 light** not
heavy/promiscuous   **206 light** quick   **swain** rustic (contemptuous)   **207 as . . . be** the
right weight/of sound social standing   **208 be** puns on "bee"   **buzz** rumor—i.e. you should
hear what actually is said about you; also a noise of impatience; **wasp** then shifts sense to
insect noise   **209 ta'en** seized upon, used   **buzzard** fool (literally useless bird of prey)/
rumor-monger   **210 turtle** turtle-dove (symbol of faithful love)   **211 turtle . . . buzzard** i.e.
only a fool will take me for a faithful wife, just as the turtle-dove mistakenly swallows an insect
213 waspish spiteful/wasp-like

	PETRUCHIO	Who knows not where a wasp does wear his sting?
		In his tail.
	KATE	In his tongue.
	PETRUCHIO	Whose tongue?
	KATE	Yours, if you talk of tails, and so farewell.
220	PETRUCHIO	What, with my tongue in your tail? Nay, come
		again.
		Good Kate, I am a gentleman.
	KATE	That I'll try. *She strikes him*
	PETRUCHIO	I swear I'll cuff you, if you strike again.
	KATE	So may you lose your arms:
225		If you strike me, you are no gentleman,
		And if no gentleman, why then no arms.
	PETRUCHIO	A herald, Kate? O, put me in thy books!
	KATE	What is your crest, a coxcomb?
	PETRUCHIO	A combless cock, so Kate will be my hen.
230	KATE	No cock of mine, you crow too like a craven.
	PETRUCHIO	Nay, come, Kate, come, you must not look so sour.
	KATE	It is my fashion, when I see a crab.
	PETRUCHIO	Why, here's no crab, and therefore look not sour.
	KATE	There is, there is.
235	PETRUCHIO	Then show it me.
	KATE	Had I a glass, I would.
	PETRUCHIO	What, you mean my face?
	KATE	Well aimed of such a young one.
	PETRUCHIO	Now, by Saint George, I am too young for you.

---

216 sting plays on the sense of genitals/sexual urge   **219 tails** puns on "tales"   **220 with . . . tail** i.e. leaving me with the last word (**tail** puns on the sense of "vagina")   **come** plays on the sense of "have an orgasm"   **again** back/once more   **222 try** test   **223 cuff** hit   **224 lose your arms** waste your strength/loosen your grip/forfeit your coat of arms (the sign of being a gentleman)   **225 strike** plays on the sense of "have sex with"   **227 books** book of heraldry, where gentlemen's coats of arms were recorded (plays on the notion of "good books" and on "vagina")   **228 crest** identifying feature on a coat of arms/tuft on the head of an animal (with phallic connotations)   **coxcomb** fool's cap (similar in appearance to a cock's crest; plays on "cock"—i.e. penis)   **229 combless** i.e. unthreatening   **cock** cockerel/penis   **so** provided that   **hen** i.e. wife/harlot   **230 craven** cock with no fighting spirit   **232 fashion** manner   **crab** sour crab-apple   **236 glass** mirror   **238 Well . . . one** well guessed for one so inexperienced   **239 young** youthful/strong

240   KATE   Yet you are withered.

PETRUCHIO   'Tis with cares.

KATE   I care not.

PETRUCHIO   Nay, hear you, Kate. In sooth you scape not so.

KATE   I chafe you, if I tarry. Let me go.

245   PETRUCHIO   No, not a whit. I find you passing gentle.
              'Twas told me you were rough and coy and sullen,
              And now I find report a very liar,
              For thou are pleasant, gamesome, passing courteous,
              But slow in speech, yet sweet as spring-time flowers.
250   Thou canst not frown, thou canst not look askance,
              Nor bite the lip, as angry wenches will,
              Nor hast thou pleasure to be cross in talk.
              But thou with mildness entertain'st thy wooers,
              With gentle conference, soft and affable.
255   Why does the world report that Kate doth limp?   *Kicks her?*
              O sland'rous world! Kate like the hazel twig
              Is straight and slender and as brown in hue
              As hazelnuts and sweeter than the kernels.
              O, let me see thee walk: thou dost not halt.

260   KATE   Go, fool, and whom thou keep'st command.

PETRUCHIO   Did ever Dian so become a grove
              As Kate this chamber with her princely gait?
              O, be thou Dian, and let her be Kate,
              And then let Kate be chaste and Dian sportful!

265   KATE   Where did you study all this goodly speech?

PETRUCHIO   It is extempore, from my mother-wit.

KATE   A witty mother, witless else her son.

---

241 cares troubles   243 scape escape   244 chafe annoy, inflame   246 rough harsh/
unmanageable   coy disdainful, unresponsive   248 pleasant merry   gamesome sportive,
playful   249 slow easygoing, without a quick tongue   250 askance scornfully   252 cross
combative/ill-tempered   253 entertain'st receive   254 conference conversation   259 halt
limp   260 whom . . . command order you servants about (rather than me)   261 Dian Diana,
goddess of chastity, the moon and hunting   become suit, enhance   262 gait manner,
bearing, way of walking   264 sportful lively/playful/amorous   265 study learn/practice
goodly splendid (sarcastic)   266 extempore spontaneous, improvised   mother-wit natural
intelligence   267 A . . . son your mother must have had some wit, as left to yourself you
would have none at all

	PETRUCHIO	Am I not wise?
	KATE	Yes, keep you warm.
270	PETRUCHIO	Marry, so I mean, sweet Katherine, in thy bed.

And therefore, setting all this chat aside,
Thus in plain terms: your father hath consented
That you shall be my wife; your dowry 'greed on,
And, will you, nill you, I will marry you.

275   Now, Kate, I am a husband for your turn,
For by this light, whereby I see thy beauty,
Thy beauty that doth make me like thee well,
Thou must be married to no man but me,

Enter Baptista, Gremio, Tranio [disguised as Lucentio]

For I am he am born to tame you, Kate,
280   And bring you from a wild Kate to a Kate
Conformable as other household Kates.
Here comes your father. Never make denial,
I must and will have Katherine to my wife.

BAPTISTA   Now, Signior Petruchio, how speed you with my
daughter?

285   PETRUCHIO   How but well, sir? How but well?
It were impossible I should speed amiss.

BAPTISTA   Why, how now, daughter Katherine? In your
dumps?

KATE   Call you me 'daughter'? Now, I promise you
You have showed a tender fatherly regard,
290   To wish me wed to one half-lunatic,
A mad-cap ruffian and a swearing Jack
That thinks with oaths to face the matter out.

PETRUCHIO   Father, 'tis thus: yourself and all the world
That talked of her, have talked amiss of her:
295   If she be curst, it is for policy,

---

268 **wise . . . warm** "he is wise enough that can keep himself warm" (proverbial)   270 **mean**
intend to   274 **will . . . you** whether you will or not   275 **for your turn** right for you (plays on
the sense of "for sex with you")   280 **wild Kate** puns on "wild-cat"   281 **Conformable**
pliant, obedient   282 **Never make denial** do not refuse me   284 **speed you** do you succeed,
fare   286 **amiss** adversely, without progress   287 **In your dumps?** Down-hearted?
292 **face . . . out** brazenly get his own way   295 **policy** strategic purposes

For she's not froward, but modest as the dove,
She is not hot, but temperate as the morn,
For patience she will prove a second Grissel,
And Roman Lucrece for her chastity.

300 And to conclude, we have 'greed so well together
That upon Sunday is the wedding day.

KATE   I'll see thee hanged on Sunday first.

GREMIO   Hark, Petruchio, she says she'll see thee hanged
first.

TRANIO   Is this your speeding? Nay then, goodnight our part!

305 PETRUCHIO   Be patient, gentlemen, I choose her for myself.
If she and I be pleased, what's that to you?
'Tis bargained 'twixt us twain, being alone,
That she shall still be curst in company.
I tell you, 'tis incredible to believe

310 How much she loves me: O, the kindest Kate!
She hung about my neck, and kiss on kiss
She vied so fast, protesting oath on oath,
That in a twink she won me to her love.
O, you are novices! 'Tis a world to see

315 How tame, when men and women are alone,
A meacock wretch can make the curstest shrew.
Give me thy hand, Kate. I will unto Venice
To buy apparel gainst the wedding day;
Provide the feast, father, and bid the guests.

320 I will be sure my Katherine shall be fine.

BAPTISTA   I know not what to say, but give me your hands.
God send you joy, Petruchio! 'Tis a match.

GREMIO and TRANIO   Amen, say we. We will be witnesses.

PETRUCHIO   Father, and wife, and gentlemen, adieu.

325   I will to Venice. Sunday comes apace.

We will have rings and things and fine array,

And kiss me, Kate, we will be married o'Sunday.

Exeunt Petruchio and Katherine [separately]

GREMIO   Was ever match clapped up so suddenly?

BAPTISTA   Faith, gentlemen, now I play a merchant's part,

330   And venture madly on a desperate mart.

TRANIO   'Twas a commodity lay fretting by you:

'Twill bring you gain, or perish on the seas.

BAPTISTA   The gain I seek is quiet in the match.

GREMIO   No doubt but he hath got a quiet catch.

335   But now, Baptista, to your younger daughter.

Now is the day we long have lookèd for.

I am your neighbour, and was suitor first.

TRANIO   And I am one that love Bianca more

Than words can witness, or your thoughts can guess.

340   GREMIO   Youngling, thou canst not love so dear as I.

TRANIO   Greybeard, thy love doth freeze.

GREMIO   But thine doth fry.

Skipper, stand back, 'tis age that nourisheth.

TRANIO   But youth in ladies' eyes that flourisheth.

345   BAPTISTA   Content you, gentlemen, I will compound this strife.

'Tis deeds must win the prize, and he of both

That can assure my daughter greatest dower

Shall have my Bianca's love.

Say, Signior Gremio, what can you assure her?

350   GREMIO   First, as you know, my house within the city

Is richly furnishèd with plate and gold,

Basins and ewers to lave her dainty hands:

---

325 apace swiftly   328 clapped up settled   330 desperate mart risky business endeavor
331 'Twas . . . you it (Kate) was a piece of merchandise that was losing its value (fretting plays
on the sense of "aggravating")   333 quiet peace of mind   334 quiet catch (ironic)
341 freeze possibly implies impotence   342 fry burn lecherously   343 Skipper frivolous
wastrel   nourisheth sustains life   345 compound settle   346 deeds actions/legal deeds
he of both whichever of the two of you   347 dower settlement made to the wife on the death
of the husband   351 plate gold or silver tableware   352 lave wash

My hangings all of Tyrian tapestry:
In ivory coffers I have stuffed my crowns:
355   In cypress chests my arras counterpoints,
Costly apparel, tents, and canopies,
Fine linen, Turkey cushions bossed with pearl,
Valance of Venice gold in needlework:
Pewter and brass and all things that belongs
360   To house or housekeeping. Then, at my farm
I have a hundred milch-kine to the pail,
Sixscore fat oxen standing in my stalls,
And all things answerable to this portion.
Myself am struck in years, I must confess,
365   And if I die tomorrow, this is hers,
If whilst I live she will be only mine.

TRANIO   That 'only' came well in. Sir, list to me:
I am my father's heir and only son.
If I may have your daughter to my wife,
370   I'll leave her houses three or four as good,
Within rich Pisa walls, as any one
Old Signior Gremio has in Padua,
Besides two thousand ducats by the year
Of fruitful land, all which shall be her jointure.
375   What, have I pinched you, Signior Gremio?

GREMIO   Two thousand ducats by the year of land?
My land amounts not to so much in all.—   *Aside*
That she shall have, besides an argosy
That now is lying in Marseillis' road.
380   What, have I choked you with an argosy?   *To Tranio*

---

353 hangings wall coverings   **Tyrian** from Tyre, an ancient trading city on the Mediterranean
354 coffers chests   **355 cypress** made from cypress wood   **arras counterpoints** tapestried
bed coverings from Arras   **356 tents** hangings for a bed   **357 Turkey** Turkish   **bossed**
embossed, adorned   **358 Valance . . . needlework** valences (borders on the sides or canopy of
a bed) embroidered with Venetian gold thread   **361 milch-kine** dairy cows   **to the pail**
(specifically) for milking   **363 answerable . . . portion** appropriate to an estate of this size
364 struck old   **367 came well in** is to the point   **list** listen   **371 walls** i.e. the walls forming
the city limits   **373 two . . . land** i.e. the land brings in an annual income of two thousand
ducats (gold coins)   **374 jointure** widow's settlement   **375 pinched** distressed/belittled
378 argosy large merchant ship   **379 Marseillis' road** the harbor at Marseilles

TRANIO   Gremio, 'tis known my father hath no less
Than three great argosies, besides two galliases,
And twelve tight galleys. These I will assure her,
And twice as much, whate'er thou offer'st next.

385 GREMIO   Nay, I have offered all, I have no more,
And she can have no more than all I have.
If you like me, she shall have me and mine.   *To Baptista*

TRANIO   Why then the maid is mine from all the world,
By your firm promise. Gremio is out-vied.

390 BAPTISTA   I must confess your offer is the best,
And let your father make her the assurance,
She is your own, else, you must pardon me.
If you should die before him, where's her dower?

TRANIO   That's but a cavil. He is old, I young.

395 GREMIO   And may not young men die, as well as old?

BAPTISTA   Well, gentlemen,
I am thus resolved: on Sunday next, you know
My daughter Katherine is to be married.
Now on the Sunday following, shall Bianca

400 Be bride to you, if you make this assurance.
If not, to Signior Gremio.
And so, I take my leave, and thank you both.   *Exit*

GREMIO   Adieu, good neighbour.— Now I fear thee not.
Sirrah young gamester, your father were a fool

405 To give thee all, and in his waning age
Set foot under thy table. Tut, a toy!
An old Italian fox is not so kind, my boy.   *Exit*

TRANIO   A vengeance on your crafty withered hide!
Yet I have faced it with a card of ten.

410 'Tis in my head to do my master good:
I see no reason but supposed Lucentio

---

382 **galliases** heavy low-built vessels   383 **tight** efficient, seaworthy   389 **out-vied** outbid
(card-playing term)   391 **let** providing   **assurance** (financial) guarantee   392 **else**
otherwise   394 **cavil** quibble   404 **gamester** gambler, foolish adventurer   **were** would be
406 **Set . . . table** i.e. become dependent upon you   **toy** piece of nonsense   409 **faced . . .
ten** bluffed, brazened it out with a card only worth ten   410 **'Tis . . . head** I have a plan

Must get a father, called 'supposed Vincentio',
And that's a wonder. Fathers commonly
Do get their children, but in this case of wooing,
415 A child shall get a sire, if I fail not of my cunning. *Exit*

Act 3 [Scene 1]

running scene 3 continues

Enter Lucentio [disguised as Cambio], Hortensio [disguised as Litio] and Bianca

LUCENTIO   Fiddler, forbear. You grow too forward, sir.
Have you so soon forgot the entertainment
Her sister Katherine welcomed you withal?
HORTENSIO   But, wrangling pedant, this is
5 The patroness of heavenly harmony:
Then give me leave to have prerogative,
And when in music we have spent an hour,
Your lecture shall have leisure for as much.
LUCENTIO   Preposterous ass, that never read so far
10 To know the cause why music was ordained!
Was it not to refresh the mind of man
After his studies or his usual pain?
Then give me leave to read philosophy,
And while I pause, serve in your harmony.
15 HORTENSIO   Sirrah, I will not bear these braves of thine.
BIANCA   Why, gentlemen, you do me double wrong
To strive for that which resteth in my choice.
I am no breeching scholar in the schools,
I'll not be tied to hours nor 'pointed times,
20 But learn my lessons as I please myself.
And, to cut off all strife, here sit we down.

---

412 **get** beget, conceive   415 **sire** father   **3.1**   1 **Fiddler . . . sir** implies that Hortensio is holding Bianca's fingers as he teaches her the lute   2 **entertainment** reception   3 **withal** with   6 **prerogative** priority   8 **lecture** lesson   9 **Preposterous** unreasonable/placing last what should be first   10 **ordained** created   12 **usual pain** habitual labor   14 **serve in** serve up (contemptuous)   15 **braves** blustering threats   17 **resteth . . . choice** is up to me   18 **breeching . . . schools** schoolboy liable to be whipped (breeched)   19 **'pointed** appointed

Take you your instrument, play you the whiles.   *To Hortensio*
His lecture will be done ere you have tuned.

HORTENSIO   You'll leave his lecture when I am in tune?

25   LUCENTIO   That will be never. Tune your instrument.

BIANCA   Where left we last?

LUCENTIO   Here, madam:
'*Hic ibat Simois. Hic est Sigeia tellus.*   *Reads*
Hic steterat Priami regia celsa senis.'

30   BIANCA   Conster them.

LUCENTIO   '*Hic ibat*', as I told you before, '*Simois*', I am Lucentio,
'*hic est*', son unto Vincentio of Pisa, '*Sigeia tellus*', disguised
thus to get your love, '*Hic steterat*', and that Lucentio that
comes a-wooing, '*Priami*', is my man Tranio, '*regia*', bearing
35   my port, '*celsa senis*', that we might beguile the old pantaloon.

HORTENSIO   Madam, my instrument's in tune.

BIANCA   Let's hear. O fie! The treble jars.   *He plays*

LUCENTIO   Spit in the hole, man, and tune again.

BIANCA   Now let me see if I can conster it: '*Hic ibat Simois*', I
40   know you not, '*hic est Sigeia tellus*', I trust you not, '*Hic steterat
Priami*', take heed he hear us not, '*regia*', presume not, '*celsa
senis*', despair not.

HORTENSIO   Madam, 'tis now in tune.   *He plays again*

LUCENTIO   All but the bass.

45   HORTENSIO   The bass is right: 'tis the base knave that jars.
How fiery and forward our pedant is.   *Aside*
Now, for my life, the knave doth court my love.
Pedascule, I'll watch you better yet.

BIANCA   In time I may believe, yet I mistrust.   *To Lucentio*

---

22 **the whiles** in the meantime   28 '*Hic . . . senis*' "here ran the [river] Simois; here is the
Sigeian land [Troy]; here stood the lofty palace of old Priam [King of Troy]" (from Ovid's
Heroides)   30 **Conster** translate/analyze grammatically/expound   35 **port** station, dignity
pantaloon foolish old man (i.e. Gremio)   37 **fie** expression of impatience or disgust   **jars**
sounds discordant   38 **Spit . . . again** possibly a perversion of the proverb "spit in your hands
and take a better hold" (sequence **instrument's . . . spit in the hole . . . tune . . . fingering**
may have sexual connotations)   45 **jars** quarrels   46 **pedant** schoolmaster/quibbler
48 **Pedascule** little pedant

50   LUCENTIO   Mistrust it not, for, sure, Aeacides
Was Ajax, called so from his grandfather.
BIANCA   I must believe my master, else, I promise you,
I should be arguing still upon that doubt.
But let it rest.— Now, Litio, to you:
55   Good master, take it not unkindly, pray,
That I have been thus pleasant with you both.
HORTENSIO   You may go walk, and give me leave a
while.   *To Lucentio*
My lessons make no music in three parts.
LUCENTIO   Are you so formal, sir? Well, I must wait —
60   And watch withal, for, but I be deceived,   *Aside*
Our fine musician groweth amorous.   *He stands aside*
HORTENSIO   Madam, before you touch the instrument,
To learn the order of my fingering,
I must begin with rudiments of art,
65   To teach you gamut in a briefer sort,
More pleasant, pithy and effectual,
Than hath been taught by any of my trade.
And there it is in writing, fairly drawn.   *Gives Bianca a paper*
BIANCA   Why, I am past my gamut long ago.
70   HORTENSIO   Yet read the gamut of Hortensio.
BIANCA   '*Gamut* I am, the ground of all accord,   *Reads*
A re, to plead Hortensio's passion.
B mi, Bianca, take him for thy lord,
C fa ut, that loves with all affection.
75   *D sol re*, one clef, two notes have I,
E la mi, show pity, or I die.'
Call you this gamut? Tut, I like it not.

---

50 Aeacides . . . grandfather the Greek hero Ajax was also known as Aeacides, after his
grandfather Aeacus (Lucentio has moved to the next line of Ovid's *Heroides*)   **52 master** tutor
53 doubt point   **56 pleasant** merry, playful   **57 give me leave** leave me   **58 three parts** i.e.
the company of three people   **59 formal** punctilious   **60 withal** at the same time   **but**
unless   **63 order** method   **65 gamut** the musical scale   **briefer sort** quicker way   **68 fairly
drawn** neatly set out   **71 ground . . . accord** basis of all harmony   **75 one . . . I** perhaps
Hortensio's love (**one clef**) and his real and assumed personalities (**two notes**); may also have
sexual connotations ("one vagina," "two testicles"—**notes** playing on "nuts") leading to play
on **die** in next line

Old fashions please me best. I am not so nice
To change true rules for old inventions.

Enter a Messenger

80   MESSENGER   Mistress, your father prays you leave your books
And help to dress your sister's chamber up.
You know tomorrow is the wedding day.

BIANCA   Farewell, sweet masters both, I must be gone.

[Exeunt Bianca and Messenger]

LUCENTIO   Faith, mistress, then I have no cause to stay.   *[Exit]*

85   HORTENSIO   But I have cause to pry into this pedant.
Methinks he looks as though he were in love.
Yet if thy thoughts, Bianca, be so humble
To cast thy wand'ring eyes on every stale,
Seize thee that list. If once I find thee ranging,

90   Hortensio will be quit with thee by changing.   *Exit*

[Act 3 Scene 2]   *running scene 4*

Enter Baptista, Gremio, Tranio, Katherina, Bianca, [Lucentio] and others, Attendants

BAPTISTA   Signior Lucentio, this is the 'pointed day.   *To Tranio*
That Katherine and Petruchio should be married,
And yet we hear not of our son-in-law.
What will be said? What mockery will it be,

5   To want the bridegroom when the priest attends
To speak the ceremonial rites of marriage?
What says Lucentio to this shame of ours?

KATE   No shame but mine: I must forsooth be forced
To give my hand opposed against my heart

10   Unto a mad-brain rudesby full of spleen,
Who wooed in haste and means to wed at leisure.

---

78 **Old** established   **nice** capricious   79 **true** legitimate, constant   85 **pry into** spy on, investigate   88 **stale** decoy (specifically, one that distracts a poorly trained hawk) 89 **Seize . . . list** let those who want you have you   **ranging** straying (like a hawk)/unfaithful 90 **quit with** rid of/even with   **3.2   5 want** lack   8 **forsooth** in truth   10 **rudesby** insolent ruffian   **spleen** temper, passion   11 **wooed . . . leisure** varies the proverbial "he who marries in haste repents at leisure"

I told you, I, he was a frantic fool,
Hiding his bitter jests in blunt behaviour.
And to be noted for a merry man,
He'll woo a thousand, 'point the day of marriage,
Make feasts, invite friends, and proclaim the banns,
Yet never means to wed where he hath wooed.
Now must the world point at poor Katherine,
And say, 'Lo, there is mad Petruchio's wife,
If it would please him come and marry her.'

TRANIO   Patience, good Katherine, and Baptista too.
Upon my life, Petruchio means but well,
Whatever fortune stays him from his word.
Though he be blunt, I know him passing wise,
Though he be merry, yet withal he's honest.

KATE   Would Katherine had never seen him though!

Exit weeping [followed by Bianca and others]

BAPTISTA   Go, girl. I cannot blame thee now to weep,
For such an injury would vex a very saint,
Much more a shrew of thy impatient humour.

Enter Biondello

BIONDELLO   Master, master, news! Old news, and such news as
you never heard of!

BAPTISTA   Is it new and old too? How may that be?

BIONDELLO   Why, is it not news to hear of Petruchio's coming?

BAPTISTA   Is he come?

BIONDELLO   Why, no, sir.

BAPTISTA   What then?

BIONDELLO   He is coming.

BAPTISTA   When will he be here?

BIONDELLO   When he stands where I am and sees you there.

TRANIO   But say, what to thine old news?

BIONDELLO   Why, Petruchio is coming in a new hat and an old
jerkin: a pair of old breeches thrice turned: a pair of boots

---

12 **frantic** insane, frenzied   14 **noted for** known as   19 **Lo** look   23 **fortune . . . word** event
prevents him from keeping his word   29 **humour** temperament   30 **Old** plentiful (Baptista
plays on the more familiar sense)   40 **to** of   42 **jerkin** close-fitting jacket   **turned** i.e. inside
out (to make them last longer)

that have been candle-cases, one buckled, another laced, an
old rusty sword ta'en out of the town armoury, with a
45   broken hilt, and chapeless: with two broken points: his horse
hipped, with an old mothy saddle and stirrups of no kindred:
besides, possessed with the glanders and like to mose in the
chine, troubled with the lampass, infected with the fashions,
full of windgalls, sped with spavins, rayed with yellows, past
50   cure of the fives, stark spoiled with the staggers, begnawn
with the bots, swayed in the back and shoulder-shotten, near-
legged before and with a half-checked bit and a head-stall of
sheep's leather which, being restrained to keep him from
stumbling, hath been often burst and now repaired with
55   knots, one girth six times pieced, and a woman's crupper of
velure, which hath two letters for her name fairly set down in
studs, and here and there pieced with packthread.

BAPTISTA   Who comes with him?

BIONDELLO   O, sir, his lackey, for all the world caparisoned like
60   the horse: with a linen stock on one leg and a kersey boot-
hose on the other, gartered with a red and blue list; an old hat
and the humour of forty fancies pricked in't for a feather —

---

43 candle-cases containers for candle ends (i.e. too worn out to wear)   **45 chapeless**
without a sheath   **points** laces for fastening the doublet to the hose   **46 hipped** lame, with
an injured hip   **of no kindred** that do not match   **47 glanders** horse disease affecting the
nostrils and jaws   **like . . . chine** of unclear meaning; perhaps a corruption of "like to mourn
in the chine"—i.e. likely to be in the final stages of the **glanders**—or possibly "likely to have a
weak spine (**chine**)"   **48 lampass** horse disease affecting the mouth   **fashions** farcins (horse
disease causing tumors)   **49 windgalls** tumors on a horse's leg   **sped with spavins** rendered
useless by swelling of the leg joints   **rayed** disfigured   **yellows** jaundice   **50 fives** horse
disease affecting the parotid glands   **stark** utterly   **staggers** horse disease marked by a
staggering movement   **begnawn** gnawed at   **51 bots** intestinal worms   **swayed . . . back**
with a bowed spine   **shoulder-shotten** with a dislocated shoulder   **near-legged before**
knock-kneed in the front legs   **52 half-checked bit** restraining bit with a broken side-ring (so,
ineffective)   **head-stall** part of the horse's bridle that goes over the head   **53 sheep's leather**
i.e. weak leather   **restrained** pulled tight   **55 girth** leather band that goes under the horse's
stomach to hold the saddle in place   **pieced** mended   **crupper** leather strap that prevents
the saddle from slipping   **56 velure** velvet   **hath . . . studs** is adorned with her initials in
(brass or silver) studs   **57 packthread** string   **59 lackey** servant   **caparisoned** dressed
60 stock stocking   **kersey** coarse cloth   **boot-hose** over-stocking covering the whole of the
lower leg   **61 list** strip of cloth   **62 humour . . . fancies** unclear; possibly refers to an old
ballad, or to a fanciful ornament—the general sense is that the hat is adorned in an elaborate
and whimsical manner   **pricked . . . feather** pinned in it in place of

a monster, a very monster in apparel, and not like a Christian
footboy or a gentleman's lackey.

65 TRANIO   'Tis some odd humour pricks him to this fashion.

Yet oftentimes he goes but mean-apparelled.

BAPTISTA   I am glad he's come, howsoe'er he comes.

BIONDELLO   Why, sir, he comes not.

BAPTISTA   Didst thou not say he comes?

70 BIONDELLO   Who? That Petruchio came?

BAPTISTA   Ay, that Petruchio came.

BIONDELLO   No, sir, I say his horse comes, with him on his back.

BAPTISTA   Why, that's all one.

BIONDELLO   Nay, by Saint Jamy,

75   I hold you a penny,
     A horse and a man
     Is more than one,
     And yet not many.

Enter Petruchio and Grumio

PETRUCHIO   Come, where be these gallants? Who's at home?

80 BAPTISTA   You are welcome, sir.

PETRUCHIO   And yet I come not well.

BAPTISTA   And yet you halt not.

TRANIO   Not so well apparelled as I wish you were.

PETRUCHIO   Were it better, I should rush in thus.

85   But where is Kate? Where is my lovely bride?
     How does my father? Gentles, methinks you frown.
     And wherefore gaze this goodly company,
     As if they saw some wondrous monument,
     Some comet or unusual prodigy?

90 BAPTISTA   Why, sir, you know this is your wedding day.

First were we sad, fearing you would not come,

---

64 **footboy** page, servant on foot   65 **pricks** spurs   66 **mean-apparelled** dressed humbly/
moderately   74 **Saint Jamy** probably Saint James of Compostella, whose shrine was a popular
object of pilgrimage   75 **hold** bet   79 **gallants** fashionable, fine young gentlemen   81 **come
not well** am not welcome (Baptista responds to the sense of "walk with difficulty")   82 **halt**
limp   86 **Gentles** gentlemen   87 **wherefore** why   **goodly** fine   88 **monument** portent
89 **comet** thought to be a bad omen   **prodigy** omen

Now sadder that you come so unprovided.
Fie, doff this habit, shame to your estate,
An eyesore to our solemn festival!

95 TRANIO   And tell us what occasion of import
Hath all so long detained you from your wife,
And sent you hither so unlike yourself?

PETRUCHIO   Tedious it were to tell, and harsh to hear:
Sufficeth I am come to keep my word,

100   Though in some part enforcèd to digress,
Which at more leisure I will so excuse
As you shall well be satisfied withal.
But where is Kate? I stay too long from her.
The morning wears, 'tis time we were at church.

105 TRANIO   See not your bride in these unreverent robes.
Go to my chamber, put on clothes of mine.

PETRUCHIO   Not I, believe me. Thus I'll visit her.

BAPTISTA   But thus, I trust, you will not marry her.

PETRUCHIO   Good sooth, even thus: therefore ha' done with
words.

110   To me she's married, not unto my clothes.
Could I repair what she will wear in me,
As I can change these poor accoutrements,
'Twere well for Kate and better for myself.
But what a fool am I to chat with you,

115   When I should bid good morrow to my bride,
And seal the title with a lovely kiss!

                    Exeunt [Petruchio and Grumio]

TRANIO   He hath some meaning in his mad attire.
We will persuade him, be it possible,
To put on better ere he go to church.

120 BAPTISTA   I'll after him, and see the event of this.

                    Exeunt [Baptista, Gremio and Attendants]

---

92 **unprovided** ill-dressed, unprepared   93 **doff** take off   **habit** clothing   **estate** rank
94 **solemn** ceremonious   95 **occasion of import** important event   104 **wears** is passing,
being wasted   105 **unreverent** disrespectful   109 **Good sooth** truly   **ha'** have   111 **wear**
wear out (with sexual connotations)   112 **accoutrements** clothes   116 **lovely** loving
120 **event** outcome

TRANIO   But, sir, love concerneth us to add   *To Lucentio*
Her father's liking, which to bring to pass,
As before I imparted to your worship,
I am to get a man — whate'er he be,
125   It skills not much, we'll fit him to our turn —
And he shall be Vincentio of Pisa,
And make assurance here in Padua
Of greater sums than I have promisèd.
So shall you quietly enjoy your hope,
130   And marry sweet Bianca with consent.

LUCENTIO   Were it not that my fellow schoolmaster
Doth watch Bianca's steps so narrowly,
'Twere good, methinks, to steal our marriage,
Which once performed, let all the world say no,
135   I'll keep mine own, despite of all the world.

TRANIO   That by degrees we mean to look into,
And watch our vantage in this business.
We'll overreach the greybeard, Gremio,
The narrow-prying father, Minola,
140   The quaint musician, amorous Litio,
All for my master's sake, Lucentio.

Enter Gremio

Signior Gremio, came you from the church?

GREMIO   As willingly as e'er I came from school.

TRANIO   And is the bride and bridegroom coming home?

145   GREMIO   A bridegroom, say you? 'Tis a groom indeed,
A grumbling groom, and that the girl shall find.

TRANIO   Curster than she? Why, 'tis impossible.

GREMIO   Why he's a devil, a devil, a very fiend.

TRANIO   Why, she's a devil, a devil, the devil's dam.

150   GREMIO   Tut, she's a lamb, a dove, a fool to him.
I'll tell you, Sir Lucentio, when the priest

---

122 liking approval   **to pass** about   **125 skills** matters   **fit** adapt   **132 steps** movements
narrowly closely   **133 steal our marriage** marry secretly   **137 watch our vantage** look for a
favorable opportunity   **138 overreach** outwit   **139 narrow-prying** inquisitive   **140 quaint**
crafty   **145 groom** lowly character/servingman   **147 Curster** more quarrelsome   **150 a**
fool to innocent compared to   **151 Sir** respectful term of address

Should ask if Katherine should be his wife,
'Ay, by gogs-wouns', quoth he, and swore so loud
That all amazed the priest let fall the book,
155 And as he stooped again to take it up,
This mad-brained bridegroom took him such a cuff
That down fell priest and book and book and priest.
'Now take them up,' quoth he, 'if any list.'

TRANIO   What said the wench when he rose again?

160 GREMIO   Trembled and shook, for why, he stamped and
swore,
As if the vicar meant to cozen him.
But after many ceremonies done,
He calls for wine: 'A health!' quoth he, as if
He had been aboard, carousing to his mates
165 After a storm, quaffed off the muscadel
And threw the sops all in the sexton's face,
Having no other reason
But that his beard grew thin and hungerly
And seemed to ask him sops as he was drinking.
170 This done, he took the bride about the neck
And kissed her lips with such a clamorous smack
That at the parting all the church did echo.
And I seeing this came thence for very shame,
And after me, I know, the rout is coming.
175 Such a mad marriage never was before.
Hark, hark! I hear the minstrels play.   *Music plays*

*Enter Petruchio, Kate, Bianca, Hortensio [disguised as Litio], Baptista,
[Grumio and others]*

PETRUCHIO   Gentlemen and friends, I thank you for your pains.
I know you think to dine with me today,
And have prepared great store of wedding cheer,

---

153 **gogs-wouns** God's wounds (a common oath)   154 **book** i.e. Bible   156 **took** gave
158 **them** probably refers to the priest and his book; possibly refers to the hem of Kate's skirt
with Petruchio claiming to suspect the priest of peeping at her undergarments   **any list**
anyone is listening/wants to   160 **for why** because   161 **cozen** cheat   162 **many** various
165 **quaffed off** drank up, drained   **muscadel** a sweet wine   166 **sops** pieces of bread or
cake placed in wine   168 **hungerly** sparsely   169 **him** him for   174 **rout** company
176 **minstrels** musicians   178 **think** expect   179 **cheer** food and drink

180   But so it is, my haste doth call me hence,
       And therefore here I mean to take my leave.
BAPTISTA   Is't possible you will away tonight?
PETRUCHIO   I must away today, before night come.
       Make it no wonder. If you knew my business,
185   You would entreat me rather go than stay.
       And honest company, I thank you all,
       That have beheld me give away myself
       To this most patient, sweet and virtuous wife.
       Dine with my father, drink a health to me,
190   For I must hence, and farewell to you all.
TRANIO   Let us entreat you stay till after dinner.
PETRUCHIO   It may not be.
GREMIO   Let me entreat you.
PETRUCHIO   It cannot be.
195   KATE   Let me entreat you.
PETRUCHIO   I am content.
KATE   Are you content to stay?
PETRUCHIO   I am content you shall entreat me stay,
       But yet not stay, entreat me how you can.
200   KATE   Now, if you love me, stay.
PETRUCHIO   Grumio, my horse.
GRUMIO   Ay, sir, they be ready, the oats have eaten the horses.
KATE   Nay, then,
       Do what thou canst, I will not go today,
205   No, nor tomorrow, not till I please myself.
       The door is open, sir, there lies your way,
       You may be jogging whiles your boots are green.
       For me, I'll not be gone till I please myself.
       'Tis like you'll prove a jolly surly groom,
210   That take it on you at the first so roundly.
PETRUCHIO   O Kate, content thee. Prithee be not angry.

---

184 **Make . . . wonder** don't be surprised   186 **honest** worthy, kind   199 **not stay** not
content to stay   202 **oats . . . horses** i.e. the horses are more than ready to gallop (as they
have been so well fed)   207 **be . . . green** go while your boots are still fresh   209 **jolly** self-
confident, arrogant   210 **take . . . roundly** behaves so presumptuously from the start

KATE   I will be angry. What hast thou to do?—
            Father, be quiet. He shall stay my leisure.
GREMIO   Ay, marry, sir, now it begins to work.
215 KATE   Gentlemen, forward to the bridal dinner.
            I see a woman may be made a fool,
            If she had not a spirit to resist.
PETRUCHIO   They shall go forward, Kate, at thy command.—
            Obey the bride, you that attend on her.
220   Go to the feast, revel and domineer,
            Carouse full measure to her maidenhead,
            Be mad and merry, or go hang yourselves.
            But for my bonny Kate, she must with me.—
            Nay, look not big, nor stamp, nor stare, nor fret.
225   I will be master of what is mine own:
            She is my goods, my chattels, she is my house,
            My household stuff, my field, my barn,
            My horse, my ox, my ass, my anything,
            And here she stands, touch her whoever dare.
230   I'll bring mine action on the proudest he
            That stops my way in Padua.— Grumio,
            Draw forth thy weapon, we are beset with thieves.
            Rescue thy mistress, if thou be a man.
            Fear not, sweet wench, they shall not touch thee, Kate.
235   I'll buckler thee against a million.
                        Exeunt Petruchio, Katherina [and Grumio]
BAPTISTA   Nay, let them go, a couple of quiet ones.
GREMIO   Went they not quickly, I should die with laughing.
TRANIO   Of all mad matches never was the like.
LUCENTIO   Mistress, what's your opinion of your sister?

---

212 hast . . . do is it to do with you   213 stay my leisure wait until I'm ready   214 it . . .
work things are beginning to happen   220 domineer feast riotously   221 Carouse full
measure drink heartily   maidenhead virginity   222 mad high-spirited   224 big
threatening, irate   226 my . . . anything an echo of the Tenth Commandment, which lists the
possessions one should not covet   chattels movable possessions   227 stuff furnishings
230 bring mine action take legal action against/respond with physical force   proudest he
bravest/most self-assured man   235 buckler defend (a buckler was a small round shield)
237 Went they not if they had not gone

240 BIANCA	That, being mad herself, she's madly mated.
GREMIO	I warrant him, Petruchio is Kated.
BAPTISTA	Neighbours and friends, though bride and

bridegroom wants
For to supply the places at the table,
You know there wants no junkets at the feast.
245 Lucentio, you shall supply the bridegroom's place,
And let Bianca take her sister's room.

TRANIO   Shall sweet Bianca practise how to bride it?
BAPTISTA   She shall, Lucentio. Come, gentlemen, let's go.

Exeunt

[Act 3 Scene 3]   *running scene 5*

Enter Grumio

GRUMIO   Fie, fie on all tired jades, on all mad masters, and all
foul ways! Was ever man so beaten? Was ever man so rayed?
Was ever man so weary? I am sent before to make a fire, and
they are coming after to warm them. Now, were not I a little
5   pot and soon hot, my very lips might freeze to my teeth, my
tongue to the roof of my mouth, my heart in my belly, ere I
should come by a fire to thaw me. But I with blowing the fire
shall warm myself, for, considering the weather, a taller man
than I will take cold. Holla, ho, Curtis!

Enter Curtis

10   CURTIS   Who is that calls so coldly?
GRUMIO   A piece of ice: if thou doubt it, thou mayst slide
from my shoulder to my heel with no greater a run but my
head and my neck. A fire, good Curtis.
CURTIS   Is my master and his wife coming, Grumio?

---

241 **Kated mated** with Kate/infected with "the Kate"   242 **wants For to** are lacking to
244 **junkets** sweetmeats   246 **room** place   247 **bride it** play the bride   **3.3** *Location: a
country estate*   2 **foul ways** muddy roads   **rayed** dirtied   4 **little . . . hot** small pot that
boils rapidly—i.e. small man who is quick to become angry (proverbial)   8 **taller** braver/
nobler/less short   10 **coldly** unenthusiastically/like one who is physically chilly   12 **run**
running start

15 GRUMIO   O, ay, Curtis, ay, and therefore fire, fire, cast on no water.

CURTIS   Is she so hot a shrew as she's reported?

GRUMIO   She was, good Curtis, before this frost. But, thou know'st, winter tames man, woman and beast, for it hath tamed my old master and my new mistress and myself, fellow
20 Curtis.

CURTIS   Away, you three-inch fool! I am no beast.

GRUMIO   Am I but three inches? Why, thy horn is a foot, and so long am I at the least. But wilt thou make a fire, or shall I complain on thee to our mistress, whose hand, she being
25 now at hand, thou shalt soon feel, to thy cold comfort, for being slow in thy hot office?

CURTIS   I prithee, good Grumio, tell me how goes the world?

GRUMIO   A cold world, Curtis, in every office but thine, and therefore fire: do thy duty, and have thy duty, for my master
30 and mistress are almost frozen to death.

CURTIS   There's fire ready, and therefore, good Grumio, the news.

GRUMIO   Why, 'Jack, boy! Ho, boy!' and as much news as wilt thou.

35 CURTIS   Come, you are so full of cony-catching!

GRUMIO   Why, therefore fire, for I have caught extreme cold. Where's the cook? Is supper ready, the house trimmed, rushes strewed, cobwebs swept, the servingmen in their new fustian, the white stockings, and every officer his wedding-

---

15 fire . . . water refers to the musical round "Scotland's burning, Scotland's burning / See yonder! See yonder! / Fire, fire! Fire, fire! / Cast on water! Cast on water!"   16 hot fiery tempered   18 winter . . . beast "winter and wedlock tame both man and beast" (proverbial)   21 beast Curtis objects to the implication that he is Grumio's **fellow** after Grumio compares himself to a beast   22 horn cuckold's horn (the sign of a man with an unfaithful wife)   23 so . . . least i.e. I/my penis must be at least as long to have made you a cuckold (picking up on the **three-inch** insult)   26 hot office fire-making duty   29 do . . . duty do your duty and take your dues (wages)   33 Jack . . . news alludes to the musical round "Jack boy, ho boy, News: / The cat is in the well"   35 cony-catching trickery (puns on "catch"—i.e. a musical round, such as that quoted by Grumio)   37 trimmed decked out, prepared   38 strewed i.e. on the floor, the usual Elizabethan practice   39 fustian type of coarse cloth

40   garment on? Be the jacks fair within, the jills fair without,
the carpets laid, and everything in order?

CURTIS   All ready, and therefore, I pray thee, news.

GRUMIO   First know my horse is tired, my master and mistress
fallen out.

45   CURTIS   How?

GRUMIO   Out of their saddles into the dirt, and thereby hangs
a tale.

CURTIS   Let's ha't, good Grumio.

GRUMIO   Lend thine ear.

50   CURTIS   Here.

GRUMIO   There.   *Strikes him*

CURTIS   This 'tis to feel a tale, not to hear a tale.

GRUMIO   And therefore 'tis called a sensible tale, and this cuff
was but to knock at your ear, and beseech listening. Now I
55   begin: *Imprimis*, we came down a foul hill, my master riding
behind my mistress—

CURTIS   Both of one horse?

GRUMIO   What's that to thee?

CURTIS   Why, a horse.

60   GRUMIO   Tell thou the tale. But hadst thou not crossed me,
thou shouldst have heard how her horse fell and she under
her horse: thou shouldst have heard in how miry a place,
how she was bemoiled, how he left her with the horse upon
her, how he beat me because her horse stumbled, how she
65   waded through the dirt to pluck him off me, how he swore,
how she prayed that never prayed before, how I cried, how
the horses ran away, how her bridle was burst, how I lost my
crupper, with many things of worthy memory, which now
shall die in oblivion and thou return unexperienced to thy
70   grave.

---

40 **jacks** male servants/leather drinking vessels   **jills** female servants/metal drinking vessels
(which would need polishing **without**)   41 **laid** usually on tables or hung on walls   48 **ha't**
have it, hear it   53 **sensible** felt by the senses/easily understood   55 *Imprimis* first (Latin)
57 **of** on   60 **crossed** interrupted/irritated   62 **miry** boggy   63 **bemoiled** covered with mud
67 **burst** broken   68 **worthy memory** worth remembering   69 **unexperienced** in ignorance

CURTIS   By this reckoning he is more shrew than she.

GRUMIO   Ay, and that thou and the proudest of you all shall find when he comes home. But what talk I of this? Call forth Nathaniel, Joseph, Nicholas, Philip, Walter, Sugarsop and
75   the rest. Let their heads be slickly combed, their blue coats brushed and their garters of an indifferent knit. Let them curtsy with their left legs and not presume to touch a hair of my master's horsetail till they kiss their hands. Are they all ready?

80   CURTIS   They are.

GRUMIO   Call them forth.

CURTIS   Do you hear, ho? You must meet my master to countenance my mistress.

GRUMIO   Why, she hath a face of her own.

85   CURTIS   Who knows not that?

GRUMIO   Thou, it seems, that calls for company to countenance her.

CURTIS   I call them forth to credit her.

Enter four or five Servingmen

GRUMIO   Why, she comes to borrow nothing of them.

90   NATHANIEL   Welcome home, Grumio!

PHILIP   How now, Grumio!

JOSEPH   What, Grumio!

NICHOLAS   Fellow Grumio!

NATHANIEL   How now, old lad?

95   GRUMIO   Welcome, you.— How now, you?—   *Greets each*
What, you?— Fellow, you.— And thus much for   *Servingman*
greeting. Now, my spruce companions, is all ready, and all things neat?

NATHANIEL   All things is ready. How near is our master?

---

72 **proudest** bravest   73 **what** why   75 **blue** traditional color of a servant's livery
76 **indifferent knit** modest/matching pattern   77 **curtsy** bow   **left legs** as a show of
subservience (to put your right foot forward was considered arrogant)   78 **kiss their hands** to
kiss your own hand was a mark of respect to a superior   83 **countenance** honor (in the next
line Grumio puns on the sense of "face")   88 **credit** respect (in the next line Grumio puns on
the sense of "provide financial credit for")   97 **spruce** lively/smart   98 **neat** spotless/elegant

100   GRUMIO   E'en at hand, alighted by this, and therefore be not—
Cock's passion, silence! I hear my master.

Enter Petruchio and Kate

PETRUCHIO   Where be these knaves? What, no man at door
To hold my stirrup nor to take my horse?
Where is Nathaniel, Gregory, Philip?

105   ALL SERVINGMEN   Here, here, sir, here, sir.

PETRUCHIO   Here, sir, here, sir, here, sir, here, sir!
You logger-headed and unpolished grooms!
What, no attendance? No regard? No duty?
Where is the foolish knave I sent before?

110   GRUMIO   Here, sir, as foolish as I was before.

PETRUCHIO   You peasant swain. You whoreson malt-horse
    drudge.
Did I not bid thee meet me in the park,
And bring along these rascal knaves with thee?

GRUMIO   Nathaniel's coat, sir, was not fully made,

115   And Gabriel's pumps were all unpinked i'th'heel.
There was no link to colour Peter's hat,
And Walter's dagger was not come from sheathing.
There were none fine but Adam, Rafe and Gregory,
The rest were ragged, old, and beggarly.

120   Yet, as they are, here are they come to meet you.

PETRUCHIO   Go, rascals, go, and fetch my supper in.

Exeunt Servingmen

'Where is the life that late I led?   *Sings*
Where are those—'
Sit down, Kate, and welcome.— Soud, soud, soud,
soud!   *They sit*

---

100 this this time   **101 Cock's passion** by God's passion   **107 logger-headed** stupid
111 swain yokel   **whoreson** rogue, son-of-a-whore   **malt-horse drudge** plodding idiot
(literally, heavy brewer's horse used to grind malt by working a treadmill)   **112 park** enclosed
hunting ground   **114 made** finished   **115 unpinked** lacking ornamentation   **116 link**
blacking (from a burnt torch)   **117 come from sheathing** returned from being fitted with a
scabbard   **118 fine** properly dressed   **122 "Where . . . those—"** lines from of an old (lost)
ballad   **124 Soud** unclear; possibly an exclamation of impatience or despair (many editors
emend to "Food")

Enter Servants with supper

125   Why, when, I say? Nay, good sweet Kate, be merry.—
       Off with my boots, you rogues! You villains, when?

A Servant takes off his boots

           'It was the friar of orders grey,   *Sings*
           As he forth walkèd on his way—'
       Out, you rogue! You pluck my foot awry.
130   Take that, and mend the plucking of the other.   *Kicks him*
       Be merry, Kate.— Some water, here. What, ho!

Enter one with water

       Where's my spaniel Troilus? Sirrah, get you hence,
       And bid my cousin Ferdinand come hither.—
       One, Kate, that you must kiss, and be acquainted with.—
135   Where are my slippers? Shall I have some water?
       Come, Kate, and wash, and welcome
           heartily.—   *Servant spills water*
       You whoreson villain, will you let it fall?   *Strikes the Servant*

KATE   Patience, I pray you. 'Twas a fault unwilling.

PETRUCHIO   A whoreson beetle-headed, flap-eared knave!—
140   Come, Kate, sit down, I know you have a stomach.
       Will you give thanks, sweet Kate, or else shall I?
       What's this? Mutton?

FIRST SERVANT   Ay.

PETRUCHIO   Who brought it?

145   PETER   I.

PETRUCHIO   'Tis burnt, and so is all the meat.
       What dogs are these? Where is the rascal cook?
       How durst you, villains, bring it from the dresser
       And serve it thus to me that love it not?

---

126 when exclamation of impatience   **127 "It . . . way"** fragment of a ballad (possibly bawdy,
now lost)   **friar . . . grey** Gray friar or Franciscan   **129 Out** exclamation of anger   **pluck . . .
awry** pull my foot the wrong way (as you remove my boot)   **130 mend** make a better job of
131 water for handwashing   **132 Troilus** a name associated with fidelity   **133 Ferdinand** no
such character ever appears   **139 beetle-headed** thick-headed (a "beetle" is a heavy wooden
mallet)   **flap-eared** with long hanging ears   **140 stomach** appetite   **141 give thanks** say
grace   **148 dresser** kitchen table on which food was prepared/sideboard from which food was
served

150   There, take it to you, trenchers, cups, and all.   *Throws the meat and*
       You heedless joltheads and unmannered slaves!   *dishes at them*
       What, do you grumble? I'll be with you straight.
KATE   I pray you, husband, be not so disquiet.
       The meat was well, if you were so contented.
155 PETRUCHIO   I tell thee, Kate, 'twas burnt and dried away,
       And I expressly am forbid to touch it,
       For it engenders choler, planteth anger,
       And better 'twere that both of us did fast,
       Since, of ourselves, ourselves are choleric,
160   Than feed it with such over-roasted flesh.
       Be patient, tomorrow't shall be mended,
       And for this night we'll fast for company.
       Come, I will bring thee to thy bridal chamber.   *Exeunt*
Enter Servants severally
NATHANIEL   Peter, didst ever see the like?
165 PETER   He kills her in her own humour.
GRUMIO   Where is he?
Enter Curtis, a servant
CURTIS   In her chamber, making a sermon of continency
       to her,
       And rails and swears and rates that she, poor soul,
170   Knows not which way to stand, to look, to speak,
       And sits as one new-risen from a dream.
       Away, away, for he is coming hither.   [*Exeunt*]
Enter Petruchio
PETRUCHIO   Thus have I politicly begun my reign,
       And 'tis my hope to end successfully.
175   My falcon now is sharp and passing empty,
       And till she stoop she must not be full-gorged,

---

150 **trenchers** plates   151 **joltheads** blockheads   **unmannered** insolent   152 **be . . .
straight** deal with you immediately   154 **well** satisfactory   157 **choler** anger (associated
with heat and dryness)   159 **of ourselves** by our natures   162 **for company** together
165 **kills . . . humour** defeats her with her own temperament   167 **continency** moderation,
self-restraint   169 **rates** scolds   171 **new-risen** newly woken   173 **politicly** shrewdly,
strategically   175 **falcon** i.e. Kate; methods used in training a wild hawk involved continual
observation, sleep deprivation and hunger   **sharp** keenly hungry   176 **stoop** swoops
directly to the prey/submits   **full-gorged** fully fed

For then she never looks upon her lure.
Another way I have to man my haggard,
To make her come and know her keeper's call,
180   That is, to watch her, as we watch these kites
That bate and beat and will not be obedient.
She eat no meat today, nor none shall eat.
Last night she slept not, nor tonight she shall not.
As with the meat, some undeservèd fault
185   I'll find about the making of the bed,
And here I'll fling the pillow, there the bolster,
This way the coverlet, another way the sheets.
Ay, and amid this hurly I intend
That all is done in reverend care of her.
190   And in conclusion she shall watch all night,
And if she chance to nod I'll rail and brawl
And with the clamour keep her still awake.
This is a way to kill a wife with kindness,
And thus I'll curb her mad and headstrong humour.
195   He that knows better how to tame a shrew,
Now let him speak. 'Tis charity to show.   *Exit*

[Act 3 Scene 4]   *running scene 6*

Enter Tranio and Hortensio

TRANIO   Is't possible, friend Litio, that Mistress Bianca
Doth fancy any other but Lucentio?
I tell you, sir, she bears me fair in hand.
HORTENSIO   Sir, to satisfy you in what I have said,
5   Stand by and mark the manner of his teaching.
Enter Bianca [and Lucentio]

---

177 **looks upon** takes notice of   **lure** bait used in training a hawk   178 **man** control
haggard female hawk/wild woman   180 **watch her** keep her awake   **kites** birds of prey
181 **bate and beat** flutter and flap   182 **eat** ate   188 **hurly** commotion   **intend** pretend
190 **watch** remain awake   196 **charity to show** public duty to reveal it   **3.4** *Location:*
Padua   3 **bears . . . hand** encourages me   4 **satisfy** convince

	LUCENTIO	Now, mistress, profit you in what you read?
	BIANCA	What, master, read you? First resolve me that.
	LUCENTIO	I read that I profess, the *Art to Love*.
	BIANCA	And may you prove, sir, master of your art.
10	LUCENTIO	While you, sweet dear, prove mistress of my heart.

Lucentio and Bianca talk aside

HORTENSIO   Quick proceeders, marry! Now tell me, I pray,
You that durst swear that your mistress Bianca
Loved none in the world so well as Lucentio.

TRANIO   O despiteful love, unconstant womankind!
15   I tell thee, Litio, this is wonderful.

HORTENSIO   Mistake no more, I am not Litio,
Nor a musician, as I seem to be,
But one that scorn to live in this disguise,
For such a one as leaves a gentleman,
20   And makes a god of such a cullion;
Know, sir, that I am called Hortensio.

TRANIO   Signior Hortensio, I have often heard
Of your entire affection to Bianca,
And since mine eyes are witness of her lightness,
25   I will with you, if you be so contented,
Forswear Bianca and her love forever.

HORTENSIO   See how they kiss and court! Signior Lucentio,
Here is my hand, and here I firmly vow
Never to woo her more, but do forswear her,
30   As one unworthy all the former favours
That I have fondly flattered her withal.

TRANIO   And here I take the like unfeignèd oath,
Never to marry with her though she would entreat.
Fie on her! See how beastly she doth court him!

---

7 **resolve** answer   8 **I profess** which I practice/claim knowledge of   *Art to Love* Ovid's erotic poem *Ars Amatoria*   11 **Quick proceeders** apt/rapid students (plays on the scholarly sense of to "proceed" from a bachelor's to a master's degree)   15 **wonderful** extraordinary   19 **such a one** i.e. Bianca   20 **cullion** wretch   23 **entire** wholehearted   24 **lightness** inconstancy/ promiscuity   26 **Forswear** reject   31 **fondly** foolishly/dotingly   32 **unfeignèd** genuine   34 **beastly** abominably/lecherously

35 HORTENSIO   Would all the world but he had quite forsworn!
For me, that I may surely keep mine oath,
I will be married to a wealthy widow,
Ere three days pass, which hath as long loved me
As I have loved this proud disdainful haggard.
40 And so farewell, Signior Lucentio.
Kindness in women, not their beauteous looks,
Shall win my love. And so I take my leave,
In resolution as I swore before.   [*Exit*]

TRANIO   Mistress Bianca, bless you with such grace
45 As 'longeth to a lover's blessèd case!
Nay, I have ta'en you napping, gentle love,
And have forsworn you with Hortensio.

BIANCA   Tranio, you jest. But have you both forsworn me?

TRANIO   Mistress, we have.

50 LUCENTIO   Then we are rid of Litio.

TRANIO   I'faith, he'll have a lusty widow now,
That shall be wooed and wedded in a day.

BIANCA   God give him joy!

TRANIO   Ay, and he'll tame her.

55 BIANCA   He says so, Tranio.

TRANIO   Faith, he is gone unto the taming school.

BIANCA   The taming school? What, is there such a place?

TRANIO   Ay, mistress, and Petruchio is the master,
That teacheth tricks eleven and twenty long,
60 To tame a shrew and charm her chatt'ring tongue.

Enter Biondello

BIONDELLO   O master, master, I have watched so long
That I am dog-weary, but at last I spied
An ancient angel coming down the hill
Will serve the turn.

65 TRANIO   What is he, Biondello?

---

35 **Would . . . forsworn!** If only the whole world, other than he, would forsake her!   36 **that** so that   43 **In resolution** determinedly   45 **'longeth** belongs   46 **ta'en you napping** caught you off guard   51 **lusty** lively/eager/merry/lustful   59 **eleven . . . long** i.e. exactly right (alludes to the card game "thirty-one")   60 **charm** silence with a spell   62 **dog-weary** exhausted   63 **ancient angel** old guardian angel

BIONDELLO Master, a mercatante, or a pedant,
I know not what, but formal in apparel,
In gait and countenance surely like a father.

LUCENTIO And what of him, Tranio?

70 TRANIO If he be credulous and trust my tale,
I'll make him glad to seem Vincentio,
And give assurance to Baptista Minola
As if he were the right Vincentio.
Take in your love, and then let me alone.

[*Exeunt Lucentio and Bianca*]

Enter a Pedant

75 PEDANT God save you, sir!

TRANIO And you, sir! You are welcome.
Travel you far on, or are you at the furthest?

PEDANT Sir, at the furthest for a week or two,
But then up further, and as far as Rome,

80 And so to Tripoli, if God lend me life.

TRANIO What countryman, I pray?

PEDANT Of Mantua.

TRANIO Of Mantua, sir? Marry, God forbid!
And come to Padua, careless of your life?

85 PEDANT My life, sir? How, I pray? For that goes hard.

TRANIO 'Tis death for anyone in Mantua
To come to Padua. Know you not the cause?
Your ships are stayed at Venice, and the duke,
For private quarrel 'twixt your duke and him,

90 Hath published and proclaimed it openly.
'Tis marvel, but that you are but newly come,
You might have heard it else proclaimed about.

PEDANT Alas, sir, it is worse for me than so,
For I have bills for money by exchange

95 From Florence and must here deliver them.

---

66 **mercatante** merchant (Italian)   **pedant** schoolmaster   71 **seem** pretend to be   74 **let me
alone** i.e. rely on me   81 **What countryman** where are you from   85 **goes hard** is significant
88 **stayed** detained   89 **For** on account of a   90 **published** publicly announced   91 **marvel**
remarkable   **newly come** have only just arrived   93 **than so** even than this   94 **bills . . .
exchange** money orders, promissory notes

TRANIO   Well, sir, to do you courtesy,
This will I do, and this I will advise you:
First tell me, have you ever been at Pisa?
PEDANT   Ay, sir, in Pisa have I often been,
100   Pisa renownèd for grave citizens.
TRANIO   Among them know you one Vincentio?
PEDANT   I know him not, but I have heard of him,
A merchant of incomparable wealth.
TRANIO   He is my father, sir, and sooth to say,
105   In count'nance somewhat doth resemble you.
BIONDELLO   As much as an apple doth an oyster, and all
one.   *Aside*
TRANIO   To save your life in this extremity,
This favour will I do you for his sake,
And think it not the worst of all your fortunes
110   That you are like to Sir Vincentio.
His name and credit shall you undertake,
And in my house you shall be friendly lodged.
Look that you take upon you as you should.
You understand me, sir. So shall you stay
115   Till you have done your business in the city.
If this be court'sy, sir, accept of it.
PEDANT   O, sir, I do, and will repute you ever
The patron of my life and liberty.
TRANIO   Then go with me to make the matter good.
120   This, by the way, I let you understand.
My father is here looked for every day,
To pass assurance of a dower in marriage
'Twixt me and one Baptista's daughter here.
In all these circumstances I'll instruct you.
125   Go with me to clothe you as becomes you.   *Exeunt*

---

106 and all one but never mind   111 credit reputation   undertake assume   113 Look . . .
should make sure that you play your part properly   117 repute consider, esteem
119 make . . . good put the plan into action   121 looked for expected   125 becomes befits

Act 4 Scene 1

Enter Katherina and Grumio

GRUMIO   No, no, forsooth, I dare not for my life.

KATE   The more my wrong, the more his spite appears.
What, did he marry me to famish me?
Beggars that come unto my father's door

5   Upon entreaty have a present alms,
If not, elsewhere they meet with charity.
But I, who never knew how to entreat,
Nor never needed that I should entreat,
Am starved for meat, giddy for lack of sleep,

10   With oaths kept waking and with brawling fed.
And that which spites me more than all these wants,
He does it under name of perfect love,
As who should say, if I should sleep or eat,
'Twere deadly sickness or else present death.

15   I prithee go and get me some repast,
I care not what, so it be wholesome food.

GRUMIO   What say you to a neat's foot?

KATE   'Tis passing good, I prithee let me have it.

GRUMIO   I fear it is too choleric a meat.

20   How say you to a fat tripe finely broiled?

KATE   I like it well, good Grumio, fetch it me.

GRUMIO   I cannot tell, I fear 'tis choleric.
What say you to a piece of beef and mustard?

KATE   A dish that I do love to feed upon.

25 GRUMIO   Ay, but the mustard is too hot a little.

KATE   Why then, the beef, and let the mustard rest.

GRUMIO   Nay then, I will not. You shall have the mustard,
Or else you get no beef of Grumio.

KATE   Then both, or one, or anything thou wilt.

30 GRUMIO   Why then, the mustard without the beef.

4.1 *Location: a country estate*   **2 my wrong** injustice I undergo   **5 present** immediate
9 meat food   **11 spites** mortifies, vexes   **13 who** one who   **16 so** so long as   **17 neat's** ox's
19 choleric likely to induce choler (anger)   **20 broiled** grilled   **22 cannot tell** am not sure

KATE   Go, get thee gone, thou false deluding slave

Beats him

That feed'st me with the very name of meat.

Sorrow on thee and all the pack of you

That triumph thus upon my misery.

35   Go, get thee gone, I say.

Enter Petruchio and Hortensio with meat

PETRUCHIO   How fares my Kate? What, sweeting, all amort?

HORTENSIO   Mistress, what cheer?

KATE   Faith, as cold as can be.

PETRUCHIO   Pluck up thy spirits, look cheerfully upon me.

40   Here love, thou see'st how diligent I am

To dress thy meat myself and bring it thee.

I am sure, sweet Kate, this kindness merits thanks.

What, not a word? Nay then thou lov'st it not,

And all my pains is sorted to no proof.

45   Here, take away this dish.

KATE   I pray you let it stand.

PETRUCHIO   The poorest service is repaid with thanks,

And so shall mine, before you touch the meat.

KATE   I thank you, sir.

50   HORTENSIO   Signior Petruchio, fie, you are to blame.

Come, mistress Kate, I'll bear you company.

PETRUCHIO   Eat it up all, Hortensio, if thou lovest me.   *Aside*

Much good do it unto thy gentle heart!—   *Hortensio takes plate*

Kate, eat apace. And now, my honey love,   *and does not let*

55   Will we return unto thy father's house   *Kate eat*

And revel it as bravely as the best,

With silken coats and caps and golden rings,

With ruffs and cuffs and farthingales and things,

With scarfs and fans and double change of bravery,

---

32 very mere   **36 sweeting** sweetheart   **amort** dispirited   **37 what cheer** how are you (in the next line Kate plays on the sense of "food/hospitality" and Petruchio continues the wordplay with cheerfully)   **38 cold** poor, inadequate   **44 pains . . . proof** efforts are wasted   **46 stand** remain   **50 to blame** at fault   **54 apace** quickly   **56 bravely** splendidly   **58 ruffs** elaborate starched neck-wear   **cuffs** decorative bands sewn onto the sleeves   **farthingales** boned petticoats worn underneath the back of the dress

60   With amber bracelets, beads and all this knavery.
        What, hast thou dined? The tailor stays thy leisure,
        To deck thy body with his ruffling treasure.
        Enter Tailor [with a gown]
        Come, tailor, let us see these ornaments.
        Enter Haberdasher [with a hat]
        Lay forth the gown.— What news with you, sir?
65 HABERDASHER   Here is the cap your worship did bespeak.
    PETRUCHIO   Why, this was moulded on a porringer,
        A velvet dish. Fie, fie, 'tis lewd and filthy.
        Why, 'tis a cockle or a walnut-shell,
        A knack, a toy, a trick, a baby's cap.
70   Away with it! Come, let me have a bigger.
    KATE   I'll have no bigger. This doth fit the time,
        And gentlewomen wear such caps as these.
    PETRUCHIO   When you are gentle, you shall have one too,
        And not till then.
75 HORTENSIO   That will not be in haste.   *Aside*
    KATE   Why, sir, I trust I may have leave to speak,
        And speak I will. I am no child, no babe.
        Your betters have endured me say my mind,
        And if you cannot, best you stop your ears.
80   My tongue will tell the anger of my heart,
        Or else my heart concealing it will break,
        And rather than it shall, I will be free
        Even to the uttermost, as I please, in words.
    PETRUCHIO   Why, thou say'st true. It is a paltry cap,
85   A custard-coffin, a bauble, a silken pie.
        I love thee well in that thou lik'st it not.
    KATE   Love me or love me not, I like the cap,
        And it I will have, or I will have none.   *[Exit Haberdasher]*

---

60 **knavery** showy adornment   62 **ruffling treasure** frilled, lacy clothing   65 **bespeak** order
66 **porringer** porridge bowl   67 **lewd** vile, cheap   **filthy** contemptible   68 **cockle** cockleshell
69 **A . . . trick** i.e. trinkets, trifles   71 **fit the time** is fashionable   73 **gentle** mild   78 **endured me** permitted me to   85 **custard-coffin** pastry crust for custard

PETRUCHIO   Thy gown? Why, ay. Come, tailor, let us see't.

90   O mercy, God! What masquing stuff is here?

What's this? A sleeve? 'Tis like a demi-cannon.

What, up and down, carved like an apple tart?

Here's snip and nip and cut and slish and slash,

Like to a censer in a barber's shop.

95   Why, what o'devil's name, tailor, call'st thou this?

HORTENSIO   I see she's like to have neither cap nor gown.   *Aside*

TAILOR   You bid me make it orderly and well,

According to the fashion and the time.

PETRUCHIO   Marry, and did. But if you be remembered,

100   I did not bid you mar it to the time.

Go, hop me over every kennel home,

For you shall hop without my custom, sir:

I'll none of it. Hence, make your best of it.

KATE   I never saw a better-fashioned gown,

105   More quaint, more pleasing, nor more commendable.

Belike you mean to make a puppet of me.

PETRUCHIO   Why, true, he means to make a puppet of thee.

TAILOR   She says your worship means to make a puppet

of her.

PETRUCHIO   O monstrous arrogance! Thou liest, thou thread,

thou thimble,

110   Thou yard, three-quarters, half-yard, quarter, nail!

Thou flea, thou nit, thou winter-cricket thou!

Braved in mine own house with a skein of thread?

Away, thou rag, thou quantity, thou remnant,

Or I shall so be-mete thee with thy yard

115   As thou shalt think on prating whilst thou liv'st!

I tell thee, I, that thou hast marred her gown.

---

90 masquing stuff clothes fit for a masque (i.e. elaborate, theatrical)   **91 demi-cannon** large
cannon   **92 up and down** in every respect   **carved . . . tart** i.e. slashed to reveal a different
fabric beneath (like the slits on tart crusts)   **94 censer** perfuming vessel with a perforated lid
99 did I did   **100 mar** ruin   **101 hop . . . home** hop home over every street gutter (**kennel**)
103 make . . . it do what you can with it   **105 quaint** elegant, skillfully made   **106 Belike**
perhaps   **puppet** i.e. fool   **110 yard** yardstick, measuring rod   **nail** measure of length for cloth
(two and a quarter inches)   **112 Braved** defied   **113 quantity** scrap   **114 be-mete** measure
(quibbles on "mete out punishment")   **115 on prating** of prattling like this again

TAILOR   Your worship is deceived. The gown is made
     Just as my master had direction.
     Grumio gave order how it should be done.

120 GRUMIO   I gave him no order, I gave him the stuff.

TAILOR   But how did you desire it should be made?

GRUMIO   Marry, sir, with needle and thread.

TAILOR   But did you not request to have it cut?

GRUMIO   Thou hast faced many things.

125 TAILOR   I have.

GRUMIO   Face not me. Thou hast braved many men, brave
     not me; I will neither be faced nor braved. I say unto thee, I
     bid thy master cut out the gown, but I did not bid him cut it
     to pieces. *Ergo*, thou liest.

130 TAILOR   Why, here is the note of the fashion to
     testify.   *Shows bill*

PETRUCHIO   Read it.

GRUMIO   The note lies in's throat, if he say I said so.

TAILOR   'Imprimis, a loose-bodied gown.'   *Reads*

GRUMIO   Master, if ever I said loose-bodied gown, sew me in
135 the skirts of it, and beat me to death with a bottom of brown
     thread: I said a gown.

PETRUCHIO   Proceed.

TAILOR   'With a small compassed cape.'   *Reads*

GRUMIO   I confess the cape.

140 TAILOR   'With a trunk sleeve.'   *Reads*

GRUMIO   I confess two sleeves.

TAILOR   'The sleeves curiously cut.'   *Reads*

PETRUCHIO   Ay, there's the villainy.

GRUMIO   Error i'th'bill, sir, error i'th'bill. I commanded the
145 sleeves should be cut out and sewed up again, and that I'll

---

120 **stuff** material   124 **faced** adorned (Grumio's next usage puns on the sense of "confront")
126 **braved** provided clothes for/defied   129 *Ergo* "therefore" (Latin)   132 **The . . . throat** the
note lies outrageously (punning on the sense of a musical note that emanates from the throat)
133 **loose-bodied gown** loose-fitting/designed for sexually "loose" women   135 **bottom** ball
138 **compassed** cut with a curved edge   140 **trunk** full, puffed   142 **curiously** elaborately/
skillfully   144 **bill** the note detailing the nature of the dress

prove upon thee, though thy little finger be armed in a thimble.

TAILOR   This is true that I say, an I had thee in place where, thou shouldst know it.

150   GRUMIO   I am for thee straight. Take thou the bill, give me thy mete-yard, and spare not me.

HORTENSIO   God-a-mercy, Grumio, then he shall have no odds.

PETRUCHIO   Well, sir, in brief, the gown is not for me.

GRUMIO   You are i'th'right, sir, 'tis for my mistress.

155   PETRUCHIO   Go, take it up unto thy master's use.

GRUMIO   Villain, not for thy life. Take up my mistress' gown for thy master's use!

PETRUCHIO   Why, sir, what's your conceit in that?

GRUMIO   O, sir, the conceit is deeper than you think for:

160   Take up my mistress' gown to his master's use!
O, fie, fie, fie!

PETRUCHIO   Hortensio, say thou wilt see the
tailor paid.—   *Aside to Hortensio*
Go take it hence. Be gone, and say no more.   *To the Tailor*

HORTENSIO   Tailor, I'll pay thee for thy gown tomorrow.   *Aside to*
165   Take no unkindness of his hasty words.   *the Tailor*
Away, I say, commend me to thy master.   *Exit Tailor*

PETRUCHIO   Well, come, my Kate. We will unto your father's
Even in these honest mean habiliments:
Our purses shall be proud, our garments poor,
170   For 'tis the mind that makes the body rich,
And as the sun breaks through the darkest clouds,
So honour peereth in the meanest habit.
What, is the jay more precious than the lark,
Because his feathers are more beautiful?
175   Or is the adder better than the eel

---

146 **prove upon thee** i.e. by fighting you   148 **an** if   **place where** suitable place   150 **for thee straight** ready for you now   151 **mete-yard** yardstick   152 **odds** advantage   155 **take . . . use** take it away and let your master use it how he will (in his response, Grumio interprets **take up** as "pull up" and **use** as "sexual usage")   158 **conceit** idea (puns on "con"—i.e. "vagina")   159 **think for** think   165 **of** from   168 **mean habiliments** poor, humble clothes   169 **proud** bulging   172 **peereth** appears/peeps through

Because his painted skin contents the eye?
O no, good Kate, neither art thou the worse
For this poor furniture and mean array.
If thou account'st it shame, lay it on me.
180   And therefore frolic. We will hence forthwith,
To feast and sport us at thy father's house.—
Go, call my men, and let us straight to him,   *To Grumio*
And bring our horses unto Long-lane end.—
There will we mount, and thither walk on foot.
185   Let's see, I think 'tis now some seven o'clock,
And well we may come there by dinnertime.
KATE   I dare assure you, sir, 'tis almost two,
And 'twill be suppertime ere you come there.
PETRUCHIO   It shall be seven ere I go to horse.
190   Look, what I speak, or do, or think to do,
You are still crossing it. Sirs, let't alone.
I will not go today, and ere I do,
It shall be what o'clock I say it is.
HORTENSIO   Why, so this gallant will command the sun.   *Aside*

                                                    [*Exeunt*]

[Act 4 Scene 2]   *running scene 8*

Enter Tranio [disguised as Lucentio], and the Pedant dressed like
Vincentio, booted and bareheaded

TRANIO   Sir, this is the house. Please it you that I call?
PEDANT   Ay, what else? And but I be deceived,
Signior Baptista may remember me,
Near twenty years ago, in Genoa,
5   Where we were lodgers at the Pegasus.
TRANIO   'Tis well, and hold your own, in any case,
With such austerity as 'longeth to a father.

---

176 painted colored, patterned   178 furniture clothing   179 lay blame   180 frolic be joyous
181 sport us make merry   186 dinnertime noon   188 suppertime i.e. about six   190 what
whatever   191 crossing contradicting   let't alone leave it   4.2 *Location: Padua*   2 but
unless   5 Pegasus i.e. at an inn with the sign of Pegasus, the winged horse of classical
mythology   6 hold your own play your part   7 'longeth belongs

Enter Biondello

PEDANT   I warrant you. But, sir, here comes your boy.
'Twere good he were schooled.

10   TRANIO   Fear you not him.— Sirrah Biondello,
Now do your duty throughly, I advise you:
Imagine 'twere the right Vincentio.

BIONDELLO   Tut, fear not me.

TRANIO   But hast thou done thy errand to Baptista?

15   BIONDELLO   I told him that your father was at Venice,
And that you looked for him this day in Padua.

TRANIO   Thou'rt a tall fellow. Hold thee that to   *Gives money*
drink.
Here comes Baptista: set your countenance, sir.

Enter Baptista and Lucentio

Signior Baptista, you are happily met.

20   Sir, this is the gentleman I told you of.   *To the Pedant*
I pray you stand good father to me now,
Give me Bianca for my patrimony.

PEDANT   Soft son!
Sir, by your leave, having come to Padua

25   To gather in some debts, my son Lucentio
Made me acquainted with a weighty cause
Of love between your daughter and himself:
And, for the good report I hear of you,
And for the love he beareth to your daughter,

30   And she to him, to stay him not too long,
I am content, in a good father's care,
To have him matched. And if you please to like
No worse than I, upon some agreement
Me shall you find ready and willing

35   With one consent to have her so bestowed,

---

9 **schooled** instructed/practiced (in his part)   11 **throughly** thoroughly   12 **right** real
16 **looked for** expected   17 **tall** fine   **hold . . . drink** take this to buy a drink   18 **set your**
countenance assume the appearance (of a father)   21 **stand** show yourself a   22 **patrimony**
inheritance   23 **Soft** wait a moment   28 **for** because of   30 **stay** delay   32 **please . . . I** are as
satisfied as I am   35 **one consent** absolute agreement   **bestowed** given in marriage

For curious I cannot be with you,
Signior Baptista, of whom I hear so well.

BAPTISTA   Sir, pardon me in what I have to say.
Your plainness and your shortness please me well.

40   Right true it is, your son Lucentio here
Doth love my daughter and she loveth him,
Or both dissemble deeply their affections.
And therefore if you say no more than this,
That like a father you will deal with him

45   And pass my daughter a sufficient dower,
The match is made and all is done.
Your son shall have my daughter with consent.

TRANIO   I thank you, sir. Where then do you know best
We be affied and such assurance ta'en

50   As shall with either part's agreement stand?

BAPTISTA   Not in my house, Lucentio, for you know
Pitchers have ears, and I have many servants.
Besides, old Gremio is heark'ning still,
And haply we might be interrupted.

55   TRANIO   Then at my lodging, an it like you.
There doth my father lie, and there, this night,
We'll pass the business privately and well.
Send for your daughter by your servant here.   *Indicates Lucentio,*
My boy shall fetch the scriv'ner presently.   *and winks at him*

60   The worst is this, that at so slender warning
You are like to have a thin and slender pittance.

BAPTISTA   It likes me well. Cambio, hie you home,
And bid Bianca make her ready straight.
And, if you will, tell what hath happened:

65   Lucentio's father is arrived in Padua,
And how she's like to be Lucentio's wife.   [*Exit Lucentio*]

---

36 **curious** particular, awkward   45 **pass** confirm   48 **know** deem, think   49 **affied** betrothed
formally   **assurance . . . stand** pledges made as will be agreeable to both parties   52 **Pitchers
have ears** i.e. there may be eavesdroppers (proverbial)   **Pitchers** jugs with large handles ("ears")
on either side   53 **heark'ning still** continues to wait for his opportunity   54 **haply** perhaps
56 **lie** lodge   57 **pass** settle   59 **scriv'ner** scribe authorized to draw up legal contracts
61 **pittance** sustenance, food   62 **hie** hurry   66 **like** soon, likely

BIONDELLO   I pray the gods she may with all my heart!   *Exit*

TRANIO   Dally not with the gods, but get thee gone.

Enter Peter

Signior Baptista, shall I lead the way?

70   Welcome! One mess is like to be your cheer.

Come, sir, we will better it in Pisa.

BAPTISTA   I follow you.   *Exeunt [Tranio, Pedant and Baptista]*

Enter Lucentio [disguised as Cambio] and Biondello

BIONDELLO   Cambio!

LUCENTIO   What say'st thou, Biondello?

75   BIONDELLO   You saw my master wink and laugh upon you?

LUCENTIO   Biondello, what of that?

BIONDELLO   Faith, nothing. But has left me here behind to
expound the meaning or moral of his signs and tokens.

LUCENTIO   I pray thee moralize them.

80   BIONDELLO   Then thus: Baptista is safe, talking with the
deceiving father of a deceitful son.

LUCENTIO   And what of him?

BIONDELLO   His daughter is to be brought by you to the supper.

LUCENTIO   And then?

85   BIONDELLO   The old priest at Saint Luke's church is at your
command at all hours.

LUCENTIO   And what of all this?

BIONDELLO   I cannot tell, except they are busied about a
counterfeit assurance. Take you assurance of her, *cum*

90   *privilegio ad imprimendum solum.* To th'church, take the
priest, clerk and some sufficient honest witnesses. If this be
not that you look for, I have no more to say, but bid Bianca
farewell forever and a day.

LUCENTIO   Hear'st thou, Biondello?

95   BIONDELLO   I cannot tarry: I knew a wench married in an
afternoon as she went to the garden for parsley to stuff a

---

70 mess dish, basic meal   77 has he has   78 tokens signals   79 moralize explain
86 command service   89 counterfeit assurance invalid legal settlement   assurance pledge
cum . . . solum "with the sole right to print" (Latin), a copyright phrase found in the title pages of
books but here applied to the idea of marriage and reproduction   91 sufficient right amount/
competent   92 that . . . for what you want

rabbit, and so may you, sir. And so, adieu, sir. My master
hath appointed me to go to Saint Luke's to bid the priest be
ready to come against you come with your appendix.   *Exit*

100   LUCENTIO   I may, and will, if she be so contented.
She will be pleased, then wherefore should I doubt?
Hap what hap may, I'll roundly go about her.
It shall go hard if Cambio go without her.   *Exit*

[Act 4 Scene 3]

Enter Petruchio, Kate, Hortensio [and Servants]

PETRUCHIO   Come on, a God's name, once more toward our
father's.
Good Lord, how bright and goodly shines the moon!

KATE   The moon? The sun: it is not moonlight now.

PETRUCHIO   I say it is the moon that shines so bright.

5   KATE   I know it is the sun that shines so bright.

PETRUCHIO   Now, by my mother's son, and that's myself,
It shall be moon, or star, or what I list,
Or ere I journey to your father's house.—
Go on, and fetch our horses back again.—   *To the Servants*

10   Evermore crossed and crossed, nothing but crossed!

HORTENSIO   Say as he says, or we shall never go.   *To Kate*

KATE   Forward, I pray, since we have come so far,
And be it moon, or sun, or what you please.
An if you please to call it a rush-candle,

15   Henceforth I vow it shall be so for me.

PETRUCHIO   I say it is the moon.

KATE   I know it is the moon.

PETRUCHIO   Nay, then you lie. It is the blessèd sun.

KATE   Then, God be blessed, it is the blessèd sun.

20   But sun it is not, when you say it is not,

---

99 **against you come** in anticipation of your arrival   **appendix** appendage (i.e. Bianca; also
continues the printing metaphor)   102 **Hap** happen   **roundly . . . her** approach her plainly,
without further ado (may also have sexual connotations)   103 **go hard** be unfortunate (plays on
the sense of "get erect")   **4.3   *Location: on the road*   2 goodly** splendidly   **7 list** please
8 Or ere before   **14 rush-candle** candle dipped in tallow wax, which gave a dim light

And the moon changes even as your mind.
What you will have it named, even that it is,
And so it shall be so for Katherine.

HORTENSIO   Petruchio, go thy ways, the field is won.   *Aside*

25   PETRUCHIO   Well, forward, forward! Thus the bowl should run,
And not unluckily against the bias.
But, soft, company is coming here.

Enter Vincentio

Good morrow, gentle mistress. Where away?   *To Vincentio*
Tell me, sweet Kate, and tell me truly too,   *To Kate*
30   Hast thou beheld a fresher gentlewoman?
Such war of white and red within her cheeks!
What stars do spangle heaven with such beauty,
As those two eyes become that heav'nly face?—
Fair lovely maid, once more good day to thee.—   *To Vincentio*
35   Sweet Kate, embrace her for her beauty's sake.   *To Kate*

HORTENSIO   A will make the man mad, to make the woman
of him.   *Aside*

KATE   Young budding virgin, fair and fresh and sweet,
Whither away, or where is thy abode?
Happy the parents of so fair a child;
40   Happier the man, whom favourable stars
Allots thee for his lovely bedfellow!

PETRUCHIO   Why, how now, Kate? I hope thou art not mad.
This is a man, old, wrinkled, faded, withered,
And not a maiden, as thou say'st he is.

45   KATE   Pardon, old father, my mistaking eyes,
That have been so bedazzled with the sun
That everything I look on seemeth green.
Now I perceive thou art a reverend father.
Pardon, I pray thee, for my mad mistaking.

---

24 **go thy ways** well-done/carry on   **field** battle   25 **bowl should run** refers to the game of bowls in which balls are rolled toward a central ball   26 **against the bias** against its natural course (the **bias** is the weight in the ball that enables it to be bowled in a curve)   28 **Where away?** Where are you going?   30 **fresher** more blooming   32 **spangle** shine, adorn   36 **A** he   40 **whom** to whom   47 **green** young, fresh (also alludes to the optical effect of looking at and then away from the sun)

50 PETRUCHIO   Do, good old grandsire, and withal make known
        Which way thou travellest: if along with us,
        We shall be joyful of thy company.
    VINCENTIO   Fair sir, and you my merry mistress,
        That with your strange encounter much amazed me,
55   My name is called Vincentio, my dwelling Pisa,
        And bound I am to Padua, there to visit
        A son of mine, which long I have not seen.
    PETRUCHIO   What is his name?
    VINCENTIO   Lucentio, gentle sir.
60 PETRUCHIO   Happily met, the happier for thy son.
        And now by law, as well as reverend age,
        I may entitle thee my loving father.
        The sister to my wife, this gentlewoman,
        Thy son by this hath married. Wonder not,
65   Nor be not grieved: she is of good esteem,
        Her dowry wealthy, and of worthy birth;
        Beside, so qualified as may beseem
        The spouse of any noble gentleman.
        Let me embrace with old Vincentio,
70   And wander we to see thy honest son,
        Who will of thy arrival be full joyous.
    VINCENTIO   But is this true? Or is it else your pleasure,
        Like pleasant travellers, to break a jest
        Upon the company you overtake?
75 HORTENSIO   I do assure thee, father, so it is.
    PETRUCHIO   Come, go along, and see the truth hereof,
        For our first merriment hath made thee jealous.
                                    Exeunt [all but Hortensio]
    HORTENSIO   Well, Petruchio, this has put me in heart.
        Have to my widow! And if she be froward,
80   Then hast thou taught Hortensio to be untoward.   *Exit*

54 encounter greeting   62 father father-in-law   64 this this time   65 esteem reputation
67 beseem befit   70 honest virtuous, noble (ironically plays on the sense of "truthful")
73 pleasant jovial   break a jest play a joke   77 jealous suspicious   78 put . . . heart
encouraged me   79 Have to now for/here's to   80 untoward stubborn, perverse

[Act 4 Scene 4]   *running scene 10*

Enter Biondello, Lucentio and Bianca. Gremio is out before

BIONDELLO   Softly and swiftly, sir, for the priest is ready.

LUCENTIO   I fly, Biondello; but they may chance to need thee at
home, therefore leave us.   *Exit [Lucentio with Bianca]*

BIONDELLO   Nay, faith, I'll see the church o'your back, and then

5   come back to my master's as soon as I can.   *[Exit]*

GREMIO   I marvel Cambio comes not all this while.

Enter Petruchio, Kate, Vincentio, Grumio, with Attendants

PETRUCHIO   Sir, here's the door, this is Lucentio's house.
My father's bears more toward the marketplace.
Thither must I, and here I leave you, sir.

10   VINCENTIO   You shall not choose but drink before you go.
I think I shall command your welcome here;
And by all likelihood, some cheer is toward.   *Knock*

GREMIO   They're busy within: you were best knock louder.

Pedant looks out of the window

PEDANT   What's he that knocks as he would beat down the

15   gate?

VINCENTIO   Is Signior Lucentio within, sir?

PEDANT   He's within, sir, but not to be spoken withal.

VINCENTIO   What if a man bring him a hundred pound or two
to make merry withal?

20   PEDANT   Keep your hundred pounds to yourself. He shall
need none, so long as I live.

PETRUCHIO   Nay, I told you your son was well beloved in Padua.
Do you hear, sir? To leave frivolous circumstances, I pray you
tell Signior Lucentio that his father is come from Pisa, and is

25   here at the door to speak with him.

PEDANT   Thou liest. His father is come from Padua and here
looking out at the window.

4.4 *Location: Padua*   **4** o'your back behind you (i.e. I'll see you safely into the church)
8 father's i.e. Baptista's house   **bears** lies   **10 You . . . but** i.e. I insist that   **11 command**
authorize, ascertain   **12 cheer is toward** entertainment is in place   **23 frivolous**
circumstances trivial matters   **26 from Padua** i.e. where we are right now (some editors emend
to "from Mantua," or "to Padua")

VINCENTIO   Art thou his father?

PEDANT   Ay, sir, so his mother says, if I may believe her.

30   PETRUCHIO   Why, how now, gentleman! Why, this   *To Vincentio*
is flat knavery to take upon you another man's name.

PEDANT   Lay hands on the villain. I believe a means to cozen
somebody in this city under my countenance.

Enter Biondello

BIONDELLO   I have seen them in the church together.   *Aside*
35   God send 'em good shipping! But who is here? Mine old master
Vincentio! Now we are undone and brought to nothing.

VINCENTIO   Come hither, crack-hemp.   *Seeing Biondello*

BIONDELLO   I hope I may choose, sir.

VINCENTIO   Come hither, you rogue. What, have you forgot me?

40   BIONDELLO   Forgot you? No, sir: I could not forget you, for I never
saw you before in all my life.

VINCENTIO   What, you notorious villain, didst thou never see
thy master's father, Vincentio?

BIONDELLO   What, my old worshipful old master? Yes, marry, sir,
45   see where he looks out of the window.

VINCENTIO   Is't so, indeed?   *He beats Biondello*

BIONDELLO   Help, help, help! Here's a madman will murder me.
[*Exit*]

PEDANT   Help, son! Help, Signior Baptista!   [*Exit from above*]

PETRUCHIO   Prithee, Kate, let's stand aside and see the end of
50   this controversy.   *They stand aside*

Enter Pedant [below] with servants, Baptista, Tranio

TRANIO   Sir, what are you that offer to beat my servant?

VINCENTIO   What am I, sir? Nay, what are you, sir? O immortal
gods! O fine villain! A silken doublet, a velvet hose, a scarlet
cloak and a copatain hat! O, I am undone, I am undone!
55   While I play the good husband at home, my son and my
servant spend all at the university.

---

32 **cozen** cheat   33 **under my countenance** by pretending to be me   35 **good shipping** happy
fortune, a good journey (perhaps also "good sex")   36 **undone** ruined   37 **crack-hemp** rogue
who deserves to be hanged (literally, who causes the hempen rope to strain)   38 **choose** do as I
choose/have a choice when it comes to being hanged   51 **offer** attempt   53 **fine** richly dressed
54 **copatain** high-crowned

TRANIO   How now? What's the matter?

BAPTISTA   What, is the man lunatic?

TRANIO   Sir, you seem a sober ancient gentleman by your
60   habit, but your words show you a madman. Why, sir, what
'cerns it you if I wear pearl and gold? I thank my good father,
I am able to maintain it.

VINCENTIO   Thy father! O villain! He is a sailmaker in Bergamo.

BAPTISTA   You mistake, sir, you mistake, sir. Pray, what do you
65   think is his name?

VINCENTIO   His name? As if I knew not his name: I have
brought him up ever since he was three years old, and his
name is Tranio.

PEDANT   Away, away, mad ass! His name is Lucentio and he is
70   mine only son, and heir to the lands of me, Signior Vincentio.

VINCENTIO   Lucentio! O, he hath murdered his master! Lay hold
on him, I charge you in the duke's name. O, my son, my son!
Tell me, thou villain, where is my son Lucentio?

TRANIO   Call forth an officer.   [*Enter an Officer*]
75   Carry this mad knave to the jail. Father Baptista,
I charge you see that he be forthcoming.

VINCENTIO   Carry me to the jail?

GREMIO   Stay, officer, he shall not go to prison.

BAPTISTA   Talk not, Signior Gremio, I say he shall go to prison.

80   GREMIO   Take heed, Signior Baptista, lest you be cony-catched
in this business. I dare swear this is the right Vincentio.

PEDANT   Swear, if thou dar'st.

GREMIO   Nay, I dare not swear it.

TRANIO   Then thou wert best say that I am not Lucentio.

85   GREMIO   Yes, I know thee to be Signior Lucentio.

BAPTISTA   Away with the dotard! To the jail with him!

Enter Biondello, Lucentio and Bianca

VINCENTIO   Thus strangers may be hailed and abused. O
monstrous villain!

---

61 **'cerns it you** does it concern you   62 **maintain** afford   63 **Bergamo** town near Milan
76 **forthcoming** available to stand trial   80 **cony-catched** tricked   86 **dotard** old fool
87 **hailed** dragged about/greeted

BIONDELLO   O, we are spoiled and— yonder he is. Deny him,
90   forswear him, or else we are all undone.

Exeunt Biondello, Tranio and Pedant,
as fast as may be

LUCENTIO   Pardon, sweet father.   *Kneels*

VINCENTIO   Lives my sweet son?

BIANCA   Pardon, dear father.

BAPTISTA   How hast thou offended? Where is Lucentio?

95   LUCENTIO   Here's Lucentio,
     Right son to the right Vincentio,
     That have by marriage made thy daughter mine,
     While counterfeit supposes bleared thine eyne.

GREMIO   Here's packing, with a witness to deceive us all!

100   VINCENTIO   Where is that damnèd villain Tranio,
     That faced and braved me in this matter so?

BAPTISTA   Why, tell me, is not this my Cambio?

BIANCA   Cambio is changed into Lucentio.

LUCENTIO   Love wrought these miracles. Bianca's love
105   Made me exchange my state with Tranio,
     While he did bear my countenance in the town,
     And happily I have arrived at the last
     Unto the wishèd haven of my bliss.
     What Tranio did, myself enforced him to;
110   Then pardon him, sweet father, for my sake.

VINCENTIO   I'll slit the villain's nose, that would have sent me to
     the jail.

BAPTISTA   But do you hear, sir? Have you married my daughter
     without asking my good will?

115   VINCENTIO   Fear not, Baptista, we will content you, go to. But I
     will in, to be revenged for this villainy.   *Exit*

BAPTISTA   And I, to sound the depth of this knavery.   *Exit*

LUCENTIO   Look not pale, Bianca, thy father will not frown.

Exeunt [Lucentio and Bianca]

---

89 **spoiled** ruined   98 **counterfeit supposes** false appearances   **eyne** eyes   99 **packing**
plotting, conspiracy   **with a witness** that's for certain   103 **changed** plays on the meaning of
cambio ("change")   105 **state** situation/status   115 **go to** exclamation of mild impatience and
dismissal   117 **sound** probe

GREMIO   My cake is dough, but I'll in among the rest,
120   Out of hope of all but my share of the feast.   [*Exit*]
KATE   Husband, let's follow, to see the end of this ado.
PETRUCHIO First kiss me, Kate, and we will.
KATE   What, in the midst of the street?
PETRUCHIO What, art thou ashamed of me?
125 KATE No, sir, God forbid, but ashamed to kiss.
PETRUCHIO Why, then let's home again.— Come, sirrah, let's
           away.
KATE   Nay, I will give thee a kiss. Now pray thee, love,
           stay.   *They kiss*
PETRUCHIO Is not this well? Come, my sweet Kate.
           Better once than never, for never too late.   *Exeunt*

Act 5 [Scene 1]   *running scene 11*

Enter Baptista, Vincentio, Gremio, the Pedant, Lucentio and Bianca,
[Petruchio, Katherina, Hortensio,] Tranio, Biondello, Grumio and
Widow. The Servingmen with Tranio bringing in a banquet

LUCENTIO   At last, though long, our jarring notes agree,
           And time it is, when raging war is done,
           To smile at scapes and perils overblown.
           My fair Bianca, bid my father welcome,
5   While I with selfsame kindness welcome thine.
           Brother Petruchio, sister Katherina,
           And thou, Hortensio, with thy loving widow,
           Feast with the best, and welcome to my house.
           My banquet is to close our stomachs up
10   After our great good cheer. Pray you sit down,
           For now we sit to chat as well as eat.
PETRUCHIO Nothing but sit and sit, and eat and eat!
BAPTISTA   Padua affords this kindness, son Petruchio.

---

119 cake is dough i.e. I've failed   120 Out . . . all with no hope of anything   129 once at some
time   5.1 *banquet* fruit, sweetmeats and wine, served after the main meal   1 long after a
long time   3 scapes escapes   overblown now past   5 kindness kinship/good will   8 with on
9 close fill   10 great good cheer presumably the main wedding feast at Baptista's

	PETRUCHIO	Padua affords nothing but what is kind.
15	HORTENSIO	For both our sakes, I would that word were true.
	PETRUCHIO	Now, for my life, Hortensio fears his widow.
	WIDOW	Then never trust me if I be afeard.
	PETRUCHIO	You are very sensible, and yet you miss my sense:

I mean, Hortensio is afeard of you.

	WIDOW	He that is giddy thinks the world turns round.
20	PETRUCHIO	Roundly replied.
	KATE	Mistress, how mean you that?
	WIDOW	Thus I conceive by him.
	PETRUCHIO	Conceives by me! How likes Hortensio that?
25	HORTENSIO	My widow says, thus she conceives her tale.
	PETRUCHIO	Very well mended. Kiss him for that, good widow.
	KATE	'He that is giddy thinks the world turns round.'

I pray you tell me what you meant by that.

	WIDOW	Your husband, being troubled with a shrew,
30		Measures my husband's sorrow by his woe:

And now you know my meaning.

	KATE	A very mean meaning.
	WIDOW	Right, I mean you.
	KATE	And I am mean indeed, respecting you.
35	PETRUCHIO	To her, Kate!
	HORTENSIO	To her, widow!
	PETRUCHIO	A hundred marks, my Kate does put her down.
	HORTENSIO	That's my office.
	PETRUCHIO	Spoke like an officer. Ha' to thee, lad!

Drinks to Hortensio

	BAPTISTA	How likes Gremio these quick-witted folks?
40	GREMIO	Believe me, sir, they butt together well.

---

16 **fears** is frightened of/frightens   17 **Then . . . afeard** i.e. I can assure you I am not frightened
18 **sensible** perceptive   20 **He . . . round** i.e. you attribute your own feelings to others—you,
Petruchio, are afraid of *your* wife   21 **Roundly** boldly, soundly   23 **Thus . . . him** that's how I
understand him (Petruchio picks up on **roundly** and **conceive** to make a joke about pregnancy)
25 **conceives her tale** interprets her remark/is impregnated (tale puns on "tail"—i.e. vagina)
26 **mended** retorted/rectified   32 **mean** average/poor   34 **mean . . . you** moderate compared
to you   35 **To her** attack her (a cry used to urge on animals in hunting or fighting)   37 **marks**
coins, each worth two thirds of a pound   **put her down** outdo her (Hortensio plays on the sense
of "have sex with her")   38 **office** role/sexual duty   41 **butt** lock horns/thrust sexually

BIANCA   Head, and butt! An hasty-witted body
Would say your head and butt were head and horn.

VINCENTIO   Ay, mistress bride, hath that awakened you?

45   BIANCA   Ay, but not frighted me: therefore I'll sleep again.

PETRUCHIO   Nay, that you shall not. Since you have begun,
Have at you for a bitter jest or two.

BIANCA   Am I your bird? I mean to shift my bush,
And then pursue me as you draw your bow.

50   You are welcome all.   *Exeunt Bianca, [Katherina and Widow]*

PETRUCHIO   She hath prevented me. Here, Signior Tranio,
This bird you aimed at, though you hit her not:
Therefore a health to all that shot and missed.   *Makes a toast*

TRANIO   O, sir, Lucentio slipped me like his greyhound,

55   Which runs himself and catches for his master.

PETRUCHIO   A good swift simile, but something currish.

TRANIO   'Tis well, sir, that you hunted for yourself:
'Tis thought your deer does hold you at a bay.

BAPTISTA   O, O, Petruchio! Tranio hits you now.

60   LUCENTIO   I thank thee for that gird, good Tranio.

HORTENSIO   Confess, confess, hath he not hit you here?

PETRUCHIO   A has a little galled me, I confess.
And as the jest did glance away from me,
'Tis ten to one it maimed you two outright.

65   BAPTISTA   Now, in good sadness, son Petruchio,
I think thou hast the veriest shrew of all.

PETRUCHIO   Well, I say no: and therefore for assurance
Let's each one send unto his wife,
And he whose wife is most obedient

---

42 **butt** bottom   **hasty-witted body** quick-witted person   43 **head and horn** a horned head (i.e. that of a cuckold; horn plays on the sense of "penis/hunting horn")   47 **Have at you** be prepared for   **bitter** shrewd, keen   48 **bird** prey   **shift my bush** fly to another bush to hide in (plays on the idea of pubic hair)   49 **bow** refers to fowling—hunting sitting birds with bow and arrow (with phallic connotations)   51 **prevented** thwarted   52 **hit** shot with an arrow/penetrated sexually   53 **health** toast   54 **slipped** unleashed   56 **currish** ignoble/dog-like   58 **deer** puns on "dear"   **does . . . bay** turns on you and holds you off with its horns/denies you sex   60 **gird** taunt   62 **galled** scratched, irritated   63 **glance away from** bounce off   65 **good sadness** all seriousness   66 **veriest** truest   67 **assurance** proof

70   To come at first when he doth send for her,
        Shall win the wager which we will propose.
HORTENSIO   Content. What's the wager?
LUCENTIO   Twenty crowns.
PETRUCHIO   Twenty crowns?
75   I'll venture so much of my hawk or hound,
        But twenty times so much upon my wife.
LUCENTIO   A hundred then.
HORTENSIO   Content.
PETRUCHIO   A match! 'Tis done.
80 HORTENSIO   Who shall begin?
LUCENTIO   That will I.
        Go, Biondello, bid your mistress come to me.
BIONDELLO   I go.   *Exit*
BAPTISTA   Son, I'll be your half, Bianca comes.
85 LUCENTIO   I'll have no halves. I'll bear it all myself.
Enter Biondello
        How now? What news?
BIONDELLO   Sir, my mistress sends you word
        That she is busy and she cannot come.
PETRUCHIO   How? She's busy and she cannot come?
90   Is that an answer?
GREMIO   Ay, and a kind one too.
        Pray God, sir, your wife send you not a worse.
PETRUCHIO   I hope better.
HORTENSIO   Sirrah Biondello, go and entreat my wife
95   To come to me forthwith.   *Exit Biondello*
PETRUCHIO   O, ho, entreat her?
        Nay, then she must needs come.
HORTENSIO   I am afraid, sir,
        Do what you can,
Enter Biondello   yours will not be entreated.
100   Now, where's my wife?
BIONDELLO   She says you have some goodly jest in hand.
        She will not come. She bids you come to her.

PETRUCHIO   Worse and worse, she will not come! O, vile,
Intolerable, not to be endured!
105   Sirrah Grumio, go to your mistress,
Say, I command her come to me.   *Exit [Grumio]*

HORTENSIO   I know her answer.

PETRUCHIO   What?

HORTENSIO   She will not.

110   PETRUCHIO   The fouler fortune mine, and there an end.

Enter Katherina

BAPTISTA   Now, by my holidame, here comes Katherina!

KATE   What is your will, sir, that you send for me?

PETRUCHIO   Where is your sister, and Hortensio's wife?

KATE   They sit conferring by the parlour fire.

115   PETRUCHIO   Go fetch them hither. If they deny to come,
Swinge me them soundly forth unto their husbands.
Away, I say, and bring them hither straight.   [*Exit Katherina*]

LUCENTIO   Here is a wonder, if you talk of a wonder.

HORTENSIO   And so it is: I wonder what it bodes.

120   PETRUCHIO   Marry, peace it bodes, and love and quiet life,
And awful rule and right supremacy,
And, to be short, what not that's sweet and happy.

BAPTISTA   Now, fair befall thee, good Petruchio;
The wager thou hast won, and I will add
125   Unto their losses twenty thousand crowns,
Another dowry to another daughter,
For she is changed, as she had never been.

PETRUCHIO   Nay, I will win my wager better yet
And show more sign of her obedience,
130   Her new-built virtue and obedience.

Enter Kate, Bianca and Widow

See where she comes and brings your froward wives
As prisoners to her womanly persuasion.—

---

110 The . . . mine then I have the worst luck   111 by my holidame by Our Lady/by all that I
hold holy   114 conferring chatting   116 Swinge thrash   121 awful worthy of respect   right
rightful   122 what not everything   123 fair befall thee good luck to you   127 as . . . been as
if the former Kate had never existed

Katherine, that cap of yours becomes you not.
Off with that bauble, throw it underfoot.   *Kate throws the cap*
135 WIDOW   Lord, let me never have a cause to sigh,   *on the ground*
Till I be brought to such a silly pass!

BIANCA   Fie! What a foolish duty call you this?

LUCENTIO   I would your duty were as foolish too:
The wisdom of your duty, fair Bianca,
140   Hath cost me five hundred crowns since suppertime.

BIANCA   The more fool you for laying on my duty.

PETRUCHIO   Katherine, I charge thee tell these headstrong
women
What duty they do owe their lords and husbands.

WIDOW   Come, come, you're mocking. We will have no
telling.

145 PETRUCHIO   Come on, I say, and first begin with her.

WIDOW   She shall not.

PETRUCHIO   I say she shall, and first begin with her.

KATE   Fie, fie! Unknit that threat'ning unkind   *To the Widow*
brow,
And dart not scornful glances from those eyes,
150   To wound thy lord, thy king, thy governor.
It blots thy beauty as frosts do bite the meads,
Confounds thy fame as whirlwinds shake fair buds,
And in no sense is meet or amiable.
A woman moved is like a fountain troubled,
155   Muddy, ill-seeming, thick, bereft of beauty,
And while it is so, none so dry or thirsty
Will deign to sip or touch one drop of it.
Thy husband is thy lord, thy life, thy keeper,
Thy head, thy sovereign: one that cares for thee,
160   And for thy maintenance commits his body
To painful labour both by sea and land,
To watch the night in storms, the day in cold,

---

136 **pass** state of affairs   137 **foolish** stupid (Lucentio shifts the sense to "fond, doting")
141 **laying** betting   148 **Unknit** relax   **unkind** harsh/unnatural   151 **meads** meadows
152 **Confounds thy fame** destroys your reputation   153 **meet** appropriate   154 **moved** angered   155 **ill-seeming** ugly   161 **painful** grueling   162 **watch** be awake during

Whilst thou liest warm at home, secure and safe,
And craves no other tribute at thy hands
165   But love, fair looks and true obedience;
Too little payment for so great a debt.—
Such duty as the subject owes the prince   *To all?*
Even such a woman oweth to her husband.
And when she is froward, peevish, sullen, sour,
170   And not obedient to his honest will,
What is she but a foul contending rebel
And graceless traitor to her loving lord?
I am ashamed that women are so simple
To offer war where they should kneel for peace,
175   Or seek for rule, supremacy and sway,
When they are bound to serve, love and obey.
Why are our bodies soft and weak and smooth,
Unapt to toil and trouble in the world,
But that our soft conditions and our hearts
180   Should well agree with our external parts?—
Come, come, you froward and unable worms,   *To all the Women*
My mind hath been as big as one of yours,
My heart as great, my reason haply more,
To bandy word for word and frown for frown;
185   But now I see our lances are but straws,
Our strength as weak, our weakness past compare,
That seeming to be most which we indeed least are.
Then vail your stomachs, for it is no boot,
And place your hands below your husband's foot:
190   In token of which duty, if he please,
My hand is ready, may it do him ease.
PETRUCHIO   Why, there's a wench! Come on, and kiss me, Kate.

They kiss

---

169 **peevish** stubborn, perverse   170 **honest** virtuous, upright   172 **graceless** sinful
173 **simple** foolish   175 **sway** authority, influence   176 **bound** i.e. by duty/in marriage
178 **Unapt** not designed   179 **soft** gentle, fragile   **conditions** constitutions/qualities
181 **unable** incapable   182 **big** strong/contentious/determined/proud   183 **haply** perhaps
184 **bandy** exchange   187 **That . . . be** seeming to be that   188 **vail your stomachs** lower your
pride/surrender your inclinations   **boot** use   191 **do him ease** give him pleasure/ease his
burden

LUCENTIO	Well, go thy ways, old lad, for thou shalt ha't.	
VINCENTIO	'Tis a good hearing when children are toward.	
195 LUCENTIO	But a harsh hearing when women are froward.	
PETRUCHIO	Come, Kate, we'll to bed.	

We three are married, but you two are sped.
'Twas I won the wager, though you hit the white.   *To Lucentio*
And being a winner, God give you goodnight!

Exeunt Petruchio [and Katherina]

200 HORTENSIO	Now, go thy ways. Thou hast tamed a curst shrew.	
LUCENTIO	'Tis a wonder, by your leave, she will be tamed so.	

[Exeunt]

193 go thy ways well-done   **ha't** have it (win the wager)   **194 'Tis . . . toward** it is a good thing to hear when children are compliant   **197 three** three men   **you . . . sped** you two (Lucentio and Hortensio) are done for   **198 white** center of the target (puns on Bianca's name, "white" in Italian)   **200 shrew** pronounced "shrow," the word provides the rhyme for this final couplet

TEXTUAL NOTES

Q = First Quarto text of *The Taming of a Shrew* (1594)
F = First Folio text of 1623
F2 = a correction introduced in the Second Folio text of 1632
F3 = a correction introduced in the Third Folio text of 1664
Ed = a correction introduced by a later editor
SD = stage direction
SH = speech heading (i.e. speaker's name)

List of parts = Ed

Ind.1.0 SD *Christopher* = Ed. F = *Christophero* **1 SH SLY** = Ed. F = *Begger*
9 thirdborough = Ed. F = Headborough **18 SH FIRST HUNTSMAN** =
Ed. F = *Hunts.* **85 SH FIRST PLAYER** = Ed. F = *Sincklo* **97 SH FIRST
PLAYER** = Ed. F = *Plai.*
Ind.2.2 lordship = Q. F = Lord **21 fourteen pence** = Ed. F = xiiii d. **97 SH
PAGE** = Ed. F = *Lady. or La. (throughout)* **133 play it. Is** = Ed. F = play, it
is **137 a** = F2. F = a a
1.1.0 SD *Tranio* = F2. F = *Triano* **13 Vincentio** = Ed. F = *Vincentio's*
14 brought = Q. F = brough **25** *Mi* = Ed. F = *Me* **47 SD** *Katherina* = F2.
F = *Katerina* **SD** *suitor* = F2 *(spelled* shuiter*).* F = *sister* **159 captum** =
F2. F = *captam* **207 coloured** = F2. F = Conlord **244 your** = F2. F = you
1.2.23 *Con tutto il cuore, ben trovato* = Ed. F = *contutti le core bene trobatto*
24 *molto honorata* = Ed. F = *multo honorato* **31 pip** = Ed. F = peepe
70 she as = F2. F = she is as **115 me and other** = Ed. F = me. Other
166 me to = Ed. F = one to **184 Antonio's** = Ed. F = *Butonios* **264 feat** =
Ed. F = seeke
2.1.8 thee tell = F2. F = tel **76 Neighbour** = Ed. F = neighbors **78 unto
you** = Ed. F = vnto **199 joint** = Ed. F = ioyn'd **250 askance** = Ed. F = a
sconce **333 in** = Ed. F = me **379 Marseillis** = Ed. F = Marcellus
3.1.28 *Sigeia* = F2. F = *sigeria* **46–48** *assigned to Lucentio in* F **49 SH
BIANCA** = Ed. *Not in* F **50 SH LUCENTIO** = Ed. F = *Bian.* **52 SH
BIANCA** = Ed. F = *Hort.* **65 gamut** = Ed. F = gamoth *or* gamouth
(throughout scene) **79 change** = F2. F = charge **80 SH MESSENGER** =
Ed. F = *Nicke.*
3.2.16 Make feasts, invite friends = Ed. F = Make friends, inuite **29 of thy**
= F2. F = of **30 Old news** = Ed. F = newes **33 hear** = Q. F = heard
51 swayed = Ed. F = Waid **123 before I** = F2. F = before **146 grumbling** = F2. F = grumlling **193 SH GREMIO** = F2 *(Gre.).* F = Gra.

3.3.21 SH CURTIS = Q. F = *Gru.*

3.4.4 SH HORTENSIO = F2. F = *Luc.*   **6 SH LUCENTIO** = F2. F = *Hor.*
   7 you? First = Ed. F = you first,   **8 SH LUCENTIO** = F2. F = *Hor.*
   13 none = Ed. F = me   **31 her** = F3. F = them   **74 Take** = F2. F = *Par.*
   Take   **in** = Ed. *Not in* F

4.1.65 SH HABERDASHER = Ed. F = *Fel.*   **84 is a** = Q. F = is   **91 like a** = Q.
   F = like   **179 account'st** = Ed. F = accountedst

4.2.0 SD *Enter Tranio . . . bareheaded* = Ed. F = Enter Tranio, and the Pedant
   dressed (drest) like Vincentio   **1 Sir** = Ed. F = Sirs   **5 Where** = Ed. F = *Tra.*
   Where   **18 SD** *Enter . . . Lucentio* F *mistakenly repeats an entrance direc-*
   tion for the Pedant—Pedant booted and bareheaded—moved to SD 4.2.0
   54 haply = Ed. F = happilie   **88 except** = F2. F = expect

4.3.19 is = Q. F = in   **39 where** = F2. F = whether   **79 she be** = F2. F = she

4.4.5 master's = Ed. F = mistris   **43 master's** = F2. F = Mistris   **68 Tranio** =
   F2. F = *Tronio*   **125 No** = Q. F = Mo

5.1.2 done = Ed. F = come   **39 thee** = Q. F = the   **64 two** = Ed. F = too
   67 for = F2. F = sir

ADDITIONAL SLY SCENES AND KATE'S SUBMISSION SPEECH FROM *THE TAMING OF A SHREW* (1594)

Following a scene for which there is no equivalent in Shakespeare, roughly corresponding in the structure to the end of 2.1 (the "fool" is Sander, who plays a role similar to that of Grumio):

Then Sly speaks

SLY   Sim, when will the fool come again?

LORD   He'll come again, my lord, anon.

SLY   Giz some more drink here. Zounds, where's the tapster? Here, Sim, eat some of these things.

LORD   So I do, my lord.

SLY   Here, Sim, I drink to thee.

LORD   My lord, here comes the players again.

SLY   O brave, here's two fine gentlewomen.

Enter Valeria with a Lute and Kate with him.

In the equivalent position to between 4.2 and 4.3:

Exeunt All.

SLY   Sim, must they be married now?

LORD   Ay, my lord.

Enter Ferando and Kate and Sander.

SLY   Look, Sim, the fool is come again now.

Interrupting the action at the equivalent point to the exit at 4.4.101:

Phylotus and Valeria runs away. Then Sly speaks.

SLY   I say we'll have no sending to prison.

LORD   My lord, this is but the play, they're but in jest.

SLY   I tell thee, Sim, we'll have no sending to prison, that's flat: why, Sim, am not I Don Christo Vary? Therefore I say they shall not go to prison.

LORD   No more they shall not, my lord, they be run away.

SLY   Are they run away, Sim? That's well, then giz some more drink, and let them play again.

LORD   Here, my lord.

Sly drinks and then falls asleep.

In the equivalent position to between 4.4 and 5.1:

Exeunt All.

Sly sleeps.

LORD   Who's within there? Come hither, sirs, my lord's
            Asleep again: go take him easily up,
            And put him in his own apparel again,
            And lay him in the place where we did find him,
            Just underneath the ale-house side below.
            But see you wake him not in any case.

BOY   It shall be done, my lord. Come help to bear him hence.

Exit.

At the end of the play:

Exit Polidor and Emelia.
Then enter two bearing of Sly in his own apparel again, and leaves him where they found him, and then goes out.
Then enter the Tapster.

TAPSTER   Now that the darksome night is overpast,
            And dawning day appears in crystal sky,
            Now must I haste abroad: but soft, who's this?
            What, Sly! O wondrous, hath he lain here all night?
            I'll wake him. I think he's starved by this,
            But that his belly was so stuffed with ale.
            What ho, Sly, awake, for shame!

SLY   Sim, giz some more wine: what, 's all the players gone? Am not I a lord?

TAPSTER   A lord with a murrain! Come, art thou drunken still?

SLY   Who's this? Tapster, O lord, sirrah, I have had
   The bravest dream tonight that ever thou
   Heardest in all thy life.

TAPSTER   Ay, marry, but you had best get you home,
   For your wife will course you for dreaming here tonight.

SLY   Will she? I know now how to tame a shrew,
   I dreamt upon it all this night till now,
   And thou hast waked me out of the best dream
   That ever I had in my life. But I'll to my
   Wife presently and tame her too
   An if she anger me.

TAPSTER   Nay, tarry, Sly, for I'll go home with thee,
   And hear the rest that thou hast dreamt to night.

                                    Exeunt All.
                                    FINIS.

Kate's submission speech near the end of the play:

FERANDO   Now, lovely Kate before their husbands here,
   I prithee tell unto these headstrong women
   What duty wives do owe unto their husbands.

KATE   Then you that live thus by your pampered wills,
   Now list to me and mark what I shall say:
   Th'eternal power that with his only breath,
   Shall cause this end and this beginning frame,
   Not in time nor before time, but with time, confused,
   For all the course of years, of ages, months,
   Of seasons temperate, of days and hours,
   Are tuned and stopped by measure of his hand,
   The first world was a form without a form,
   A heap confused, a mixture all deformed,
   A gulf of gulfs, a body bodiless,
   Where all the elements were orderless,
   Before the great commander of the world,
   The King of Kings, the glorious God of heaven
   Who in six days did frame his heavenly work,
   And made all things to stand in perfect course,
   Then to his image he did make a man,

Old Adam, and from his side asleep,
A rib was taken, of which the Lord did make
The woe of man, so termed by Adam then,
Woman, for that by her came sin to us,
And for her sin was Adam doomed to die,
As Sara to her husband, so should we
Obey them, love them, keep and nourish them,
If they by any means do want our helps,
Laying our hands under their feet to tread,
If that by that we might procure their ease,
And for a precedent I'll first begin
And lay my hand under my husband's feet.

She lays her hand under her husband's feet.

SCENE-BY-SCENE ANALYSIS

INDUCTION SCENE 1

The induction scenes function as a "frame" for the wider play, although this is not sustained beyond the end of Act 1. Themes of the wider play, such as social status and identity, are established, and there are repeated images of clothing and other external indicators of these factors. Wealth, "value," artifice, illusion, and deception are also introduced and there is a clear sense of theatrical self-awareness.

Lines 1–69: A drunken Christopher Sly and the Hostess of an ale-house argue and, when she goes to fetch the constable, he falls asleep. He is discovered by a lord out hunting, raising another set of images from the wider play relating to hunting and hawking. As a joke, he arranges to have Sly conveyed to his own house, where he will be "Wrapped in sweet clothes," and, when he wakes, treated as if he is a "mighty lord" who has been "lunatic" and consequently believed himself to be Christopher Sly. The references to "pictures," "dreams," and "fancy" reinforce the theme of illusion, and the hunters' promise to "play our part" raises awareness of acting and theater. Sly is carried off.

Lines 70–135: A trumpet announces the arrival of a troupe of players, whose presence makes the theatrical self-awareness explicit. The lord discusses past performances and tells them that they are going to perform before a lord who has "never heard a play" and, no matter how odd his behavior, they must not laugh or they will offend him. The lord instructs that his page, Bartholomew, be dressed "like a lady" and play the part of Sly's noble wife. He directs how the page is to speak and act, "With soft low tongue and lowly courtesy," raising issues of "appropriate" female behavior that are explored throughout the play, and emphasizing the link between appearance and perceived identity.

INDUCTION SCENE 2

Lines 1–96: Sly wakes and is greeted by servants bearing wine and fine clothes. When he claims that he is not a lord but Christopher Sly, "by . . . profession a tinker," they insist that has been insane for fifteen years. They describe his wife, "a lady far more beautiful / Than any woman," and Sly becomes convinced that he is "a lord indeed" who has "dreamed till now."

Lines 97–139: Bartholomew enters, dressed as Sly's "wife." Sly dismisses the servants and tells "her" to come to bed, but Bartholomew makes the excuse that the physicians have said that "she" must not, in case it sends Sly mad again. News is brought of the players and Sly calls his wife to sit with him to watch. The presence of this additional "audience" reinforces our awareness of the theater and associated themes.

ACT 1 SCENE 1

Lines 1–47: Lucentio arrives in Padua from Pisa, accompanied by his servant, Tranio. He outlines his plans for studying but Tranio reminds him that he must also enjoy himself. As they wait for Lucentio's other servant, Biondello, a crowd arrives and they stand aside to watch, creating yet another "audience" on the stage.

Lines 48–142: Baptista is being "importuned" by Gremio and Hortensio for his younger daughter, Bianca, but he will not allow her to marry before he has "a husband for the elder," Katherina. He permits them to court Katherina, but Gremio says, "She's too rough," and Hortensio says she will never marry unless she is "of gentler, milder mould." Katherina retorts that she is not interested in marriage and threatens them with violence. Aside, Tranio observes that Katherina is either "stark mad" or willful, but Lucentio is more interested in Bianca, attracted by her "silence" and "mild behaviour." The differences between the sisters are established as Bianca agrees to "humbly . . . subscribe" to her father's wishes, but Katherina questions why she must be "appointed hours" as though she did not have her own mind and will. It is also clear which pattern of female behavior the men prefer. Baptista asks Gremio and Hortensio if they know of any schoolmasters to instruct Bianca "In music, instruments and poetry."

Gremio and Hortensio declare their intentions to find a teacher for Bianca. Hortensio suggests they unite, temporarily, to find a husband for Katherina so that Bianca becomes "free for a husband." Gremio agrees, but protests that Katherina needs "a devil" and argues that even though her dowry will be high (a reminder of the financial aspects of marriage) a man would be "a fool to be married to hell."

Lines 143–247: Lucentio declares his love for Bianca, saying that he will "burn," "pine," and "perish" if he cannot "achieve" her. Tranio suggests that Lucentio is so blinded by Bianca that he has not seen "the pith of all," that is, that until Katherina is married, Bianca must "live a maid at home." Lucentio intends to disguise himself as a schoolmaster, gaining access to Bianca, while Tranio masquerades as Lucentio. They exchange clothes, reinforcing the themes of identity and theater, as they don "costumes" to denote their roles. Biondello arrives and is confused by the switch, but agrees to behave as if Tranio were his master.

Lines 248–253: Sly claims to enjoy the play, but is clearly bored and anxious for it to finish.

ACT 1 SCENE 2

Lines 1–131: Petruchio arrives from Verona to visit Hortensio. He orders his servant, Grumio, to knock, and Grumio's misunderstanding of his instructions generates comedy, although the physical nature of the exchange foreshadows the violence within the play. Petruchio explains to Hortensio that his father has died and he is now looking for a wife. Hortensio suggests "a shrewd ill-favoured wife" who is "very rich," thinking of his plan to find a husband for Katherina, but says that Petruchio is too much of a friend to wish her upon him. Petruchio is caught by the reference to Katherina's fortune, and reveals his mercenary nature, claiming that "wealth is burden of [his] wooing dance." He claims that it would not matter if a woman were "foul" or "old" as long as she had money. Grumio agrees that if Petruchio were given "gold enough" he would marry a "puppet." Hortensio describes Katherina: wealthy, "young and beauteous," but also "curst" and "shrewd." Petruchio claims that he will woo Katherina nonetheless. Hortensio explains about Bianca, and suggests disguising himself as a schoolmaster for Petruchio to offer to Baptista.

Lines 132–213: Gremio boasts of finding a tutor for Bianca, unaware that it is Lucentio in disguise. Hortensio replies that he has also found a tutor. Both talk of their "duty" and "deeds" to their "beloved," although Grumio's prosaic aside about money "bags" strikes a more realistic note. Hortensio announces that he has found someone who "Will undertake to woo curst Katherine." Gremio skeptically asks if he will really woo "this wild-cat." Petruchio boasts that he has heard "lions roar" and the "Loud 'larums" of "pitchèd battle," against which a "woman's tongue" can be nothing. Hortensio and Gremio agree to pay Petruchio if he succeeds.

Lines 214–279: Tranio, dressed as Lucentio, inquires after the house of Baptista and announces his intention of wooing Bianca. Hortensio and Gremio assert their prior claims, but Tranio argues that they can all be Bianca's suitors. Initially, the exchange is in careful, deliberate rhyme, which is comic, but also suggests artifice. Tranio has changed his speech as well as his costume, suggesting that language is as much part of identity as physical appearance. Tranio "learns" of the need to find a husband for Katherina and agrees to join in paying Petruchio.

ACT 2 SCENE 1

Lines 1–34: Katherina has tied Bianca's hands and bullies her to say which of her suitors she prefers, striking Bianca when she cannot. Baptista separates them and Katherina claims that he loves Bianca more: "She is your treasure."

Lines 35–110: Gremio arrives with Lucentio (now calling himself "Cambio"). Petruchio arrives bringing Hortensio (now called "Litio"). Tranio (as Lucentio) brings a lute and books. Petruchio asks immedi-

ately for Katherina and Gremio accuses him of being "too blunt,"
but he demonstrates his command of language as he explains to
Baptista that he has come from Verona to see Katherina and offers
him Hortensio/Litio. Baptista says that Katherina is not for Petruchio, but welcomes him for his father's sake. Gremio interrupts, presenting Baptista with Lucentio/Cambio. Baptista notices "a stranger,"
and asks why he is there. Tranio introduces himself as Lucentio, a
suitor to Bianca, and presents the lute and books. He reveals his
parentage and Baptista is duly impressed: Vincentio of Pisa is "a
mighty man."

Lines 111–168: Baptista suggests they "walk a little" before dinner,
but Petruchio insists on discussing "What dowry" he shall have with
Katherina. Baptista offers "twenty thousand crowns" and half of his
lands after his death, in return for which Petruchio agrees to settle
on Katherina all of his "lands and leases" in widowhood. Baptista
says that Petruchio must, however, obtain Katherina's love and
warns him to be "armed for some unhappy words," but Petruchio
confidently boasts that Katherina's words will have little effect on
him. Hortensio appears, injured, having been beaten by Katherina
with the lute, a visual representation of the play's intrinsic links
between comedy and violence. Petruchio claims that Katherina is "a
lusty wench" and Baptista agrees to send her to meet him.

Lines 169–287: Petruchio outlines his plan to contradict Katherina,
pleasantly, over everything. She arrives, and he addresses her as
"Kate," raising the issue of identity as he names her according to his
wishes, not hers. The exchange that follows is fast-paced and quick-
witted, showing them to be well-matched in this respect, but the verbal encounter becomes physical as Katherina loses her temper and
hits him. Petruchio does not retaliate, but exasperates her with his
constant disregard of her insults. He declares "in plain terms" that it
has been agreed with her father, her dowry is agreed on, and, "will
you, nill you," he will marry her. He intends to "tame" her and make
her into a "Conformable" wife.

Lines 288–327: Katherina claims Baptista has shown no "fatherly
regard" in marrying her to a "half-lunatic," but she is ignored. Petru-

chio announces that Katherina has agreed to marry him on Sunday, and the characterization of Katherina becomes problematic as she remains silent while Petruchio reveals his plans and leads her out.

Lines 328–415: The pecuniary aspect of marriage is emphasized as Baptista declares that he must "play a merchant's part," also emphasizing the amount of "acting" that is currently under way. Gremio and Tranio/Lucentio both ask for Bianca now that Katherina is to be married. As they quarrel, Baptista announces that the one with the most money to settle on her shall marry Bianca. Tranio offers more and Baptista agrees, provided that his father makes an assurance of his offer. Once alone, Tranio realizes that he must get someone to act as Vincentio, Lucentio's father.

ACT 3 SCENE 1

Lucentio and Hortensio vie for Bianca's attentions as they tutor her, but Bianca shows a distinct preference for Lucentio. Under the pretense of translating a passage of Latin, Lucentio tells Bianca his true identity and intentions. Ignoring Hortensio's interruptions, she replies that, while she does not know or trust Lucentio, he must not despair. During Bianca's music lesson, Hortensio gives her a musical scale that he has devised containing a message to her. Bianca rejects it and a servant arrives, calling her to help prepare for Katherina's wedding the next day. Hortensio reveals his suspicions of Lucentio and his disgust that Bianca seems to return the affections of a mere tutor. He describes Bianca as a hawk who will stoop to any "stale," reinforcing the earlier hunting imagery.

ACT 3 SCENE 2

Lines 1–120: The wedding day has arrived but there is no sign of the groom. Katherina claims that Petruchio is "a mad-brain rudesby" who makes a habit of leaving women at the altar, and she leaves, weeping. Biondello brings news that Petruchio has arrived, dressed in shabby, uncoordinated clothing and riding an old, diseased horse, much to everyone's confusion: for once, clothes are not a clear indicator of identity. Petruchio refuses to change or explain why, claiming that "To me she's married, not unto my clothes," making a distinction between external appearance and true identity. He insists on seeing Katherina.

Lines 121–176: Tranio informs Lucentio of the need to find someone to play the role of his father, although Lucentio suggests it might be easier to elope. Gremio describes the wedding, particularly Petruchio's "mad-brained" behavior, which included striking the priest and calling for wine.

Lines 177–248: Petruchio declares they cannot stay for the wedding feast, but Katherina refuses to leave until it pleases her, insisting that a woman must have "spirit to resist" or "be made a fool." Petruchio announces that he "will be master" of what he owns: Katherina is as much his "goods" and "chattels" as "household stuff" or an ox. He leads her away, leaving the others to speculate on the "mad" match.

ACT 3 SCENE 3

Lines 1–172: Grumio arrives at Petruchio's house, cold and tired. He instructs Curtis to make sure that everything is ready and that the servants are smart to receive their master and new mistress. He describes the terrible journey from Padua: Katherina's horse fell and she landed in the mud, so Petruchio beat Grumio while Katherina tried to stop him. Cold and dirty, Petruchio and Katherina arrive. Petruchio is furious that his servants were not outside to meet him. Supper arrives, and he shifts between apparent pleasantries to his wife, encouraging her to sit and eat and "be merry," and violent verbal and physical abuse of his servants, which makes it impossible for Katherina to do anything. Petruchio claims that the food is burnt and throws it at the servants, despite Katherina's efforts to placate him: an action that presents her in a more gentle light. He takes her to bed, still hungry, and Curtis reports later that Petruchio is still railing at Katherina, "poor soul," so that she "knows not which way to stand, to look, to speak."

Lines 172–196: Petruchio outlines his plan to "tame" Katherina by depriving her of food and sleep, while claiming he is doing it out of "reverend care." He uses the metaphor of a wild hunting hawk, a "haggard," who will learn to come to her "keeper's call."

ACT 3 SCENE 4

Lines 1–43: In Padua, Hortensio/Litio convinces Tranio/Lucentio that Bianca favors "Cambio" and reveals his true identity. Tranio feigns shock and announces his intention to "Forswear Bianca and her love forever," encouraging Hortensio to do the same. Hortensio agrees and announces that he will marry "a wealthy widow" instead.

Lines 44–125: Tranio informs Bianca she is free from Hortensio, who has gone to Petruchio's "taming school" to learn how to tame his "lusty widow." Biondello has found someone to play Vincentio, a "Pedant" who has a "gait and countenance surely like a father." Tranio greets the Pedant and asks where he is from and pretends to be shocked, inventing a quarrel between the Dukes of Padua and Mantua, making it "death" for the Pedant to be there. He offers sanctuary in his home, where the Pedant will be safely disguised as Lucentio's father. As part of this disguise, he will need to pass "assurance of a dower" with Baptista.

ACT 4 SCENE 1

There are tensions in the character of Katherina in this scene as she shifts between desperate attempts to assert herself, sometimes through reasoning, sometimes aggression, and an imposed submissiveness to Petruchio. She complains that she is "starved for meat, giddy for lack of sleep" and asks Grumio to bring her food. He taunts her by suggesting various dishes and then inventing excuses why she may not have them, until Katherina strikes him. Hortensio and Petruchio arrive with food, which Katherina may have only when she thanks her husband. He secretly instructs Hortensio to eat it, and Hortensio shows some discomfort at the situation, saying that Petruchio is "to blame." Petruchio tells Katherina that they are to visit her father, lavishly describing the new clothes she will have for the occasion.

The arrival of the tailor provides visual emphasis of the play's clothing imagery and associated themes. He displays a cap and gown for Katherina, but Petruchio rejects both, on the grounds that they are not good enough for his wife to wear. Katherina attempts to express her opinion, claiming that she will "be free . . . in words," and claims that Petruchio means to "make a puppet" of her, but she is thwarted every time. The tailor is dismissed and Petruchio announces that they will go in their "honest mean habiliments," asserting that " 'tis the mind that makes the body rich," implying that true identity is more important than external appearance.

ACT 4 SCENE 2

Lines 1–72: Tranio and the Pedant (disguised as Vincentio) arrive at Baptista's. They "rehearse" what he is to say, and when Baptista arrives they agree to make the transactions at Lucentio's lodgings. Baptista sends Cambio to fetch Bianca.

Lines 73–103: Biondello informs Lucentio that while Tranio has Baptista safely at his house, a church and priest have been arranged so that he may elope with Bianca.

ACT 4 SCENE 3

Petruchio asserts his will over Katherina by forcing her to agree with him and refusing to continue the journey to Baptista's unless she does so, despite asserting deliberate and contradictory untruths, such as the brightness of the moon in bright daylight. Katherina is forced to agree that it is the moon, even though she says, "I know it is the sun," and thus contradicts Petruchio's earlier assertions concerning appearance and identity, as he denies Katherina external expression of her internal self and her personal conviction. Hortensio comments that Petruchio has "won," but Katherina is tested once more when they meet the real Vincentio and Petruchio makes her greet him as if he were a young girl. Vincentio tells them that he is

going to visit his son, Lucentio, in Padua, and Petruchio congratu-
lates him on the marriage of his son to Bianca. Hortensio leaves to
woo his widow, vowing to use the techniques he has learned from
Petruchio.

ACT 4 SCENE 4

Lines 1–50: Lucentio and Bianca leave for the church as Petruchio
and Katherina arrive with Vincentio. They knock at Lucentio's door
and the Pedant looks out the window, demanding to know who is
there. Petruchio says that it is Lucentio's father, but the Pedant
claims that he is Vincentio. When Biondello arrives he exclaims that
they are "undone," but denies recognizing the real Vincentio. Petruchio draws Katherina aside to watch, forming another onstage "audience."

Lines 51–129: Baptista, Tranio, and the Pedant arrive, and Vincentio sees through Tranio's disguise. Enraged when Tranio refuses to
recognize him, he concludes that Lucentio has been murdered by his
servants. Tranio calls for Vincentio to be taken to prison, but Lucentio and Bianca arrive, and Tranio, Biondello, and the Pedant run
away. Lucentio begs his father's pardon, reveals his true identity to
Baptista, and announces his marriage to Bianca. Vincentio promises
to "content" Baptista, but both fathers vow revenge on Tranio.
Before they follow the others, Petruchio demands that Kate kiss him.
At first she refuses, but then complies in a romantic exchange con-
trasting with their previous encounters.

ACT 5 SCENE 1

At the wedding feast, a public ceremony marking a return to order,
Hortensio's "lusty widow" suggests that Petruchio is "troubled with
a shrew" as a wife. Katherina retaliates, but they are encouraged to
withdraw by Bianca. Once the women are gone, the men discuss
their wives, employing hunting imagery once more as Tranio suggests that Petruchio's "deer" holds him "at a bay." Petruchio proposes a wager: "he whose wife is most obedient / To come at first

when he doth send for her," will win. One hundred crowns is agreed on, and Biondello is sent to fetch Bianca, the Widow and Katherina in turn. Bianca and the Widow both refuse their husbands' commands, but Katherina obeys, much to everyone's surprise. Petruchio sends her to fetch the other two women and, again, she does as she is told. When she returns with Bianca and the Widow, Petruchio orders Katherina to remove her cap and "throw it underfoot." She obeys and the other women claim that she is "silly" and "foolish." Lucentio expresses a wish that Bianca would be more "foolish," as her disobedience has cost him one hundred crowns, but in a manner more associated with Katherina at the beginning of the play, she tells him that he is the fool. Petruchio instructs Katherina to tell the other women "What duty they do owe their lords and husbands." She gives a speech asserting that "Thy husband is thy lord, thy life, thy keeper, / Thy head, thy sovereign." This presents a problematic end to the play and the audience are left to decide for themselves whether Katherina has really changed or whether she is simply playing along with Petruchio.

THE TAMING OF THE SHREW IN PERFORMANCE: THE RSC AND BEYOND

The best way to understand a Shakespeare play is to see it or ideally to participate in it. By examining a range of productions, we may gain a sense of the extraordinary variety of approaches and interpretations that are possible—a variety that gives Shakespeare his unique capacity to be reinvented and made "our contemporary" four centuries after his death.

We begin with a brief overview of the play's theatrical and cinematic life, offering historical perspectives on how it has been performed. We then analyze in more detail a series of productions staged over the last half-century by the Royal Shakespeare Company. The sense of dialogue between productions that can only occur when a company is dedicated to the revival and investigation of the Shakespeare canon over a long period, together with the uniquely comprehensive archival resource of promptbooks, program notes, reviews, and interviews held on behalf of the RSC at the Shakespeare Birthplace Trust in Stratford-upon-Avon, allows an "RSC stage history" to become a crucible in which the chemistry of the play can be explored.

Finally, we go to the horse's mouth. Modern theater is dominated by the figure of the director, who must hold together the whole play, whereas the actor must concentrate on his or her part. The director's viewpoint is therefore especially valuable. Shakespeare's plasticity is wonderfully revealed when we hear directors of highly successful productions answering the same questions in very different ways. We also hear from a Kate about the experience of playing "the shrew."

FOUR CENTURIES OF THE SHREW: AN OVERVIEW

The early performance and textual history of *The Taming of the Shrew*, believed to be one of Shakespeare's earliest plays, are clouded with confusion over the precise nature of its relationship with *The Taming of a Shrew*. It is not clear, for example, whether the 1594 performance of *The Taming of a Shrew* recorded in Philip Henslowe's diary at Newington Butts in south London by the "Right Honourable the Earl of Pembroke's Men" (Shakespeare's Company) was Shakespeare's play therefore, although scholars believe it probably was. The title page of the 1631 Quarto of *The Shrew* which claims it was performed by the King's Men at the Globe and Blackfriars theaters and a court performance before Charles I in 1633 indicate that it continued in the company repertoire. The popularity of and interest in Shakespeare's play is also suggested by John Fletcher's sequel *The Woman's Prize* or *The Tamer Tamed* (written around 1611) in which widower Petruchio is remarried, to Maria, and subjected in turn to his new wife's taming regime.

Shakespeare's play was not produced in its entirety from then until the mid–nineteenth century. Instead audiences from the Restoration onward saw partial performances of Shakespeare's text in numerous adaptations. While these testify to the popularity and familiarity of characters and plot, they suggest unease with its complex interweaving of narrative strands. Apart from the anonymous *A Shrew* which features a complete Sly framework, none of these adaptations treats both the induction and the Katherina/Petruchio plot together. Sometimes they treat the induction material relating to Christopher Sly, in which case the focus is on class, but more commonly the induction has been ignored and the focus is on gender.

In 1698 John Lacey produced *Sauny the Scott or The Taming of the Shrew*, a bawdy farce in which the main character is a Scots servant named Sauny (the Grumio role in *The Shrew*)—from "Sander," the character's name in *A Shrew*. Written in prose, it has no induction or framework. It's set in London and most of the names are anglicized except Petruchio, Tranio, and Biancha *(sic)*. Katherina becomes Margaret/Peg; Baptista, Lord Beaufoy; Lucentio, Winlove, and so on. The rough outline of Shakespeare's play is adhered to but with an emphasis on physical violence. Petruchio threatens to beat Peg with a stick in the second act, and once in his country house she is not only deprived of food and sleep but is threatened with being undressed by Sauny and forced to sit up, drink beer, and smoke tobacco. Margaret is not tamed by this treatment though, and when she and Petruchio return to her father's, she counsels her sister to rebel against her new husband. When she refuses to speak to Petruchio a barber is brought in to extract a tooth. Petruchio pretends that Peg is dead and is going to have her buried, at which point Margaret capitulates. Her final speech is reduced to "Fy Ladys, for shame, How dare you infringe that Duty which you justly owe your Husbands, they are our Lords and we must pay 'em Service." The writing and characterization are unsophisticated, with the comic emphasis divided between Sauny's bawdy and Margaret's humiliation.

Charles Johnson's *The Cobbler of Preston* (1716) is a dramatic response to contemporary political events—the first Jacobite rebellion of the previous year (Battle of Preston, 1715). Johnson was a lawyer turned playwright through his acquaintance with the actor Robert Wilks, joint manager of Drury Lane. He uses the induction from *The Shrew*, making Kit Sly a drunken cobbler from Preston whom Sir Charles Briton decides to teach a lesson. A rival version written and produced by Christopher Bullock at Lincoln's Inn Fields proved more successful, however, and was regularly revived until 1759.

James Worsdale's *A Cure for a Scold* (1735) is an anglicized version of *Sauny the Scott,* which takes place in polite society and is brought into line with the dramatic unities. The text is stripped right down and filled out with twenty-three songs plus dancing. There is no induction or Sly frame. Baptista has become Sir William Worthy; Petruchio Mr. Manly, now an old friend of Sir William's, and Grumio Archer (Manly's friend rather than a servant); Lucentio is called Gainlove and there is no disguising subplot, although he does run off and marry Flora (Bianca); Katherina is Margaret/Peg as in *Sauny.* The Tranio role is omitted but some of his functions are taken over by Flora's maid, Lucy. The language in this version has been cleaned up—there is none of the bawdy of the original or vulgarity of *Sauny,* and there are picturesque archaisms, but despite this and the expression of egalitarian sentiments, the violent potential of the original is exploited and Margaret's physical humiliation relished.

The most famous and popular adaptation was David Garrick's *Catherine and Petruchio* (1756), frequently played in a double bill with his similarly abridged version of *The Winter's Tale, Florizel and Perdita*. Garrick cut the Sly frame and returned the play to Padua. Petruchio is a wealthy man come to Padua to woo Kate. There is no suggestion of any hostility toward her sister or indelicate suggestion that Bianca cannot marry because of Kate. In fact, Bianca is already newly married to Hortensio. Much of Petruchio and Katherina's dialogue from *The Shrew* is retained but the bawdy innuendo is removed. Garrick's Catherine keeps the line from *A Shrew/Sauny/Cure for a Scold* in which she decides to accept Petruchio as a husband. They are to be married the next day and Petruchio turns up unsuitably dressed, as in Shakespeare's play. Petruchio comes out of the church singing before taking his bride away. Grumio has gone on ahead and describes events to the female Curtis, who strikes him. The scene in Petruchio's house is much as in Shakespeare's—the line " 'Twas a fault unwilling" is one of very few to survive in all versions. With no disguised suitors or pretended fathers, it is her own father that Kate addresses as "Young budding virgin, fair and fresh and sweet" when he, Bianca, and Hortensio come to visit. Kate's speech is broken up with interjections from her father, sister, and husband. Petruchio turns down the second dowry, claims that he will "doff the lordly husband; / An honest mask, which I throw off with pleasure" and concludes the final speech himself. This is a polite, genteel, and radically simplified version with rather tame shrews, but it nevertheless evoked sufficient anxiety for Garrick to write an Epilogue for Kate in which the actor proclaims, "Thank Heav'n! I'm not the Thing I represented."

Hannah Pritchard's Catherine was celebrated for her "humour, wit and . . . sprightliness"[25] as was Henry Woodward's Petruchio. It was revived in 1756 with Kitty Clive as Catherine and enjoyed considerable success despite the notoriously ill-tempered relationship between the leads. Thomas Davies, Garrick's biographer, records how, on one occasion, "In one of his mad fits, when he and his bride are at supper, Woodward stuck a fork, it is said, in Mrs. Clive's finger; and in pushing her off the stage he was so much in earnest that he threw her down: as it is well known that they did not greatly respect one another, it was believed that something more than chance contributed to these excesses."[26]

So popular was Garrick's adaptation that *The Taming of the Shrew* was the last of Shakespeare's plays to be restored to the repertory, in 1844, when Samuel Webster and J. R. Planché produced it at the Haymarket Theatre in London. It was Garrick's rather than Shakespeare's version which was played by many of the greatest Shakespearean actors of the day including John Philip Kemble and Sarah Siddons, William Charles Macready and Helen Faucit, Henry Irving and Ellen Terry. It was Garrick's version also that crossed the Atlantic and was first performed by David Douglass and the American Company at the Southwark Theatre in Philadelphia in 1766, making it the most popular of Shakespeare's plays of the late eighteenth century there after *Romeo and Juliet* and *Richard III*.[27]

Despite the favorable reception by critics of Webster and Planché's restoration of Shakespeare's play in 1844 and the excellent performances of Louisa Nisbett as Katherina and Robert Strickland as Sly, Garrick's adaptation continued to hold the stage. Samuel Phelps produced Shakespeare's *Shrew* at Sadler's Wells in 1856, playing the part of Sly himself to great critical acclaim:

> Mr Phelps has a special aptitude for the impersonation of low-comedy characters. . . . *Sly*, under the influence of drink, is little better than a machine, and wholly moved by his instincts. His head turns mechanically from one to another when spoken to. . . . Gradually his impulses are awakened, and he then shows somewhat of his native humour; the various traits of which were so excellently delineated that the house was convulsed with laughter. We may add that the most uproarious merriment also rewarded the efforts of Mr Marston and Miss Atkinson, as *Petruchio* and *Katherine*. The effect was incomparably greater than any ever produced by the performance of the same play in its usual abridged form.[28]

But it was Augustin Daly's 1887 production at Daly's Theater, New York, in 1887 which finally "assured that Shakespeare's play would replace Garrick's afterpiece on both the English and American stages."[29] As the *New York Times* records, "It was a performance of poetic comedy, so beautiful, so graceful, and so merry that the eye was dazzled, the ear captivated, and the senses charmed."[30] The greatest praise was reserved for Ada Rehan whose Katherine "was of greater merit than any other individual performance."[31] The production and Rehan's performance met with equal success when they transferred to London's Gaiety Theatre the following year: "Miss Ada Rehan has entered into the very soul of Katherine, and furnishes a representation of the character not to be surpassed in loveliness and in originality."[32] Theater historians have been less kind to Daly's production, Stark Young called his acting version of *The Shrew* "only a patch-up of the Garrick version."[33] Nevertheless, the French comedian Constant Coquelin was so impressed when the production went to Paris that he ordered a French translation. Paul Delair's *La Mégère Apprivoisée* was produced in 1892 at Abbey's Theatre. An Italian version starring Ermete Novelli was also produced at New York's Lyric theater in 1907. Margaret Anglin's production, which opened in Melbourne in 1908, originally included Shakespeare's induction, making this its first presentation in America when the show transferred to San Francisco in 1913, but the scene was inexplicably cut before going on to New York.

In the same year John Martin Harvey produced Shakespeare's play at the Prince of Wales Theatre in collaboration with William Poel, actor-manager and founder of the Elizabethan Stage Society, with himself as Petruchio and his wife, Nina DeSilva, as Kate. *The Times* reviewer reported:

We found not only the Induction (which was given in full) but the presence of Christopher Sly in the audience a great help. We had seen the troupe of players arrive in their gaudy clothes of red and yellow. We knew they were only players. It left us free to enjoy this "pleasant conceited historie" as a piece of hearty fun, without bothering about its ethics or calculating its probability or its likeness to life.[34]

The restored text of Shakespeare's play was regarded as problematic even before feminism and critical theory turned *The Taming of the Shrew* into a problem play. Among the earliest critics to voice his objections, particularly in relation to the last scene, was George Bernard Shaw:

No man with any decency of feeling can sit it out in the company of a woman without being extremely ashamed of the lord-of-creation moral implied in the wager and the speech put into the woman's mouth.[35]

In her account of the play in performance, *From Farce to Metadrama: A Stage History of the Taming of the Shrew 1594–1983*, Tori Haring-Smith describes the various strategies directors have adopted over the years in order to make the play palatable to modern audiences.[36] As her title suggests, directors attempted to distance productions from those elements deemed problematic through emphasizing its comedy in slapstick routines and *commedia dell'arte* caricature featuring madcap shrews and ruffianly Petruchios. While these were often popular with audiences, critics were judgmental to the point of asking whether the play should in fact be performed at all. It has continued to be performed but the ideas which had brought about a cultural revolution and the revision of critical judgments were naturally to have an effect on performance. In the light of such new thinking, it was difficult to produce the old-fashioned farces or romantic wish-fulfillments. One way in which the play could be made acceptable was by emphasizing the induction which had so frequently been cut in earlier productions. This lent the play distance from the taming plot and also illuminated the relationship between class and gender oppression—if Kate was a victim of patriarchy brainwashed by Petruchio and the social structure, so was Christopher Sly. Many modern productions have focused on the play's examination of class structures in relation to Sly and the actors, most notoriously Bill Alexander's RSC productions of the early 1990s (discussed in detail below) in which the induction is used as a springboard for a more philosophical exploration of the discrepancy between appearance and reality.

In America Alfred Lunt and Lynn Fontane enjoyed great success with their "thumping picnic"[37] of a production in the 1930s. George Devine at the Shakespeare Memorial Theatre, Stratford, in 1953 was the first director to incorporate the epilogue from *A Shrew* in which the Sly framework is completed. Its *commedia dell'arte* treatment was

1. Shakespeare Memorial Theatre, 1953: a *commedia dell'arte* treatment.

much admired, as were Marius Goring's Petruchio and Yvonne Mitchell's Katherina.

John Barton's subsequent production at Stratford in 1960 with Peter O'Toole and Peggy Ashcroft took over and heightened many of Devine's effects.

Michael Langham, for the Stratford Festival, Ontario, in 1962, took the framing device beyond the conclusion of the play:

2. John Barton production, 1960: Peter O'Toole as Petruchio and Peggy Ashcroft as Katherina, a production which "heightened many of Devine's effects."

In that moment—with just a faint suspension of breath to show that something is passing—a world closes down like the last light of day. Petruchio, so triumphant over Kate only a moment ago, is now leaning against a pillar as though his energies could never be restored, his shoulders limp with an actor's weariness. Kate, the virago who has not for a moment stood still, stands alone, looking at no one as the stage properties are hustled past her, waiting for her composure to return. The supporting company, instantly characterless and briskly indifferent, cares only about packing the cart for the journey into the night. And when Petruchio has breathed out his tensions and become a mere player again, he moves past Kate without so much as a nod to her. Starting down the road that will end somewhere in another performance, he throws his arm about Bianca, who is obviously his real love. A play is a play, and even when it is well done, 'tis done.[38]

Productions in the late twentieth and early twenty-first century have continued to experiment with strategies and ideas to update *The Shrew* and render its problematic politics acceptable: "Directors have been drawn to the *Shrew* because it can withstand extensive adaptation and modification, enabling them to put their personal signatures upon their productions."[39] One of the most disturbing is Charles Marowitz's "Gothic tragedy"[40] *The Shrew* (1974) which opens with Kate tormenting Bianca "tied to a pole, bound hand and foot." There is no Christopher Sly framework but the theme of playacting becomes part of Katherina's taming as Grumio and Hortensio take all the supporting roles wearing masks of "gnarled brutish servants."[41] Petruchio is an adventurer seeking a wealthy wife, but the undercurrent of menace and violence is horrifyingly exploited. The theme of class is reinforced through a parallel modern couple—the Boy/Girl who play Bianca and Hortensio. Katherina is finally brainwashed and becomes a mindless cipher parroting the words she has been taught to speak.

Directors have set the play "in such unlikely places as Cleveland's Little Italy, the American Southwest, Nigeria, New South Wales and the American West"[42]—Tyrone Guthrie at Stratford, Ontario, in 1954 and James Dunn at the Edinburgh Festival in 1979, among others. They have played with gender roles; for example, the Medieval Players in Oxford's New College cloisters in 1986 cast men in the roles of Kate and Bianca and women as Lucentio, Tranio, and Hortensio, but the problem according to one critic was that Petruchio was not also cross-cast,

> If Petruchio had been played by a woman, the relationship between the two would have been funnier because the actors could have used the fact that they were of the opposite sex to comment on their characters' follies. . . . In addition to making the relationship between the central characters funnier, casting a woman as Petruchio would have enabled the actors to find a way of engaging constructively with the problems the play holds for us today.[43]

There have been a number of all-male productions since then in which the cross-dressed performances have successfully challenged essentialist theories of gender and highlighted its role-playing aspects. At Shakespeare's Globe in 2003 it was performed by the Women's Company directed by Phyllida Lloyd:

> Rather than struggle with this troublesome piece, however, the girls' strategy is to have fun with it. Striding about the stage in doublet and hose, the cast adopts its male personas with relish, slapping each other on the back, drumming the table and lounging with their legs apart—in short enjoying all the laddish behaviour that would still be thought unladylike today.[44]

The leading performances were much praised:

> [Janet] McTeer makes a smashing Petruchio and has a ball with the part. . . . Her swaggering bravado is absurdly comical, yet believable . . . [she] is delightfully paired with Kathryn Hunter as Kate. This Kate is a match for her man. Hunter plays her transformation beautifully and delivers the infamous final speech with such heartfelt sincerity that Petruchio actually weeps, until he realises she has beaten him at his own game.[45]

The review concludes that the production is "fun while it lasts and, as the play so ably demonstrates, it's almost impossible to tame *The Shrew* completely."[46]

There were seven silent-film versions of *The Taming of the Shrew*, including a seventeen-minute version directed by D. W. Griffith in 1908, before Sam Taylor's 1929 production for United Artists starring Mary Pickford as Katherina and Douglas Fairbanks Jr. as Petruchio. It was the first Shakespearean "talkie." Much of the focus is on the star-couple billing. As with many early talkies, it deploys a performance style associated with silent films—exaggerated movement and slow delivery. In place of the induction, there is a short Punch and Judy puppet show, which functions in a similar way to frame the action and arguably as a similarly subversive gesture. The main emphasis, though, is on the relationship between these two protagonists. Fairbanks, the notorious swashbuckling hero, swashes his buckle through Petruchio suggesting an empty, blustering braggart. He carries the whip, first used as a character prop by John Philip Kemble, but Katherina has one as well—just not as long! Making the film does not appear to have been a very happy experience for Pickford (a theme which is endlessly repeated in the accounts of other actors taking on the role of Katherina). Pickford was dissatisfied with her performance and reviewers frequently refer to her "kittenish" quality. Her performance is notable historically for the enormous wink she gives her sister and the audience in the final scene at the end of her long speech thereby ironizing Katherina's subjection.

In *Sly*, Ermanno Wolf-Ferrari's 1927 tragic opera, the main character kills himself for love of the lord's girlfriend who has pretended to love him. It later turns out that her protestations of love were sincere. Meanwhile, in 1948 Samuel and Bella Spewack and Cole Porter produced the popular Broadway musical, *Kiss Me Kate*. Franco Zeffirelli's 1967 film starred another celebrity couple with a tempestuous off-screen relationship, Elizabeth Taylor and Richard Burton. Zeffirelli goes for farce and romance and tones down realistic elements. In place of the Sly induction, the film opens with a backdrop of an Italian landscape across which Lucentio (Michael York) and Tranio (Cyril Cusack) ride into Padua. As they arrive, Lucentio announces his desire to further his studies as a solemn university ceremony for the first day of term is underway. This immediately gives way to carnival and the feast of misrule in which the natural order is turned upside down. The parade and the vitality of these scenes demonstrate Zeffirelli's work at its best—full of invention and wit, and exhilarating to watch. While Burton blusters his way lazily through the film, Taylor's Katherina seems certifiable as she smashes up her father's house. It includes the infamous chase in which Kate ends up on a woolsack/bed with Petruchio on top of her. There is also a curious interpolated scene in which she supervises the cleaning of Petruchio's country house which the critic Ann Christensen locates within postwar twentieth-century attempts to tame and domesticate women.[47] Taylor makes an unlikely housewife, but she's clearly the boss as Petruchio walks behind her—on the other hand, she can't, unfortunately, handle the meter of the poetry in her long speech. This is a Hollywood extravaganza, spectacular and enjoyable in its way.

The 1980 BBC television version directed by Jonathan Miller controversially cast the well-known comedy actor John Cleese as Petruchio, a decision which "was a huge gamble but it paid off."[48] Cleese's performance attracted most of the critical attention:

> His performance stands out from those characterisations which hew closely to naturalism, as a sustained and inspired deployment of Brechtian alienation-effect. Cleese is never entirely naturalised within his role, as other comic characters contrive to be: his delivery of the lines always preserves a certain ironic distance, as if he found difficulty not only in taking them seriously himself, but in the idea that anyone could possibly take them seriously at all. The result is a beautifully-composed detachment, which allows to the part of Petruchio a unique doubleness and self-reflexive ironical consciousness. Towering over his strange mixed company of Stanislavskian soul-searchers and music-hall comedians in creative innovation as well as height, Cleese is easily the most admirable component of the production.[49]

Gil Junger's *Ten Things I Hate About You* (1999) updates the play to a modern American high school and stars Julia Stiles as Katarina (Kat) Stratford and Heath Ledger as Patrick (Pat) Verona. Kat is smart and spiky and far too bright for her classmates and teachers, but her gynaecologist father won't let her spoiled younger sister date until Kat has a boyfriend. The boys get together to find a suitable candidate and pick on the local firebrand. It's slick and entertaining, with a lot of nice touches—such as the romantic novelist school counselor, Ms. Perky, played by Allison Janney. The comic references to romantic fiction work in a subversive, ironic, and self-reflexive manner since the film is clearly a romantic comedy but sufficiently embarrassed to want to distance itself from the genre's conventions.

AT THE RSC

A Director's Dilemma

Discussing the function of theater, director Michael Bogdanov commented:

> It's meant to provoke debate: to explore issues that are carried on into debate with a passion and a commitment to change. That makes theatre worthwhile. Theatre, when it is doing its job properly, is a more effective medium than any other for provoking thought into action: unhappily, most of the time it doesn't do its job.[50]

As a catalyst for political discussion *The Taming of the Shrew* has created a wealth of controversy in its last fifty years of performance, provoking extreme reactions at times in directors, audiences, and critics. On seeing Bogdanov's 1978 production, critic Michael Billington questioned whether "there is any reason to revive a play that seems totally offensive to our age and our society. My own feeling is that it should be put back firmly and squarely on the shelf."[51] David Ward similarly pointed out: "Shrews used to be good for a laugh. Then guilt set in: where's the joke in seeing a curst woman tamed by a macho bigmouth? Should not the play be stuffed back in the Folio and allowed to die?"[52] Misogynist fantasy, feminist critique, or both—the battle between the sexes prompts a passionate response. Nevertheless, the *Shrew*'s popularity has ensured it a regular spot in the RSC's repertoire, indicating that the audiences have no problem with what critics and directors have come to consider a "problem play."

Making the play palatable is a source of constant worry for the director, even when that director is a woman. Gale Edwards, who directed the *Shrew* in 1995, neatly summed up the dilemma:

> A woman directing *The Taming of the Shrew*, whoever she is, might as well get a loaded shotgun and put it against her temple because half the critics will be disappointed and will criticise it if the view of the play is not radical and feminist because

they expect that from a woman; then the other half will shoot you down in flames because you're doing a feminist, "limited" view of the play which is meant to be about the surrender of love. So you *cannot* possibly win. You're absolutely f—ked.[53]

The wide variety of approaches to the play by the RSC in the last fifty years has clearly demonstrated the challenges the *Shrew* poses. The induction scene has proved a crucial staging tool in the re-evaluation of the Shrew plot, that is, as a play-within-a-play. This combined with the emphasis on questions of love, money and class have given the play an added depth, moving it away from farce into far darker territory.

Plays Within Plays

Bill Alexander, who directed the *Shrew* in 1992, commented:

When I read the quarto text I was convinced that, in structural terms, it was closer to what Shakespeare had intended. The Sly plot has all sorts of proleptic ironies that anticipate the action of the central plot, which is all about performance—people in disguise or pretending—in all sorts of ways. . . . I think Shakespeare's intention was to have Sly and the others watching the play within the play the whole time, that he did intend interruptions and a final scene that reconciles the whole Sly plot. For two reasons. Artistically it's more likely, and such highly conceptualised scenes would more probably be left out than added as time went on . . . the idea of life being a performance, of people putting on characters in life to get through, to impress, to conceal themselves, to make a stand against the world. That's the subject matter of this play, a central moral . . . that until people stop pretending, confident enough to display their true selves, they will never find love that's meaningful and lasting.[54]

In his updating of the induction:

Christopher Sly collapses outside the Ugly Duckling into the arms of an unpleasant group of coke-snorting young toffs who anticipate some fun in the playing around with his mind. They lift him into their ancestral home where Sly is dressed as a lord, and the players, looking like themselves arrive to put on their play in the panelled drawing room.

The clash between reality and illusion and the nature of identity become crucial themes: Sly becomes a Lord, and Tranio, disguised as Lucentio, falls in love with both his part and Bianca.[55]

The lords and ladies watching the play had their own existence and journey throughout the play. They were dressed in contemporary costume and given updated dialogue, and the play-within-a-play was performed in Renaissance dress. Bill Alexander explained:

All I've done is modernise the language; there's a juxtaposition of times and periods on stage. It is taking a liberty indeed to rewrite the first two scenes, but I think it's worth it because you are making the play modern, but setting it in its period context. It would be inconsistent to have modern characters speaking the same language as the actors playing the sixteenth century characters. So what I've sacrificed in terms of what Shakespeare wrote, I think I've more than replaced by reclaiming the overall structure of the play.[56]

On stage throughout, watching the action of the *Taming*, the lords were also roped into the action as a means of deflating their pompous smugness:

The most disconcerting moment comes when the players enlist the yuppies to take on roles in their play. The gangly young things are shown to have no wit or imagination about them as the players outpace them easily in the bravura display of comedy.[57]

In 1985 director Di Trevis used the framing device to take the issue of class dynamics a stage further by creating a link between the victimization of Sly and Katherina and the powerlessness of the poor:

> I felt with the structure of the play within a play, I could make all the comments I wanted about the role of the women and this became intensely interesting to me. With that very sadistic trick played on the poor man, Sly, I realised that I could draw a parallel between the powerlessness of the women in the play and the powerlessness of that beggar. And I didn't have to do that terrible thing of making Katherine send up the last speech because I had a structure whereby, after the ending of the play, I could make a theatrical comment about the position of the actress playing Katherine in the inner play—she and the beggar were finally left alone on the stage together and one saw that they were fellows.[58]

The harsh realities of the dispossessed players punctuated the action. Their costumes were shabby and ripped. As the production began, out of the darkness, the audience heard the cry of a baby, which was brought on by the actress playing Katherina. Later in the production Di Trevis explained how she

> also kept showing that the players were acting; just little things like when they all danced at Kate's wedding, and it was the end of the first half, all the players came out dancing but Kate came out nursing the baby as if the baby had been woken up by the music.[59]

Gale Edwards, who was the second woman to direct the play for the RSC, used the induction to present the play as the guilt-ridden male fantasy/nightmare. The play began with Sly and the rarely seen Mrs. Sly in fierce argument, during which

> Christopher Sly, a drunken tinker, is abandoned by his wife on a blasted Warwickshire heath. In his alcoholic stupor, he imagines he is rescued by a lord who presents him with a Pad-

uan farce in which Sly himself is translated into the fortune-hunting Petruchio and his wife into Katherina. Finally shamed by the excesses of his chauvinist fantasy, Sly wakes to find his wife standing over him and leading him off into a presumably redefined marital relationship.[60]

The idea of the *Shrew* as a twisted male fantasy was taken further in Lindsay Posner's 1999 production. The induction was again in contemporary costume—the drunken Sly was picked up and cleaned off by the hunting party to awake in the lord's bedroom, believing it is somehow his own:

Logging on to "his" computer, he accesses a dodgy web-site and "becomes" Petruchio. The story is presented as the chat-room fantasy of an angry mind, and Ashley Martin-Davis's designs consist chiefly of back-wall projections of computer-screen images. At the end, Sly is again drunk and dirty in a gutter, listening to Prodigy's *Smack My Bitch Up*, which sort of puts his domination-dreams into context.[61]

As an idea it is ingenious; and the designer, Ashley Martin-Davis, cleverly uses a giant screen to show filmic images dissolving into reality, so that the two horsemen riding toward us in the opening shot turn into flesh-and-blood Lucentio and Tranio.[62]

The induction device used by Michael Bogdanov (1978) un-nerved his audience as they settled into their seats:

Before the house lights dim we become aware of an uproar in the aisle. A roughly dressed man, grasping a bottle, quarrels loudly in a prole accent with the usherette, then proceeds to clamber on to the stage and wreck the set—one of those tacky, pastel-flavoured, Italian Renaissance confections, complete with proscenium arch. . . . Much tumult accompanies the demolition: stagehands running up and down, bits and pieces of carpentry collapsing.[63]

Who was the unshaven lout in the third row, shouting and singing and struggling with an usherette? Wasn't it Jonathan Pryce, the actor billed to play Petruchio? Yes, it was, and presenting so plausible a display of alcoholic rage that I was momentarily convinced he had been given the boot and was taking an ugly revenge on the RSC hierarchy. Then he yelled, "I'm not having any bloody woman tell me what to do."[64]

The usherette getting the tirade of abuse and threats of violence was actress Paola Dionisotti, who also played Katherina. This riotous opening and the subsequent destruction of the set gave the audience a clear indication that they were not going to be witnessing a traditional approach to the play:

> The elaborate prettiness of the old-fashioned, Italianate set was literally deconstructed before the audience's eyes to reveal a network of metallic stairs and gantries, resembling the uncompromising interior of a gaol.[65]

In this one clever move, Bogdanov set up and then demolished the audiences' preconceptions, left-footing them and preparing them for a very different reading of the play. The dividing line between reality and fantasy was crossed by the leading actors, who took the audience physically into the world of the play. The Italianate set which audiences saw as they entered, set up the expectation of safe theater—the traditional approach. In destroying it to reveal the stark modern setting behind it, Bogdanov instantly installed a darker note—they are going to see beyond the façade, a break from preconceptions about the play from its stage history.

My Goods, My Chattels: Anti-Capitalist Shrews

Money, class, and status have a marked effect on the characters in *The Taming of the Shrew*. As soon as human life is evaluated as a financial commodity you devalue a person's worth, take away their humanity and individuality. Similarly, in a society where people are valued by how much wealth they have, those with less are valued as lesser human beings and open to all sorts of exploitation.

In his 1978 production:

Bogdanov was concerned to stress the continuities between the mercantile ethics of Renaissance Padua and the commercial values of modern-day British capitalism; between the oppression of women in Shakespeare's time, and the continuing exploitation of sex today; between the class-divisions of the sixteenth century and the economic inequality of the twentieth.[66]

When interviewed, Bogdanov stated:

Shakespeare shows women totally abused—like animals—bartered to the highest bidder. He shows women used as commodities, not allowed to choose for themselves. In *The Taming of the Shrew* you get that extraordinary scene between Baptista, Grumio and Tranio, where they are vying with each other to see who can offer most for Bianca, who is described as "the prize." It is a toss of the coin to see which way she will go: to the old man with a certain amount of money, or to the young man, who is boasting that he's got so many ships. She could end up with the old impotent fool, or the young "eligible" man: what sort of life is that to look forward to? There is no question of it, his sympathy is with the women, and his purpose, to expose the cruelty of a society that allows these things to happen.[67]

In this production, Baptista

sits hunched over a vast gilt desk, the epitome of the Mafioso-turned-magnate, totting up the value of one suitor's argosies on an automatic calculator and skimming through the latest digest of farm prices when another boasts of his milch-kine and oxen. And the very last image the production offers is of the servant Grumio clambering across a table to retrieve the wager that Katherine's compliance has won his master, while Petruchio himself swaggers offstage with his wife hanging off one hand and a 20,000-crown cheque from her father in the other.[68]

Padua, it seems, is that sort of place, a competitive, grasping, cynical, and really rather horrible city.[69]

In her 1985 touring production, Di Trevis claimed that the play was "not so much about the position of women as about wealth and class, about people being treated as objects by others in more powerful positions."[70] She believed it was "about power, not gender. Power resides in economic status. The main plot is a play-within-a-play which I see as a rich man's joke."[71] Set in the early to mid-nineteenth century, the play reflected a time when "women were treated as chattels, when the gulf between the agricultural poor and the city rich was widening, and there was a marked political swing to the right."[72] The play-within-the-play ended with a wedding tableau, rose petals, and music, but the performance was not over. The players took their bows and went off to change, but Sly's own fiction had not ended. After the confusion of the congratulation of the players, and their subsequent exit, Sly and his "lady" moved toward each other. Sly was gentle and loving. He believed in his role, and he had seen that respect and affection between men and women was possible. Then the page threw off his wig and ran away, laughing mockingly. Sly watched, grief-stricken, and the genuine lord contemptuously threw a few coins at his feet. Sly had fulfilled his part as entertainer. Now he was being paid.

Some of the players returned to collect props and costumes. An actress got down on her hands and knees to clean the floor. The actress who had played Kate entered. She looked humble and downtrodden now. There was no trace of her courage and vivacity as Kate. In her arms she held the baby she had carried at the beginning of the performance as she pulled the cart. As the lights faded for the final time, Sly stretched out his hand to this actress, offering her as a gift one of the coins that had been tossed to him.

A poor man had learned something through the experience of watching the play, but he was without power. He was a man, but he was not rich, and within the society the production

3. Di Trevis production, 1985: a humble and downtrodden Kate "held the baby she had carried at the beginning of the performance as she pulled the cart," very much in the manner of Brecht's Mother Courage.

depicted both qualities were necessary before a human being was considered of real worth.[73]

Birds of Prey Are Never Truly Tame[74]

Playing games is something Petruchio does throughout the play, whether the games are funny or dark, and he sets the tone as soon as he arrives.[75]

Petruchio's motivation for his actions toward Katherina radically alters what the audience feels about the more brutal scenes in the play. Likewise, Katherina's response to his behavior, her awareness and understanding, or lack of it, will determine just how funny the play remains. Because of the ambiguity inherent in the text the relationship between these two misfits can be interpreted in many ways. It offers a precarious balance in characterization which can determine whether or not the audience sees a love story or disturbing account of spousal abuse.

In 1987 Jonathan Miller turned his psychologist's eye to the play, finding the crux of the problem in the fact that Katherina was an unwanted and neglected child:

> Dr Miller . . . is interested as always in the clinical psychology underlying the text. He has been talking of the behaviour patterns of unloved children. Katherina has every reason to resent being her father's unfavourite daughter. By being as "froward" as she knows how, she is showing just how unlovable she can be if she chooses. "It's not that she needs taming, she needs releasing," reflects Fiona Shaw [who played Katherina]. "She behaves badly because of being imprisoned by her society—being offered round by a father who says, in effect, "Which of you chaps will have Kate?—otherwise nobody gets Bianca."[76]

Fiona Shaw's Katherina was a woman on the verge of a nervous breakdown, unable to be a complete person in a repressive society: "After a while, when people are calling you a shrew, you start living the name. If you're told you're ugly, you start acting ugly."[77] Her psychological state was even reflected in the stage design of Stefanos Lazaridis:

> The Shrew is also about upstarts and outsiders, an unruly woman and a subversive suitor who affront decorum and knock Padua off its level footing. Miller's set demonstrated this too. It put Padua on a steep slope, its street a vertiginous rake. . . . [Kate] finally appeared, behind the rest, self-absorbed, teetering down the steep edge of the steep verge, arms outstretched like a tightrope walker. On one side was High Street Padua, on the other, a sheer drop. This woman was on the brink. While the suitors bickered, Fiona [Shaw's] Kate ranged behind them, flashing her embroidery scissors, gouging initials into the walls and hacking off handfuls of hair.

Shaw described how she "wanted to give the effect of a woman mutilating herself like some women in prison do. I wanted to use the scissors to cut my arm—I thought about women in crisis who, far from being aggressive towards other people, are very often aggressive towards themselves."[78] When this Katherina meets Petruchio, she finds, for the first time in her life, somebody who genuinely wants her:

> It may only be for her money and services . . . but at least she will be valued for something. . . . The scene then develops between standard hostilities and moments of astonishment and delighted intoxication, which she then chokes down to renew the combat. Miss Shaw plays this beautifully; but most of her acting has to be between the lines, with many a pause for conflicting emotions to pass over her face before the action resumes.[79]

> She comes in—and is talked to by a man for the first time; that's what disorientates her. Not his violence but his gentleness.[80]

Brian Cox's Petruchio uses violence to instruct, to throw a reflection of Katherina's behavior back at herself so that she can learn that violence against others is only really violence against herself. With this damaged Kate, extreme methods were needed to break her anger and own self-destructive behavior:

> He means to be taken seriously—when Kate slaps him, there is a deadly purr in his voice which tells us she would be very unwise to do it again—but cruelty disgusts him. . . . Petruchio is usually played as an engaging sadist. Cox makes him a shrewd eccentric, a man who brawls and shouts to parody behaviour he detests.[81]

> She comes in wrecked from the journey, still in her wedding dress, and what happens next is that her expectations of normal life are totally undermined. She who has been characterized by violence now has to observe what violence really is. . . . He shouts at the servants. . . . He beats them up and says,

4. Jonathan Miller production, 1987: Fiona Shaw as Katherina and Brian Cox as Petruchio. "With this damaged Kate, extreme methods were needed to break her anger and own self-destructive behaviour."

"Nay, Kate, be merry!" . . . It's a nightmare. Because the tamer is a man who says, "You want violence? Look at this, what d'you think of this? Bang!" So much so that the only lines Kate speaks in that scene are defending the servant! "Patience, I pray you, 'twas a fault unwilling." For the first time she is the one who's tempering. For the first time Petruchio makes contact with her civilizedness.[82]

Alternatively, when the "taming" of Katherina is portrayed as Sly's twisted male fantasy the misogynistic elements of the relationship are often emphasized by the overt use of physical and mental abuse. In Michael Bogdanov's provocative modern-dress production (1978) Jonathan Pryce was a

brutish Petruchio/Sly, both of whom used violence crudely. The brutishness in men was socially unacceptable under the veneer of conventional behaviour and was indicated in the final scene, set in a traditionally male club-like setting with a

large green baize table, with men smoking, drinking port or
brandy, and casually gambling, a society "in which well-fed
men slouch indolently over their port, baying 'hear, hear'
when one of their number extracts a particularly ignominious
confession of inferiority from his woman."[83]

Paola Dionisotti, who played Katherina, found the contemporary
setting a stumbling block, as she felt a woman of her character
would simply not put up with Petruchio's behavior in the modern
world. However, many felt that the production successfully set out to
reflect the exploitation of power in our own times:

This production's contemporary setting generated a provocative and demanding relevance, presenting the taming story as
a distasteful exhibition of male chauvinism and exploitation.
The huntsmen threw a vixen's body pelt down upon the sleep-

5. Michael Bogdanov production, 1978: Jonathan Pryce as a "brutish
Petruchio/Sly" who "uses violence crudely." The final scene was set "in a
traditionally male club-like setting with a large green baize table, with men
smoking, drinking port or brandy, and casually gambling."

ing drunkard and instead of a play within a play the ensuing action took the form of Sly-as-Petruchio's fantasy of domination and power.[84]

When asked about the harshness of Petruchio's depiction, Bogdanov explained:

> The violence in my production was meant to engage the audience on an emotional level, to the extent of asking the audience to stand up and be counted. To ask what you really believe, are you really sitting comfortably in your seats, or is there something else that theatre makes you do? Makes you angry, makes you fear, challenges you, and finally makes you want to do something to change the world. Catharsis has no meaning for me. I'm not interested in people purging their emotions in the theatre and then walking away without a care in the world. I am only interested in theatre that excites people enough to make them want to cheer, or be angry enough to walk out.[85]

Stuart McQuarrie's Petruchio in Lindsay Posner's 1999 production was also repellent in his violence toward his servants and his wife, described by one reviewer as "a charming, volatile, sunken-eyed monster who will go to any lengths to assert his authority."[86] There was even a suggestion of offstage violence when Katherina appeared with a "large red weal on her arm after her marriage."[87] As his sustained campaign of abuse went on, the production became decidedly less humorous:

> Posner's key idea is that Petruchio himself is really the one with problems: transmogrifying from Sly into Petruchio, Stuart McQuarrie plays the latter as a pathologically violent figure who beats up Grumio with the same sadistic relish he shows towards Kate. . . . You don't feel this is a Petruchio whose long-range strategy is to offer Kate a mirror image of her own madness: he simply seems a charmless bully who enjoys tormenting people. . . . Posner simply leaves us with a coldly brutal tale about psychological cruelty. . . . But if Shakespeare's central

text is no more than the moral equivalent of a sexually chauvinist video, you wonder why anyone today would choose to watch it.[88]

The excruciating final scene is well done. Dolan's Katherine recites her submissive speech like a Stepford Wife (Referring to the film *The Stepford Wives* in which men in an American small town kill and replace their wives with robotic copies who act like every man's dream of the 'perfect' wife.) and the assembled guests look on in horror. Posner almost wimps out, hinting that Kate's surrender is an in-joke, that husband and wife have come to some mysterious, us-against-the-world understanding. But nothing can disguise the naked triumphalism of McQuarrie's Petruchio.[89]

When discussing his performance as Petruchio, Michael Siberry discussed the dilemma of reaching a balance between cruelty and humor:

If you really start putting on the pressure, being really cruel—for which you have the language and the structure of the speeches to support you—it becomes simply too dark and bleak. So much cruelty is implicit in what you say and do anyway, that to play it too strongly is to overstate the obvious. . . . If, on the other hand, you try to keep it light, if you look as if you are thinking "this is wonderful and I'm more and more drawn to her by the way she deals with this experience or that" (and I think that is what is happening to him), if you look as if you are enjoying yourself and not simply putting pressure on Kate in a nasty, vindictive way, the result is much more interesting . . . no matter how good your comedy techniques are, the shadows are still there; you have to acknowledge them, but play against them too.[90]

In Gregory Doran's 2003 production, Jasper Britton played Petruchio as a man as emotionally lost after the death of his father as Katherina is by the absence of love from hers:

Initially, Britton comes over as a swaggering soldier of fortune, arriving in a seedy Padua that's all peeling doors, scraggy gowns and shameless lovemaking. Yet underneath this Petruchio is also emotionally shaky, still wearing a black armband for his father's death. His first wooing scene with [Alexandra] Gilbreath is astonishingly romantic. He floors her in a childish rough-and-tumble, tickling her foot till she roars with laughter. Then he holds her face in his hand with overwhelming tenderness. She is smitten by that, not by manhandling. Her show of obedience is a game whose rules they both understand, while his later bullying is partly explained by a drink problem and falling-back on the tough falcon-training creed of his father.[91]

There was a real sense of two people finding each other with a gradual realization that they could create a world outside of the normal rules of their society. Katherina and Petruchio were more equally dependent on each other for salvation than usual. It prompted one reviewer to comment: "I have never seen the 'wooing' scene more breathtakingly played: instead of barbaric knockabout, we see a damaged couple finding mutual support."[92]

Katherina's angry scorn quickly yields to surprised interest as she realises that this new wooer will engage with her, tease her and praise her. It is their shared sense of humour that connects them, becoming most clear on Katherina's roar of ribald laughter at Petruchio's joke about his tongue being in her tail—a joke which more commonly draws shocked outrage from the lady. . . . Her earlier anger and tension, which had been painfully visible in her aggressive posture and unkempt appearance, are replaced by playfulness, laughter and a fearful joy as she falls in love.[93]

. . . in place of an offensive comedy about "curative" wife-taming, we see Kate trying to rescue a madman she genuinely loves. . . . Packed with insight, this Shrew is a life-enhancing comedy about the triumph of marriage over paternal oppression.[94]

The final submission speech was viewed with envy by all present, for it was obvious that these two outsiders had found a way of loving which far excelled anything that they could hope for within society's normal restrictions. For her final speech Gilbreath was dressed in

a strange combination of corset, petticoats, breeches and unlaced boots, unburdened by any care for how the world might judge her. Her lack of decorum echoes her husband's outrageous appearance at their wedding, which he defended with the words "To me she's married not unto my clothes." . . . Katherina enters gladly through the central door in obedience to her husband's command and delivers her speech of wifely duty with heartfelt sincerity and love. In response to her husband, she discards the cap and, with a playful care, treads it into the ground. Petruchio carefully picks it up and dusts it off, placing it beside him on the table. She proffers her hand to "do him ease" with a big gesture. He remains seated and raises his booted foot, saying "Come on" as if demanding that she publicly take her obedience to the extreme and humiliate herself by literally placing herself beneath his foot. Katherina's face betrays the cost of such a demand as, after a short pause, she moves towards him to obey, only to be intercepted as he sweeps her into an embrace and finally completes his line " . . . and kiss me, Kate."[95]

"Being a Winner" (5.1.199)

On one level *Shrew* is about the power of theatre to change people, to actually make people see themselves, and you, through seeing life reproduced on the stage.[96]

The playwright John Arden writing about *Henry V* suggested: "one is forced to wonder if the author had not written a secret play inside the official one," and it may be that one has to question *The Taming of the Shrew* in the same way. Are the problems of sexism and chauvinistic behavior a problem at all when most right-minded people watching it are genuinely appalled by them anyway?

When directing another play about the Elizabethan attitudes to marriage, Michael Bogdanov commented that whether Shakespeare is examining personal and/or sociopolitical concerns, he is,

> all the time, analysing the nature of power and the way that it corrupts man. It is as if he were trying to find another society that could exist outside of this Elizabethan one of greed and avarice. . . . As long as there is a society where fathers are allowed to barter their daughters to the highest bidder, then tragedies like *Romeo and Juliet* are going to occur.[97]

Economics and class should not enter into the realms of emotion but they still do. Money traps the humanity of both rich and poor: the rich because the world for them, including personal relationships, becomes a matter of economics, the poor, because without money they are powerless and at the mercy of those who will use them without consequence. The question which we are left with in modern productions of *The Taming of the Shrew* is whether or not two people who love each other can break free of their restrictive milieu and challenge society's perceptions, or whether they are trapped by the established order into destructive patterns of behavior. Shakespeare's text has enabled directors to explore these possibilities in a way that is entirely relevant despite our assumption that we live in more enlightened times.

THE DIRECTOR'S CUT: INTERVIEWS WITH GREGORY DORAN AND PHYLLIDA LLOYD

Gregory Doran, born in 1958, studied at Bristol University and the Bristol Old Vic theater school. He began his career as an actor, before becoming Associate Director at the Nottingham Playhouse. He played some minor roles in the RSC ensemble before directing for the company, first as a freelance, then as Associate and subsequently

Chief Associate Director. His productions, several of which have starred his partner Antony Sher, are characterized by extreme intelligence and lucidity. He has made a particular mark with several of Shakespeare's lesser-known plays and the revival of works by his Elizabethan and Jacobean contemporaries. He talks here about his 2003 RSC production of *The Taming of the Shrew*, with Alexandra Gilbreath as Kate and Jasper Britton as Petruchio.

Phyllida Lloyd, born in 1957, is a prolific freelance director of theater and opera. A graduate of Birmingham University with a degree in English and Drama, she began directing on the London fringe. She was awarded an Arts Council Trainee Director bursary and began an apprenticeship in regional theater at The Swan Theatre Worcester, The Wolsey Theatre Ipswich, Cheltenham Everyman, Bristol Old Vic and Manchester Royal Exchange. Subsequent work has included *The Way of the World, Pericles, What the Butler Saw, The Prime of Miss Jean Brodie,* and *The Duchess of Malfi* at the National Theatre in London, as well as work for the Royal Court Theatre and the Donmar, and *The Taming of the Shrew* for Shakespeare's Globe, 2003, about which she talks here. Her career spans a variety of genres, including extensive experience in opera and the worldwide hit musical production of *Mamma Mia!*

Why take on this play in an age when it is no longer acceptable to call a woman a "shrew" or to demand that she submits to her husband's will?

Doran: To begin with I decided to direct *Shrew* because I had read Fletcher's *The Tamer Tamed* and felt that somehow we had the antidote to the play; that presented in repertoire we could allow *Shrew* to end with the subjugation of Kate (if so it does) and let it be as gruesome and unpalatable as its reputation tended to suggest it was, because the women get their revenge in the sequel (in *The Tamer Tamed* the tables are turned and Petruchio's second wife, Maria, tames her husband in return). This is at any rate how we started out. However, in rehearsal, as so often happens, our opinion changed. We needed no antidote after all. *The Taming of the Shrew* emerged as a very different play from the one we expected. Possibly because we stopped approaching it as a problem play, and allowed it to speak for itself.

Lloyd: I had been asked to direct the play several times previously and had always been paralyzed by the notion of how to do it. It seemed to require so many contortions to make sense of to a modern audience. I stepped in to direct the Globe production when someone became indisposed and the crucial decision to perform it with an all female cast and without the induction had been made. These radical choices became ones that unlocked the play for a contemporary audience. By being able to exaggerate male behavior—male bonding, powerplay, need for supremacy, codes of behavior, etc., we were able to show how isolated and vulnerable women were in society.

What's going on in the induction? How did you handle it? (Or justify not handling it!)

Doran: Often directors don't so much direct *The Taming of the Shrew* as try to solve it. I felt that the induction had been responsible for excusing the play in so many productions. So we decided to cut it instead. That way, we couldn't wink at the audience as if to say, "Of course we think this is misogynistic behavior, but the people in this play-within-a-play do not!" If Shakespeare had really had faith in his framing device he would have concluded it with an epilogue, but he didn't. He inherited the device, and his play does not need it in my opinion.

The actors playing the understudy roles in our production presented a reading of *The Taming of a Shrew*, so we could see what Shakespeare had apparently inherited. (We concluded that this play is not a bad imitation of the *Shrew* but the source play.) Now there's a misogynistic play! At one point the shrew promises to tear the flesh off someone's face and eat it. (As I recall, we decided that the actor playing the Grumio character in that play had brought it to Shakespeare to expand, because it was a great part for him!)

Lloyd: We replaced the induction with a speech from one of the company members—a kind of mock apology that we were an all-female cast. "The first time this house hosted Shakespeare's Shrew, / All parts were played by men—weird, yes, but true!" "We have 'odd piece'," etc. (referring to the play and to rhyme with "codpiece"), which established an atmosphere of levity from the start.

One of the play's sources is an Italian comedy, and there is something of the *commedia dell'arte* types about many of the roles (the patriarchal father, the elderly suitor, the clever servant, and so forth): is there a case for playing some of the supporting parts almost as caricatures?

Doran: This again is an instinct which can impose upon the play a light-hearted approach which excuses the characters as types. Shakespeare may have had something of those types in mind, but he is incapable of such two-dimensionality, and the characters all emerge with much more depth and humanity. If you begin with *commedia* as your starting point you may not bother to search out this greater depth.

Lloyd: Of course one can see how these characters derived from *commedia* but we felt the play was served by giving every character as much depth as possible. What may seem superficial or "light" is underpinned by each character's desperate need to hold their places in the complex social hierarchy.

Did the fact that Shakespeare originally wrote his female parts for boys ever come across in your work on the play?

Doran: Same problem. You wouldn't approach Cleopatra or Lady Macbeth with that in mind. It just excuses Kate, and robs her of her depth and truth as a portrait of a real person, a real woman forced into her own stereotype as a Shrew, and therefore playing it to the hilt.

Lloyd: Yes, but in opposite terms since ours was an all-female cast! Everything was thrown into relief about the society in which the play took place. That men controlled everything was heightened. That women were chattels to be played for, but that a woman who broke the code was extremely hard for that society to manage or control, became even more evident.

What did you discover about Kate's relationship with her sister?

Doran: For me this was the source of Kate's trouble and pain. Though I am not sure I ever told them, I watched my own sisters go through something very similar, when they were children, and I guess it's a familiar scenario. My twin sister was always very pretty, and winning, of a sweet nature and thus the apple of my father's eye. My older sister resented this and would do things to make my father notice her; would demand his attention, sometimes by bad behavior, and when she was punished would resent my sister even more, and accuse my father of favoritism. Both sides dug their heels in and their relationship deteriorated. She came to regard herself as unloved and unlovable, and would regard any boy who expressed his interest in her as suspect. Kate isn't a stereotype, she's an accurate portrait of a woman of low self-esteem, forced to think of herself in the mercantile world of the play as a devalued chattel, until she meets a man with similar problems in his life and they recognize a like spirit.

In some productions, Kate and Petruchio form a bond early on, because they are both subversive, aggressive figures. He's the first interesting man who has come after her. Is that a line you took? It's certainly striking that something seems to click between them for the first time when they share a joke about oral sex . . .

Doran: The key to the first encounter is to watch their language and beware of editorial stage directions. If you take seriously the distinct use of the familiar "thee/thou" or more formal "you" forms, there is a clear route-map for the scene. The other revelation for us, and frankly the key to the production, was a stage direction which had been misplaced by almost every editor in nearly every edition we read. Baptista and the others return to see what is happening in the middle of Petruchio's final speech, but many editors had replaced the stage direction at the end of the speech. The fact is that, as Jasper Britton [who played Petruchio] realized, the couple have come to a kind of plateau, to the start of a negotiation, but suddenly, as Kate's father enters, Petruchio returns to the "you" form:

For by this light, whereby I see <u>thy</u> beauty,
Thy beauty that doth make me like <u>thee</u> well,
<u>Thou</u> must be married to no man but me,
Enter Baptista, Gremio, Tranio [disguised as Lucentio]
For I am he am born to tame you, Kate,
And bring <u>you</u> from a wild Kate to a Kate
Conformable as other household Kates.

Petruchio is suddenly performing for the benefit of his new father-in-law, and himself *conforming* and reverting to the stereotype of wild, violent wife-tamer that Baptista and the others think he is. He is also possibly alerting Kate to the deception. It was a crucial moment in the rehearsal process, and provided an important lesson: DON'T TRUST EDITORS!

Lloyd: We felt that there was real attraction between Kate and Petruchio from the start. They recognized each other's verbal wit and also that neither one quite fitted in to society. Kate is really battling to define herself in this patriarchal world. Petruchio is an immature baby and has such self-confidence that he thinks he can handle anything. The kind of man who has a go at all kinds of extreme sports without any experience. A real alpha male.

The consequence of that reading might be to make the whole process of the taming a kind of game—but in some productions the cruelty, mockery and sense deprivation are in deadly earnest. Where did you stand on this? Tell us about what you and your Petruchio discovered about his character.

Doran: Petruchio is full of bluff. He is as much in a trap as Kate is. He is trapped in a view of him as a wild man. But wild men may behave as they do because of some hurt in their lives, just as angry women or "Shrews" can find themselves forced to play a role in society. One of the keys for us was Petruchio's recent bereavement. His father has died. Is he in mourning? Is he unable to face up to the sudden responsibilities of running the estate he has inherited? We felt it was wrong to view his household as some sort of grotesque place filled with Gormenghast servants. It is a substantial household. Curtis has under his charge at least twelve named servants, who presumably worked for Petruchio's father until very recently. The first thing Petruchio does is to find a rich wife who can help him run this household.

In our production, having met a woman he likes, instead of shopping in Venice as he promised to buy her "rings and things and fine array," he is afflicted with second thoughts, and out of terror goes and gets roaring drunk. He arrives at the church in this state and satirizes the whole pompous edifice of matrimony, reminding the company that he can do what he likes with his wife because, according to their rules, and to their Bible, indeed,

> She is my goods, my chattels, she is my house,
> My household stuff, my field, my barn,
> My horse, my ox, my ass, my anything,
> And here she stands.

We decided that he does not have a conscious plan, and at first neglects Kate because he is embarrassed and does not know what to do next. His initial treatment of her is careless and brutal and self-defensive. As Curtis says to Grumio's story of their journey, "By this reckoning he is more shrew than she."

He is perhaps being ironic when he talks about beginning his reign in a politic manner. He is flying by the seat of his pants, unsure of quite what he has taken on. Then, however, he begins to structure a series of "games" with Kate. It is hardly torture. His intention is not to break her, but to help her transform from the angry spoilt woman ("who never knew how to entreat") she has been to someone who can see beyond the need to dress up to society's expectations of her. Together they reassess what it means to be man and wife in their world. After the sun/moon scene, when the scales fall from Katherine's eyes, they both enjoy playing the game together, "their first merriment" particularly with Vincentio whom they meet on the road.

Lloyd: We felt that Petruchio simply had no idea how to behave toward a woman. There was an inhuman and immature side to him.

6. Phyllida Lloyd production, 2003: "We fully explored Petruchio's misogyny and it was shocking to witness his cruelty toward and neglect of Kate."

We gave him a huge shaggy dog, played by an actress, and it was obvious that he found it easier to relate to his dog and show it affection than his wife. In fact, Kate became so hungry she ate the dog food from the bowl. We fully explored Petruchio's misogyny and it was shocking to witness his cruelty toward and neglect of Kate.

How does Kate relate to the other women at the end of the play?

Doran: With something approaching pity, and possibly disgust.

Kate and Petruchio have, we believed, found in each other fellow spirits, they have come to understand the negotiations required in a healthy relationship and they understand the mercenary transaction of marriage in their world, which Shakespeare is at pains to make clear (witness the satirical marriage market scene of Baptista's trading for his daughter, and Tranio and Gremio's competition for Bianca's hand).

Hortensio has certainly married the widow, not for love (he was wooing Bianca earlier, remember) but for her wealth. And she is already nagging him.

As for Bianca, she is surely not satisfied with the airheaded Lucen-

7. Greg Doran production, 2003: Alexandra Gilbreath as Kate, Jasper Britton as Petruchio: "Kate and Petruchio have, we believed, found in each other fellow spirits."

tio. We decided that Tranio has fallen for Bianca himself, while wooing her for his master, and possibly she for him. But their relationship across the class divide (apart from anything else) is doomed. Petruchio sees this, saying: "Here, Signior Tranio, / This bird you aimed at, though you hit her not." Tranio tries to excuse himself, saying: "O sir, Lucentio slipped me like his greyhound, / Which runs himself and catches for his master." However Petruchio (and we) see through his simile.

Kate has a relationship which recognizes her love and respect for her husband, while her sister and the widow have empty relationships with their husbands, which can only end in bitterness.

And the famous submission speech: it's been played straight, played ironic, played to death, played anew . . . how did you approach it?

Doran: As the conclusion to the complex process of their "wooing dance." Kate recognizes the therapeutic process she has undergone. She had been agitated, or troubled as a person; "moved" like the woman she describes, "like a fountain troubled, / Muddy, ill-seeming, thick, bereft of beauty." They have come to recognize in each other spirits who have been compromised by society and forced to play roles. Now they have discovered genuine trust and respect for each other. They won't play by society's rules, but they will love and respect each other, so much so that Kate is prepared to subjugate herself to her husband's will if he should so choose, which of course he does not. We did, however, have a rather nice tense moment when, as she offers to present her hand to place it under her husband's foot, Jasper Britton's Petruchio smiled and said, "Come on . . . ," as if expecting her to fulfill her offer. Only when she moved forward to comply did he complete the line, " . . . and kiss me Kate." And they are clearly going to complement each other sexually as a couple. We guessed they would have a great sex life, unlike their friends' arid partnerships.

Lloyd: Our key was not Kate but her onstage audience. By having women playing men we could satirize the men's need for supremacy. We let Kate play the speech completely straight. You could feel the tension in the audience—dismay almost—"Surely she has not lost her fighting spirit? What is happening ?" etc. But the egos of all the men on stage were being bolstered by her obedience. Petruchio was like a big mafia son embracing his father-in-law and both wept sentimental tears that their little lady had finally been brought to heel. The audience understood and went wild with delight and recognition. Then suddenly Kate climbed up on the table. You realized she had been "performing" and now did so more and more extravagantly, displaying her underwear, etc. As Petruchio tried to stop her, the more wild she became. The male cronies, having been made a laughing stock, began to get up and leave the table, and it ended with the couple having an explosive fight—the kind one imagined they were going to continue to have throughout their marriage.

PLAYING KATE: AN INTERVIEW WITH MICHELLE GOMEZ

Michelle Gomez (born 1971 in Glasgow) is a Scottish actor best known for her comedy roles in the television shows *Green Wing* and

The Book Group. Her performance as Kate in the RSC 2008 *Taming of the Shrew*, directed by Conall Morrison, about which she talks here, was her first role for the company.

It must be troubling to be labeled a "shrew": is Kate a part the modern woman actor should hesitate over accepting?

No. I think Kate is a hugely misunderstood character, and to me that was a huge attraction in accepting the role, not a disincentive. We know from the text she is willful and independent, but the references to her "shrew-like" behavior are all reported speech. The only time we witness anything remotely shrewish is when she is alone with Bianca trying desperately to understand why she has been effectively disowned by her father. But even at the height of her rage and frustration she speaks with impressive eloquence. I found her to be a heartbreaking character.

Did the fact that Shakespeare originally wrote the part for a boy ever come across in your work on it?

We never explored that, but she undeniably has a maleness in the way she expresses herself. She doesn't sit quietly in the corner waiting to be spoken to.

What did you discover about Kate's relationship with her sister?

I found it to be the most tragic relationship in the play. Kate receives absolutely no support from her sister. I was astounded at the ease with which Bianca sat back and watched Kate be humiliated. I suppose siblings can often be the harshest critics!

In some productions, Kate and Petruchio form a bond early on, because they are both subversive, aggressive figures. He's the first interesting man who has come after her. Is that a line you took? It's certainly striking that something seems to click between them for the first time when they share a joke about oral sex . . .

We used that as a way to get her out of the prison she was in at home. Here at last was someone that spoke her language. However, she

8. Michelle Gomez as Kate, 2008: Kate and Petruchio form a bond early on because they are both subversive and aggressive figures. But in this production the relationship darkened profoundly in the second half of the play.

unwittingly, and almost in spite of herself, flees from one form of incarceration to another. In our production, what we found most interesting to explore was the *promise* of love—a promise that was chased and hoped for, but never found. I think that hope is why she never ran away. In some sad respects, I think Kate is a slightly delusional character.

The consequence of that reading might be to make the whole process of the taming a kind of game—but in your production the cruelty, mockery, and sense deprivation were in deadly earnest, weren't they?

We hoped that by taking the game out of it, it would make the final humiliation at the end more effective and more truthful. We were determined that she genuinely try to understand why this man was behaving so monstrously—if only to make sense of her own choice to be with him.

How does Kate relate to the other women at the end of the play?

In our production she had no energy left to relate to anyone. She is a battered wife—terrified to say or do anything for fear of reprisal.

And the famous submission speech: it's been played straight, played ironic, played to death, played anew . . . how did you approach it?

Like her life depended on it. One false move in front of the court and she would receive the most horrific beating later at home. Although I felt there was a subtle defiance in this approach, because what kind of victory is this for Petruchio? She is showing the world that the very qualities that attracted Petruchio in the first place have disappeared. He can only cope with her spirit by breaking it, and what sort of a misogynist bully does that make him?

SHAKESPEARE'S CAREER IN THE THEATER

BEGINNINGS

William Shakespeare was an extraordinarily intelligent man who was born and died in an ordinary market town in the English Midlands. He lived an uneventful life in an eventful age. Born in April 1564, he was the eldest son of John Shakespeare, a glove maker who was prominent on the town council until he fell into financial difficulties. Young William was educated at the local grammar in Stratford-upon-Avon, Warwickshire, where he gained a thorough grounding in the Latin language, the art of rhetoric, and classical poetry. He married Ann Hathaway and had three children (Susanna, then the twins Hamnet and Judith) before his twenty-first birthday: an exceptionally young age for the period. We do not know how he supported his family in the mid-1580s.

Like many clever country boys, he moved to the city in order to make his way in the world. Like many creative people, he found a career in the entertainment business. Public playhouses and professional full-time acting companies reliant on the market for their income were born in Shakespeare's childhood. When he arrived in London as a man, sometime in the late 1580s, a new phenomenon was in the making: the actor who is so successful that he becomes a "star." The word did not exist in its modern sense, but the pattern is recognizable: audiences went to the theater not so much to see a particular show as to witness the comedian Richard Tarlton or the dramatic actor Edward Alleyn.

Shakespeare was an actor before he was a writer. It appears not to have been long before he realized that he was never going to grow into a great comedian like Tarlton or a great tragedian like Alleyn. Instead, he found a role within his company as the man who patched up old plays, breathing new life, new dramatic twists, into tired repertory pieces. He paid close attention to the work of the university-educated dramatists who were writing history plays and tragedies for the public stage in a style more ambitious, sweeping, and poetically grand than anything which had been seen before. But he may also have noted that what his friend and rival Ben Jonson would call "Marlowe's mighty line" sometimes faltered in the mode of comedy. Going to university, as Christopher Marlowe did, was all well and good for honing the arts of rhetorical elaboration and classical allusion, but it could lead to a loss of the common touch. To stay close to a large segment of the potential audience for public theater, it was necessary to write for clowns as well as kings and to intersperse the flights of poetry with the humor of the tavern, the privy, and the brothel: Shakespeare was the first to establish himself early in his career as an equal master of tragedy, comedy, and history. He realized that theater could be the medium to make the national past available to a wider audience than the elite who could afford to read large history books: his signature early works include not only the classical tragedy *Titus Andronicus* but also the sequence of English historical plays on the Wars of the Roses.

He also invented a new role for himself, that of in-house company dramatist. Where his peers and predecessors had to sell their plays to the theater managers on a poorly paid piecework basis, Shakespeare took a percentage of the box-office income. The Lord Chamberlain's Men constituted themselves in 1594 as a joint stock company, with the profits being distributed among the core actors who had invested as sharers. Shakespeare acted himself—he appears in the cast lists of some of Ben Jonson's plays as well as the list of actors' names at the beginning of his own collected works—but his principal duty was to write two or three plays a year for the company. By holding shares, he was effectively earning himself a royalty on his work, something no author had ever done before in England. When the Lord Chamberlain's Men collected their fee for performance at court in the Christmas season of 1594, three of them went along to the Treasurer of the Chamber: not just Richard Burbage the tragedian and Will Kempe the clown, but also Shakespeare the scriptwriter. That was something new.

The next four years were the golden period in Shakespeare's

career, though overshadowed by the death of his only son, Hamnet, age eleven, in 1596. In his early thirties and in full command of both his poetic and his theatrical medium, he perfected his art of comedy, while also developing his tragic and historical writing in new ways. In 1598, Francis Meres, a Cambridge University graduate with his finger on the pulse of the London literary world, praised Shakespeare for his excellence across the genres:

> As Plautus and Seneca are accounted the best for comedy and tragedy among the Latins, so Shakespeare among the English is the most excellent in both kinds for the stage; for comedy, witness his *Gentlemen of Verona*, his *Errors*, his *Love Labours Lost*, his *Love Labours Won*, his *Midsummer Night Dream* and his *Merchant of Venice*: for tragedy his *Richard the 2*, *Richard the 3*, *Henry the 4*, *King John*, *Titus Andronicus* and his *Romeo and Juliet*.

For Meres, as for the many writers who praised the "honey-flowing vein" of *Venus and Adonis* and *Lucrece*, narrative poems written when the theaters were closed due to plague in 1593–94, Shakespeare was marked above all by his linguistic skill, by the gift of turning elegant poetic phrases.

PLAYHOUSES

Elizabethan playhouses were "thrust" or "one-room" theaters. To understand Shakespeare's original theatrical life, we have to forget about the indoor theater of later times, with its proscenium arch and curtain that would be opened at the beginning and closed at the end of each act. In the proscenium arch theater, stage and auditorium are effectively two separate rooms: the audience looks from one world into another as if through the imaginary "fourth wall" framed by the proscenium. The picture-frame stage, together with the elaborate scenic effects and backdrops beyond it, created the illusion of a self-contained world—especially once nineteenth-century developments in the control of artificial lighting meant that the auditorium could be darkened and the spectators made to focus on the lighted stage. Shakespeare, by contrast, wrote for a bare platform stage with a standing audience gathered around it in a courtyard in full daylight. The audience were always conscious of themselves and their fellow spectators, and they shared the same "room" as the actors. A sense of immediate presence and the creation of rapport with the audience were all-important. The actor could not afford to imagine he was in a closed world, with silent witnesses dutifully observing him from the darkness.

Shakespeare's theatrical career began at the Rose Theatre in Southwark. The stage was wide and shallow, trapezoid in shape, like a lozenge. This design had a great deal of potential for the theatrical equivalent of cinematic split-screen effects, whereby one group of characters would enter at the door at one end of the tiring-house wall at the back of the stage and another group through the door at the other end, thus creating two rival tableaux. Many of the battle-heavy and faction-filled plays that premiered at the Rose have scenes of just this sort.

At the rear of the Rose stage, there were three capacious exits, each over ten feet wide. Unfortunately, the very limited excavation of a fragmentary portion of the original Globe site, in 1989, revealed nothing about the stage. The first Globe was built in 1599 with similar proportions to those of another theater, the Fortune, albeit that the former was polygonal and looked circular, whereas the latter was rectangular. The building contract for the Fortune survives and allows us to infer that the stage of the Globe was probably substantially wider than it was deep (perhaps forty-three feet wide and twenty-seven feet deep). It may well have been tapered at the front, like that of the Rose.

The capacity of the Globe was said to have been enormous, perhaps in excess of three thousand. It has been conjectured that about eight hundred people may have stood in the yard, with two thousand or more in the three layers of covered galleries. The other "public" playhouses were also of large capacity, whereas the indoor Blackfriars theater that Shakespeare's company began using in 1608—the former refectory of a monastery—had overall internal dimensions of a mere forty-six by sixty feet. It would have made for a much more intimate theatrical experience and had a much smaller capacity, probably of about six hundred people. Since they paid at least six-pence a head, the Blackfriars attracted a more select or "private" audience. The atmosphere would have been closer to that of an indoor performance before the court in the Whitehall Palace or at Richmond. That Shakespeare always wrote for indoor production at court as well as outdoor performance in the public theater should make us cautious about inferring, as some scholars have, that the opportunity provided by the intimacy of the Blackfriars led to a sig-nificant change toward a "chamber" style in his last plays—which, besides, were performed at both the Globe and the Blackfriars. After the occupation of the Blackfriars a five-act structure seems to have become more important to Shakespeare. That was because of artifi-cial lighting: there were musical interludes between the acts, while the candles were trimmed and replaced. Again, though, something similar must have been necessary for indoor court performances throughout his career.

Front of house there were the "gatherers" who collected the money from audience members: a penny to stand in the open-air yard, another penny for a place in the covered galleries, sixpence for the prominent "lord's rooms" to the side of the stage. In the indoor "private" theaters, gallants from the audience who fancied making themselves part of the spectacle sat on stools on the edge of the stage itself. Scholars debate as to how widespread this practice was in the public theaters such as the Globe. Once the audience were in place and the money counted, the gatherers were available to be extras on stage. That is one reason why battles and crowd scenes often come later rather than early in Shakespeare's plays. There was no formal prohibition upon performance by women, and there certainly were women among the gatherers, so it is not beyond the bounds of possi-bility that female crowd members were played by females.

The play began at two o'clock in the afternoon and the theater had to be cleared by five. After the main show, there would be a jig—which consisted not only of dancing, but also of knockabout comedy (it is the origin of the farcical "afterpiece" in the eighteenth-century theater). So the time available for a Shakespeare play was about two and a half hours, somewhere between the "two hours' traffic" men-tioned in the prologue to *Romeo and Juliet* and the "three hours' spectacle" referred to in the preface to the 1647 Folio of Beaumont and Fletcher's plays. The prologue to a play by Thomas Middleton refers to a thousand lines as "one hour's words," so the likelihood is that about two and a half thousand, or a maximum of three thousand lines made up the performed text. This is indeed the length of most of Shakespeare's comedies, whereas many of his tragedies and histories are much longer, raising the possibility that he wrote full scripts, possibly with eventual publication in mind, in the full knowledge that the stage version would be heavily cut. The short Quarto texts published in his lifetime—they used to be called "Bad" Quartos—provide fascinating evidence as to the kind of cutting that probably took place. So, for instance, the First Quarto of *Hamlet* neatly merges two occasions when Hamlet is overheard, the "Fishmonger" and the "nunnery" scenes.

The social composition of the audience was mixed. The poet Sir John Davies wrote of "A thousand townsmen, gentlemen and whores, / Porters and servingmen" who would "together throng" at the public playhouses. Though moralists associated female playgoing with adultery and the sex trade, many perfectly respectable citizens' wives were regular attendees. Some, no doubt, resembled the modern groupie: a story attested in two different sources has one citizen's wife making a post-show assignation with Richard Burbage and ending up in bed with Shakespeare—supposedly eliciting from the latter the quip that William the Conqueror was before Richard III. Defenders of theater liked to say that by witnessing the comeuppance of villains on the stage, audience members would repent of their own wrongdoings, but the reality is that most people went to the theater then, as they do now, for entertainment more than moral edification. Besides, it would be foolish to suppose that audiences behaved in a homogeneous way: a pamphlet of the 1630s tells of how two men went to see *Pericles* and one of them laughed while the other wept. Bishop John Hall complained that people went to church for the same reasons that they went to the theater: "for company, for custom, for recreation . . . to feed his eyes or his ears . . . or perhaps for sleep."

Men-about-town and clever young lawyers went to be seen as much as to see. In the modern popular imagination, shaped not least by *Shakespeare in Love* and the opening sequence of Laurence Olivier's *Henry V* film, the penny-paying groundlings stand in the yard hurling abuse or encouragement and hazelnuts or orange peel at the actors, while the sophisticates in the covered galleries appreciate Shakespeare's soaring poetry. The reality was probably the other way round. A "groundling" was a kind of fish, so the nickname suggests the penny audience standing below the level of the stage and gazing in silent open-mouthed wonder at the spectacle unfolding above them. The more difficult audience members, who kept up a running commentary of clever remarks on the performance and who occasionally got into quarrels with players, were the gallants. Like Hollywood movies in modern times, Elizabethan and Jacobean plays exercised a powerful influence on the fashion and behavior of the young. John Marston mocks the lawyers who would open their lips, perhaps to court a girl, and out would "flow / Naught but pure Juliet and Romeo."

THE ENSEMBLE AT WORK

In the absence of typewriters and photocopying machines, reading aloud would have been the means by which the company got to know a new play. The tradition of the playwright reading his complete script to the assembled company endured for generations. A copy would then have been taken to the Master of the Revels for licensing. The theater book-holder or prompter would then have copied the parts for distribution to the actors. A partbook consisted of the character's lines, with each speech preceded by the last three or four words of the speech before, the so-called "cue." These would have been taken away and studied or "conned." During this period of learning the parts, an actor might have had some one-to-one instruction, perhaps from the dramatist, perhaps from a senior actor who had played the same part before, and, in the case of an apprentice, from his master. A high percentage of Desdemona's lines occur in dialogue with Othello, of Lady Macbeth's with Macbeth, Cleopatra's with Antony and Volumnia's with Coriolanus. The roles would almost certainly have been taken by the apprentice of the lead actor, usually Burbage, who delivers the majority of the cues. Given that

9. Hypothetical reconstruction of the interior of an Elizabethan playhouse during a performance.

apprentices lodged with their masters, there would have been ample opportunity for personal instruction, which may be what made it possible for young men to play such demanding parts.

After the parts were learned, there may have been no more than a single rehearsal before the first performance. With six different plays to be put on every week, there was no time for more. Actors, then, would go into a show with a very limited sense of the whole. The notion of a collective rehearsal process that is itself a process of discovery for the actors is wholly modern and would have been incomprehensible to Shakespeare and his original ensemble. Given the number of parts an actor had to hold in his memory, the forgetting of lines was probably more frequent than in the modern theater. The book holder was on hand to prompt.

Backstage personnel included the property man, the tire man who oversaw the costumes, call boys, attendants, and the musicians, who might play at various times from the main stage, the rooms above and within the tiring house. Scriptwriters sometimes made a nuisance of themselves backstage. There was often tension between the acting companies and the freelance playwrights from whom they purchased scripts: it was a smart move on the part of Shakespeare and the Lord Chamberlain's Men to bring the writing process in-house.

Scenery was limited, though sometimes set pieces were brought on (a bank of flowers, a bed, the mouth of hell). The trapdoor from below, the gallery stage above, and the curtained discovery space at the back allowed for an array of special effects: the rising of ghosts and apparitions, the descent of gods, dialogue between a character at a window and another at ground level, the revelation of a statue, or a pair of lovers playing at chess. Ingenious use could be made of props, as with the ass's head in *A Midsummer Night's Dream*. In a theater that does not clutter the stage with the material paraphernalia of everyday life, those objects that are deployed may take on powerful symbolic weight, as when Shylock bears his weighing scales in one hand and knife in the other, thus becoming a parody of the figure of Justice who traditionally bears a sword and a balance. Among the more significant items in the property cupboard of Shakespeare's company, there would have been a throne (the "chair of state"), joint stools, books, bottles, coins, purses, letters (which are brought on stage, read or referred to on about eighty occasions in the complete works), maps, gloves, a set of stocks (in which Kent is put in *King Lear*), rings, rapiers, daggers, broadswords, staves, pistols, masks and vizards, heads and skulls, torches and tapers and lanterns which served to signal night scenes on the daylit stage, a buck's head, an ass's head, animal costumes. Live animals also put in appearances, most notably the dog Crab in *The Two Gentlemen of Verona* and possibly a young polar bear in *The Winter's Tale*.

The costumes were the most important visual dimension of the play. Playwrights were paid between £2 and £6 per script, whereas Alleyn was not averse to paying £20 for "a black velvet cloak with sleeves embroidered all with silver and gold." No matter the period of the play, actors always wore contemporary costume. The excitement for the audience came not from any impression of historical accuracy, but from the richness of the attire and perhaps the transgressive thrill of the knowledge that here were commoners like themselves strutting in the costumes of courtiers in effective defiance of the strict sumptuary laws whereby in real life people had to wear the clothes that befitted their social station.

To an even greater degree than props, costumes could carry symbolic importance. Racial characteristics could be suggested: a breastplate and helmet for a Roman soldier, a turban for a Turk, long robes for exotic characters such as Moors, a gabardine for a Jew. The figure of Time, as in *The Winter's Tale*, would be equipped with hourglass, scythe and wings; Rumour, who speaks the prologue of *2 Henry IV*, wore a costume adorned with a thousand tongues. The wardrobe in the tiring house of the Globe would have contained much of the same stock as that of rival manager Philip Henslowe at the Rose: green gowns for outlaws and foresters, black for melancholy men such as Jaques and people in mourning such as the Countess in *All's Well That Ends Well* (at the beginning of *Hamlet*, the prince is still in mourning black when everyone else is in festive garb for the wedding of the new king), a gown and hood for a friar (or a feigned friar like the duke in *Measure for Measure*), blue coats and tawny to distinguish the followers of rival factions, a leather apron and ruler for a carpenter (as in the opening scene of *Julius Caesar*—and in *A Midsummer Night's Dream*, where this is the only sign that Peter Quince is a carpenter), a cockle hat with staff and a pair of sandals for a pilgrim or palmer (the disguise assumed by Helen in *All's Well*), bodices and kirtles with farthingales beneath for the boys who are to be dressed as girls. A gender switch such as that of Rosalind or Jessica seems to have taken between fifty and eighty lines of dialogue—Viola does not resume her "maiden weeds," but remains in her boy's costume to the end of *Twelfth Night* because a change would have slowed down the action at just the moment it was speeding to a climax. Henslowe's inventory also included "a robe for to go invisible": Oberon, Puck, and Ariel must have had something similar.

As the costumes appealed to the eyes, so there was music for the ears. Comedies included many songs. Desdemona's willow song, perhaps a late addition to the text, is a rare and thus exceptionally poignant example from tragedy. Trumpets and tuckets sounded for ceremonial entrances, drums denoted an army on the march. Background music could create atmosphere, as at the beginning of *Twelfth Night*, during the lovers' dialogue near the end of *The Mer-*

chant of Venice, when the statue seemingly comes to life in *The Winter's Tale*, and for the revival of Pericles and of Lear (in the Quarto text, but not the Folio). The haunting sound of the hautboy suggested a realm beyond the human, as when the god Hercules is imagined deserting Mark Antony. Dances symbolized the harmony of the end of a comedy—though in Shakespeare's world of mingled joy and sorrow, someone is usually left out of the circle.

The most important resource was, of course, the actors themselves. They needed many skills: in the words of one contemporary commentator, "dancing, activity, music, song, elocution, ability of body, memory, skill of weapon, pregnancy of wit." Their bodies were as significant as their voices. Hamlet tells the player to "suit the action to the word, the word to the action": moments of strong emotion, known as "passions," relied on a repertoire of dramatic gestures as well as a modulation of the voice. When Titus Andronicus has had his hand chopped off, he asks "How can I grace my talk, / Wanting a hand to give it action?" A pen portrait of "The Character of an Excellent Actor" by the dramatist John Webster is almost certainly based on his impression of Shakespeare's leading man, Richard Burbage: "By a full and significant action of body, he charms our attention: sit in a full theater, and you will think you see so many lines drawn from the circumference of so many ears, whiles the actor is the centre . . ."

Though Burbage was admired above all others, praise was also heaped upon the apprentice players whose alto voices fitted them for the parts of women. A spectator at Oxford in 1610 records how the audience were reduced to tears by the pathos of Desdemona's death. The puritans who fumed about the biblical prohibition upon cross-dressing and the encouragement to sodomy constituted by the sight of an adult male kissing a teenage boy on stage were a small minority. Little is known, however, about the characteristics of the leading apprentices in Shakespeare's company. It may perhaps be inferred that one was a lot taller than the other, since Shakespeare often wrote for a pair of female friends, one tall and fair, the other short and dark (Helena and Hermia, Rosalind and Celia, Beatrice and Hero).

We know little about Shakespeare's own acting roles—an early allusion indicates that he often took royal parts, and a venerable tradition gives him old Adam in *As You Like It* and the ghost of old King Hamlet. Save for Burbage's lead roles and the generic part of the clown, all such castings are mere speculation. We do not even know for sure whether the original Falstaff was Will Kempe or another actor who specialized in comic roles, Thomas Pope.

Kempe left the company in early 1599. Tradition has it that he fell out with Shakespeare over the matter of excessive improvisation. He was replaced by Robert Armin, who was less of a clown and more of a cerebral wit: this explains the difference between such parts as Lancelet Gobbo and Dogberry, which were written for Kempe, and the more verbally sophisticated Feste and Lear's Fool, which were written for Armin.

One thing that is clear from surviving "plot," or story boards of plays from the period, is that a degree of doubling was necessary. *2 Henry VI* has over sixty speaking parts, but more than half of the characters only appear in a single scene and most scenes have only six to eight speakers. At a stretch, the play could be performed by thirteen actors. When Thomas Platter saw *Julius Caesar* at the Globe in 1599, he noted that there were about fifteen. Why doesn't Paris go to the Capulet ball in *Romeo and Juliet*? Perhaps because he was doubled with Mercutio, who does. In *The Winter's Tale*, Mamillius might have come back as Perdita and Antigonus been doubled by Camillo, making the partnership with Paulina at the end a very neat touch. Titania and Oberon are often played by the same pair as Hippolyta and Theseus, suggesting a symbolic matching of the rulers of the worlds of night and day, but it is questionable whether there would have been time for the necessary costume changes. As so often, one is left in a realm of tantalizing speculation.

THE KING'S MAN

On Queen Elizabeth's death in 1603, the new king, James I, who had held the Scottish throne as James VI since he had been an infant, immediately took the Lord Chamberlain's Men under his direct patronage. Henceforth they would be the King's Men, and for the rest of Shakespeare's career they were favored with far more court performances than any of their rivals. There even seem to have been rumors early in the reign that Shakespeare and Burbage were being considered for knighthoods, an unprecedented honor for mere actors—and one that in the event was not accorded to a member of the profession for nearly three hundred years, when the title was bestowed upon Henry Irving, the leading Shakespearean actor of Queen Victoria's reign.

Shakespeare's productivity rate slowed in the Jacobean years, not because of age or some personal trauma, but because there were frequent outbreaks of plague, causing the theaters to be closed for long periods. The King's Men were forced to spend many months on the road. Between November 1603 and 1608, they were to be found at various towns in the south and Midlands, though Shakespeare probably did not tour with them by this time. He had bought a large house back home in Stratford and was accumulating other property. He may indeed have stopped acting soon after the new king took the throne. With the London theaters closed so much of the time and a large repertoire on the stocks, Shakespeare seems to have focused his energies on writing a few long and complex tragedies that could have been played on demand at court: *Othello, King Lear, Antony and Cleopatra, Coriolanus,* and *Cymbeline* are among his longest and poetically grandest plays. *Macbeth* only survives in a shorter text, which shows signs of adaptation after Shakespeare's death. The bitterly satirical *Timon of Athens,* apparently a collaboration with Thomas Middleton that may have failed on the stage, also belongs to this period. In comedy, too, he wrote longer and morally darker works than in the Elizabethan period, pushing at the very bounds of the form in *Measure for Measure* and *All's Well That Ends Well.*

From 1608 onward, when the King's Men began occupying the indoor Blackfriars playhouse (as a winter house, meaning that they only used the outdoor Globe in summer?), Shakespeare turned to a more romantic style. His company had a great success with a revived and altered version of an old pastoral play called *Mucedorus.* It even featured a bear. The younger dramatist John Fletcher, meanwhile, sometimes working in collaboration with Francis Beaumont, was pioneering a new style of tragicomedy, a mix of romance and royalism laced with intrigue and pastoral excursions. Shakespeare experimented with this idiom in *Cymbeline* and it was presumably with his blessing that Fletcher eventually took over as the King's Men's company dramatist. The two writers apparently collaborated on three plays in the years 1612–14: a lost romance called *Cardenio* (based on the love madness of a character in Cervantes's *Don Quixote*), *Henry VIII* (originally staged with the title "All Is True"), and *The Two Noble Kinsmen*, a dramatization of Chaucer's "Knight's Tale." These were written after Shakespeare's two final solo-authored plays, *The Winter's Tale*, a self-consciously old-fashioned work dramatizing the pastoral romance of his old enemy Robert Greene, and *The Tempest*, which at one and the same time drew together multiple theatrical traditions, diverse reading and contemporary interest in the fate of a ship that had been wrecked on the way to the New World.

The collaborations with Fletcher suggest that Shakespeare's career ended with a slow fade rather than the sudden retirement supposed by the nineteenth-century Romantic critics who read Prospero's epilogue to *The Tempest* as Shakespeare's personal farewell to his art. In the last few years of his life Shakespeare certainly spent more of his time in Stratford-upon-Avon, where he became further involved in property dealing and litigation. But his London life also continued. In 1613 he made his first major London property purchase: a freehold house in the Blackfriars district, close to his company's indoor theater. *The Two Noble Kinsmen* may have been written as late as 1614, and Shakespeare was in London on business a little over a year before he died of an unknown cause at home in Stratford-upon-Avon in 1616, probably on his fifty-second birthday.

About half the sum of his works were published in his lifetime, in texts of variable quality. A few years after his death, his fellow actors began putting together an authorized edition of his complete *Comedies, Histories and Tragedies*. It appeared in 1623, in large "Folio" format. This collection of thirty-six plays gave Shakespeare his immortality. In the words of his fellow dramatist Ben Jonson, who contributed two poems of praise at the start of the Folio, the body of his work made him "a monument without a tomb":

> And art alive still while thy book doth live
> And we have wits to read and praise to give . . .
> He was not of an age, but for all time!

SHAKESPEARE'S WORKS: A CHRONOLOGY

1589–91	*? Arden of Faversham* (possible part authorship)
1589–92	*The Taming of the Shrew*
1589–92	*? Edward the Third* (possible part authorship)
1591	*The Second Part of Henry the Sixth*, originally called *The First Part of the Contention Betwixt the Two Famous Houses of York and Lancaster* (element of coauthorship possible)
1591	*The Third Part of Henry the Sixth*, originally called *The True Tragedy of Richard Duke of York* (element of co-authorship probable)
1591–92	*The Two Gentlemen of Verona*
1591–92; perhaps revised 1594	*The Lamentable Tragedy of Titus Andronicus* (probably cowritten with, or revising an earlier version by, George Peele)
1592	*The First Part of Henry the Sixth*, probably with Thomas Nashe and others
1592/94	*King Richard the Third*
1593	*Venus and Adonis* (poem)
1593–94	*The Rape of Lucrece* (poem)
1593–1608	*Sonnets* (154 poems, published 1609 with *A Lover's Complaint*, a poem of disputed authorship)
1592–94/ 1600–03	*Sir Thomas More* (a single scene for a play originally by Anthony Munday, with other revisions by Henry Chettle, Thomas Dekker, and Thomas Heywood)
1594	*The Comedy of Errors*
1595	*Love's Labour's Lost*

1595–97	*Love's Labour's Won* (a lost play, unless the original title for another comedy)
1595–96	*A Midsummer Night's Dream*
1595–96	*The Tragedy of Romeo and Juliet*
1595–96	*King Richard the Second*
1595–97	*The Life and Death of King John* (possibly earlier)
1596–97	*The Merchant of Venice*
1596–97	*The First Part of Henry the Fourth*
1597–98	*The Second Part of Henry the Fourth*
1598	*Much Ado About Nothing*
1598–99	*The Passionate Pilgrim* (20 poems, some not by Shakespeare)
1599	*The Life of Henry the Fifth*
1599	"To the Queen" (epilogue for a court performance)
1599	*As You Like It*
1599	*The Tragedy of Julius Caesar*
1600–01	*The Tragedy of Hamlet, Prince of Denmark* (perhaps revising an earlier version)
1600–01	*The Merry Wives of Windsor* (perhaps revising version of 1597–99)
1601	"Let the Bird of Loudest Lay" (poem, known since 1807 as "The Phoenix and Turtle" [turtledove])
1601	*Twelfth Night, or What You Will*
1601–02	*The Tragedy of Troilus and Cressida*
1604	*The Tragedy of Othello, the Moor of Venice*
1604	*Measure for Measure*
1605	*All's Well That Ends Well*
1605	*The Life of Timon of Athens*, with Thomas Middleton
1605–06	*The Tragedy of King Lear*
1605–08	? contribution to *The Four Plays in One* (lost, except for *A Yorkshire Tragedy*, mostly by Thomas Middleton)

1606	*The Tragedy of Macbeth* (surviving text has additional scenes by Thomas Middleton)
1606–07	*The Tragedy of Antony and Cleopatra*
1608	*The Tragedy of Coriolanus*
1608	*Pericles, Prince of Tyre,* with George Wilkins
1610	*The Tragedy of Cymbeline*
1611	*The Winter's Tale*
1611	*The Tempest*
1612–13	*Cardenio,* with John Fletcher (survives only in later adaptation called *Double Falsehood* by Lewis Theobald)
1613	*Henry VIII (All Is True),* with John Fletcher
1613–14	*The Two Noble Kinsmen,* with John Fletcher

FURTHER READING
AND VIEWING

CRITICAL APPROACHES

Aspinall, Dana E., *The Taming of the Shrew: Critical Essays* (2002). Excellent critical history in Part I, useful selection of important twentieth-century critical essays in Part II and performance criticism in Part III.

Bean, John C., "Comic Structure and the Humanizing of Kate in *The Taming of the Shrew*," in *The Woman's Part: Feminist Criticism of Shakespeare*, ed. Carolyn Ruth Swift Lenz, Gayle Greene, and Carol Thomas Neely (1983), pp. 65–78.

Boose, Lynda, "Scolding Brides and Bridling Scolds: Taming the Woman's Unruly Member," *Shakespeare Quarterly* 42 (1991), pp. 179–213.

Dolan, Frances E., *The Taming of the Shrew: Texts and Contexts* (1996). Useful discussion of the play's background and performance.

Fineman, Joel, "The Turn of the Shrew," in *Shakespeare and the Question of Theory*, ed. Patricia Parker and Geoffrey Hartman (1985), pp. 138–60. Complex psychoanalytic reading.

Holderness, Graham, and Brian Loughrey, eds., *A Pleasant Conceited Historie Called The Taming of a Shrew*, Shakespeare Originals (1992). Offers text of the "other" Shrew play for interest and comparison.

Kahn, Coppélia, *Man's Estate: Masculine Identity in Shakespeare* (1981). Influential feminist reading.

Kidnie, Margaret Jane, *The Taming of the Shrew*, Shakespeare Handbooks (2006). Useful guide with chapters on text and early performances, the play's sources and cultural context, as well as discussion of key productions and a detailed textual commentary.

Leggatt, Alexander, *Shakespeare's Comedy of Love* (1974). Sympathetic, humane.

Marcus, Leah, "The Shakespearean Editor as Shrew-Tamer," *English Literary Renaissance* 22 (1992), pp. 177–200. Neat combination of interpretation and textual theory.

O'Connor, John, *Shakespearean Afterlives: Ten Characters with a Life of Their Own* (2003). Historical overviews of character plus later developments: chapter 8 deals with "Kate," pp. 257–300.

THE PLAY IN PERFORMANCE

Brooke, Michael, "*The Taming of the Shrew* on Screen," BFI Screen Online, www.screenonline.org.uk/tv/id/564739/index.html. Excellent short overview of film versions.

Forster, Antonia, ed., *The Taming of the Shrew: Shakespeare in Performance* (2008). Useful introductory guide with accompanying CD.

Haring-Smith, Tori, *From Farce to Metadrama: A Stage History of the Taming of the Shrew 1594–1983* (1985). Detailed historical account tracing the course of the play in performance.

Holderness, Graham, *The Taming of the Shrew*, Shakespeare in Performance (1989). Useful introduction followed by separate chapters on four important twentieth-century productions.

Rutter, Carol, *Clamorous Voices: Shakespeare's Women Today* (1988). In chapter 1, Paola Dionisotti, Sinead Cusack and Fiona Shaw discuss their experiences of playing Kate.

Schafer, Elizabeth, *Ms-Directing Shakespeare: Women Direct Shakespeare* (1998). Introduces important contemporary women directors in Part 1; Part 2 discusses their approach to specific plays, *The Taming of the Shrew* at pp. 57–72.

Schafer, Elizabeth, ed., *The Taming of the Shrew*, Shakespeare in Production (2002). Detailed historical overview of play with annotated text which includes performance choices, cuts, and stage directions of significant historical productions.

Smallwood, Robert, ed., *Players of Shakespeare 4* (1998). Michael Siberry on playing Petruchio, pp. 45–59.

Werner, Sarah, *Shakespeare and Feminist Performance: Ideology on Stage* (2001). Exploration of feminist issues in Shakespeare's plays with *The Taming of the Shrew* as case study.

AVAILABLE ON DVD

The Taming of the Shrew, directed by Edwin J. Collins (1923). Twenty-minute silent version, the second half of which is available at www.screenonline .org.uk/film/id/1054406/index.html.

The Taming of the Shrew, directed by Sam Taylor (1929, DVD 2007). Stars Mary Pickford and Douglas Fairbanks, it was the first Shakespearean talkie and performance style retains elements of silent film—famous for Pickford's wink to camera.

The Taming of the Shrew, directed by Franco Zeffirelli (1967, DVD 2001). Exuberant and colorful, with Elizabeth Taylor and Richard Burton.

The Taming of the Shrew, directed by Jonathan Miller (1980, DVD 2005). BBC Shakespeare, rather static in comparison with Zeffirelli, it dispenses with the Sly framework; John Cleese stands out as Petruchio.

The Taming of the Shrew, directed by Aida Zyablikova (1994, DVD 2007). In the series Shakespeare: The Animated Tales. Screenplay by Leon Garfield. Charming, full of inventive detail and brilliant puppetry. Kate is voiced by Amanda Root.

Kiss Me Kate, directed by George Sidney (1953, DVD 2003). Musical update by Sam and Bella Spewack. Songs by Cole Porter. With Howard Keel and Kathryn Grayson.

Ten Things I Hate About You, directed by Gil Younger (1999, DVD 2001). Witty updating to American high school with excellent performances from Julia Stiles and Heath Ledger—enjoyable, not for purists.

REFERENCES

1. William Blackstone, *Commentaries on the Laws of England* (1778 edn), vol. 4, p. 169.
2. Lynda E. Boose, "Scolding Brides and Bridling Scolds: Taming the Woman's Unruly Member," *Shakespeare Quarterly*, 42 (1991), pp. 179–213 (pp. 184–85).
3. Boose, "Scolding Brides and Bridling Scolds," p. 189.
4. Coppélia Kahn, *Man's Estate: Masculine Identity in Shakespeare* (1981), pp. 109–10.
5. Kahn, *Man's Estate*, p. 112.
6. Karen Newman, *Fashioning Femininity and English Renaissance Drama* (1991), p. 41.
7. Newman, *Fashioning Femininity*, pp. 47–48.
8. Leah Marcus, "The Shakespearean Editor as Shrew-Tamer," *English Literary Renaissance*, 22 (1992), pp. 177–200 (p. 182).
9. J. Dennis Huston, *Shakespeare's Comedies of Play* (1981), p. 87.
10. Cecil C. Seronsy, "'Supposes' as the Unifying Theme in *The Taming of the Shrew*," *Shakespeare Quarterly* 14 (1963), pp. 15–30 (p. 19).
11. John C. Bean, "Comic Structure and the Humanizing of Kate in *The Taming of the Shrew*," in Carolyn Ruth Swift Lenz, Gayle Greene, and Carol Thomas Neely, eds., *The Woman's Part: Feminist Criticism of Shakespeare* (1980), pp. 65–78 (p. 72).
12. Alexander Leggatt, *Shakespeare's Comedy of Love* (1974), p. 59.
13. Valerie Wayne, "Refashioning the Shrew," *Shakespeare Studies* 17 (1985), pp. 159–87 (p. 173).
14. H. B. Charlton, *Shakespearian Comedy* (1938), p. 98.
15. Bean, "Comic Structure and the Humanizing of Kate," pp. 68–72.
16. Ralph Berry, *Shakespeare's Comedies: Explorations in Form* (1972), p. 70.
17. Wayne, "Refashioning the Shrew," p. 172.
18. Huston, *Shakespeare's Comedies of Play*, p. 64.
19. Wayne, "Refashioning the Shrew," p. 174.
20. Graham Holderness, *Shakespeare in Performance: The Taming of the Shrew* (1989), p. 1.
21. Kahn, *Man's Estate*, p. 104.
22. Leggatt, *Shakespeare's Comedy of Love*, pp. 48–49.

23. Newman, *Fashioning Femininity*, p. 38.
24. Leggatt, *Shakespeare's Comedy of Love*, pp. 42–43.
25. Thomas Davies, Chapter XXIV, in his *Memoirs of the Life of David Garrick*, Vol. 1 (rev. edn, 1808; reprinted 1969), pp. 311–15.
26. Davies, Chapter XXIV.
27. Tori Haring-Smith, *From Farce to Metadrama: A Stage History of the Taming of the Shrew, 1594–1983* (1985), p. 20.
28. Review of *The Taming of the Shrew, Illustrated London News*, Vol. XXIX, No. 831, 22 November 1856, p. 521.
29. Haring-Smith, *From Farce to Metadrama*, p. 72.
30. *New York Times*, 19 January 1887.
31. *New York Times*, 19 January 1887.
32. *The Athenaeum*, No. 3162, 2 June 1888, p. 706.
33. Stark Young, 1935, quoted in Haring-Smith, *From Farce to Metadrama*, p. 72.
34. *The Times*, London, 12 May 1913.
35. *Saturday Review*, 6 November 1897. Reprinted in Edwin Wilson, ed., *Shaw on Shakespeare* (1961), p. 198.
36. Haring-Smith, *From Farce to Metadrama*.
37. *Literary Digest*, New York, Vol. 120, 12 October 1935, p. 20.
38. Walter Kerr, *New York Herald Tribune*, 21 June 1962.
39. Tice L. Miller, "The Taming of the Shrew," in Samuel L. Leiter, ed., *Shakespeare Around the Globe: A Guide to Notable Postwar Revivals* (1986), pp. 661–84.
40. Charles Marowitz, *The Marowitz Shakespeare* (1978), p. 15.
41. Marowitz, *The Marowitz Shakespeare*, p. 160.
42. Miller, "The Taming of the Shrew."
43. Geraldine Cousin, *New Theatre Quarterly*, Vol. 2, No. 7, August 1986, pp. 275–81.
44. Sarah Hemming, *Financial Times*, 23 August 2003.
45. Ibid.
46. Ibid.
47. Ann Christensen, "Petruchio's House in Postwar Suburbia: Reinventing the Domestic Woman (Again)" in *Post Script* 17.1 (1997), pp. 28–42.
48. Chris Dunkley, *Financial Times*, 24 October 1980.
49. Graham Holderness, in his *Shakespeare in Performance: The Taming of the Shrew* (1989), pp. 104–11.
50. Michael Bogdanov interviewed by Christopher J. McCullough, in Graham Holderness, *The Shakespeare Myth* (1988).

51. Michael Billington, *Guardian*, 5 May 1979.

52. David Ward, *Guardian*, 11 October 1990.

53. Gale Edwards discussing "The Taming of the Shrew," in Elizabeth Schafer, *Ms-Directing Shakespeare: Women Direct Shakespeare* (1998).

54. Bill Alexander in interview with Liz Gilbey, *Plays International*, April 1992.

55. Jane Edwardes, *Time Out*, 8 April 1992.

56. Bill Alexander in interview with Liz Gilbey.

57. Brian Mairs, *Solihull Times*, 10 April 1992.

58. Di Trevis interviewed in Schafer, *Ms-Directing Shakespeare*.

59. Ibid.

60. Michael Billington, *Guardian*, 24 April 1995.

61. Nick Curtis, *Evening Standard*, 28 October 1999.

62. Michael Billington, *Guardian*, 29 October 1999.

63. Samuel Schoenbaum, *Times Literary Supplement*, 27 October 1978.

64. Benedict Nightingale, *New Statesman*, 12 May 1978.

65. Rebecca Brown, *The Taming of the Shrew in Performance*, Shakespeare Birthplace Trust Website (2006).

66. Graham Holderness, *The Taming of the Shrew*, Shakespeare in Performance (1989).

67. Michael Bogdanov in Holderness, *The Shakespeare Myth*.

68. Nightingale, *New Statesman*, 12 May 1978.

69. Ibid.

70. *Northamptonshire Evening Telegraph*, 24 August 1985.

71. *Time Out*, 12 September 1985.

72. Di Trevis (interview from the *Northamptonshire Evening Telegraph*, 28 August 1985), in Schafer, *Ms-Directing Shakespeare*.

73. Geraldine Cousin, "The Touring of the Shrew," *New Theatre Quarterly*, Vol. 2, No. 7 (August 1986).

74. Michael Siberry, "Petruccio," in Robert Smallwood, ed., *Players of Shakespeare* 4 (1998).

75. Siberry, "Petruccio."

76. Fiona Shaw in interview with Peter Lewis, *The Times*, London, 2 September 1987.

77. Fiona Shaw on Katherina, in Carol Chillington Rutter, *Clamorous Voices* (1988).

78. Ibid.

79. Irving Wardle, *The Times*, London, 10 September 1987.

80. Shaw on Katherina, in Rutter, *Clamorous Voices*.

81. Andrew Rissik, *Independent*, 10 September 1987.

180   REFERENCES

82. Shaw on Katherina, in Rutter, *Clamorous Voices*.
83. *New Statesman*, 12 May 1978, quoted in Elizabeth Schafer, *The Taming of the Shrew*, Shakespeare in Production (2002).
84. www.rsc.org.uk/explore/workspace/shrew_play_guide_3249.htm.
85. Michael Bogdanov interviewed in Holderness, *The Shakespeare Myth*.
86. Curtis, *Evening Standard*, 28 October 1999.
87. Schafer, *The Taming of the Shrew*.
88. Billington, *Guardian*, 29 October 1999.
89. Curtis, *Evening Standard*, 28 October 1999.
90. Siberry, "Petruccio."
91. Kate Bassett, *Independent on Sunday*, 13 April 2003.
92. Michael Billington, *Guardian*, 11 April 2003.
93. Rebecca Brown, Shakespeare Birthplace Trust Website, 2006.
94. Billington, *Guardian*, 11 April 2003.
95. Brown, Shakespeare Birthplace Trust Website.
96. Bill Alexander in interview with Liz Gilbey, *Plays International*, April 1992.
97. Michael Bogdanov interviewed in Holderness, *The Shakespeare Myth*.

ACKNOWLEDGMENTS AND PICTURE CREDITS

Preparation of *"The Taming of the Shrew* in Performance" was assisted by a generous grant from the CAPITAL Centre (Creativity and Performance in Teaching and Learning) of the University of Warwick for research in the RSC archive at the Shakespeare Birthplace Trust.

The second half of the introduction ("The Critics Debate") draws extensively on a longer overview of the play's critical history prepared for us by Sarah Carter.

Thanks as always to our indefatigable and eagle-eyed copy editor Tracey Day and to Ray Addicott for overseeing the production process with rigor and calmness.

Picture research by Michelle Morton. Grateful acknowledgment is made to the Shakespeare Birthplace Trust for assistance with picture research (special thanks to Helen Hargest) and reproduction fees.

Images of RSC productions are supplied by the Shakespeare Centre Library and Archive, Stratford-upon-Avon. This Library, maintained by the Shakespeare Birthplace Trust, holds the most important collection of Shakespeare material in the UK, including the Royal Shakespeare Company's official archive. It is open to the public free of charge.

For more information see www.shakespeare.org.uk.

1. Directed by George Devine (1953) Angus McBean © Royal Shakespeare Company
2. Directed by John Barton (1960) Angus McBean © Royal Shakespeare Company
3. Directed by Di Trevis (1985) © Donald Cooper/photostage.co.uk
4. Directed by Jonathan Miller (1987) Joe Cocks Studio Collection © Shakespeare Birthplace Trust

MODERN LIBRARY IS ONLINE AT
WWW.MODERNLIBRARY.COM

MODERN LIBRARY ONLINE IS YOUR GUIDE
TO CLASSIC LITERATURE ON THE WEB

THE MODERN LIBRARY E-NEWSLETTER

Our free e-mail newsletter is sent to subscribers, and features sample chapters, interviews with and essays by our authors, upcoming books, special promotions, announcements, and news. To subscribe to the Modern Library e-newsletter, visit **www.modernlibrary.com**

THE MODERN LIBRARY WEBSITE

Check out the Modern Library website at
www.modernlibrary.com for:

• The Modern Library e-newsletter

• A list of our current and upcoming titles and series

• Reading Group Guides and exclusive author spotlights

• Special features with information on the classics and
  other paperback series

• Excerpts from new releases and other titles

• A list of our e-books and information on where to buy them

• The Modern Library Editorial Board's 100 Best Novels and
  100 Best Nonfiction Books of the Twentieth Century written in
  the English language

• News and announcements

Questions? E-mail us at **modernlibrary@randomhouse.com**.
For questions about examination or desk copies, please visit
the Random House Academic Resources site at
www.randomhouse.com/academic

THE TAMING OF
THE SHREW

The RSC Shakespeare

Edited by Jonathan Bate and Eric Rasmussen

Chief Associate Editors: Héloïse Sénéchal and Jan Sewell

Associate Editors: Trey Jansen, Eleanor Lowe, Lucy Munro,
Dee Anna Phares

The Taming of the Shrew

Textual editing: Eric Rasmussen

Introduction and "Shakespeare's Career in the Theater": Jonathan Bate

Commentary: Charlotte Scott and Héloïse Sénéchal

Scene-by-Scene Analysis: Esme Miskimmin

In Performance: Karin Brown (RSC stagings) and Jan Sewell (overview)

The Director's Cut (interviews by Jonathan Bate and Kevin Wright):
Gregory Doran and Phyllida Lloyd
Playing Kate: Michelle Gomez

Editorial Advisory Board